Praise for
Learner-Centered Innovation

"In *Learner-Centered Innovation*, Katie Martin shares a compelling vision of what is possible in schools today. Filled with research and examples from leading educators, this must-read book will inspire you to create experiences that develop learners, workers, and citizens who will thrive in a changing world."

—Linda Darling-Hammond,
president, Learning Policy Institute,
and professor emeritus, Stanford University

"Despite the long shadow of standardization and high-stakes testing, Katie Martin's exploration of the innovative education landscape shines a light on teachers, schools, and districts that are exercising creative noncompliance with courage and conviction. It's a book of hope, purpose, and impact. Katie not only provides an analysis of what's (glaringly) wrong in education but she also paints a bright vision for what's possible and provides a practical roadmap for how we might get there, with case-study–like examples. It's a must-read for teachers, administrators, or anyone who seeks to cultivate a more creative vision for the future of education."

—Kaleb Rashad,
director, High Tech High, San Diego

"With all that we understand about how students learn, the predictions of the world they will face after graduation, and the education inequities that have existed for centuries, continuing to use a traditional, teacher-centric approach to teaching and learning is instructional malpractice. In *Learner-Centered Innovation*, Martin eloquently shares evidence-based, practical ways to ignite curiosity, develop passions, and unleash student genius, through the types of learning experiences that today's modern learners need to thrive in tomorrow's world. If we are going to empower future-ready students, learner-centered, innovative experiences must be the foundation."

—Thomas C. Murray,
director of innovation, Future Ready Schools, and coauthor of
Learning Transformed: 8 Keys to Designing Tomorrow's Schools, Today

"In *Learner-Centered Innovation*, Katie writes about creating a true culture of innovation and explains how schools must rethink how we "do school"—from assessments and curriculum to professional development and programming (and so much more). What you measure matters, and *Learner-Centered Innovation* serves as a true compass for anyone aiming to revamp their traditions to place a high value on innovative practices and authentic learning. Katie shares ideas, tips, strategies, and personal stories that make this book a page turner that is impossible to put down!"

—Kayla Delzer,
globally awarded teacher, author, and CEO of Top Dog Teaching Inc.

"*Learner-Centered Innovation* is a must-read for educators seeking to transform the way learning happens in their schools and classrooms. Dr. Martin provides a refreshing examination of the very real obstacles educators face, challenging us to think differently about the contradictions of many reform narratives. Rather than offer simple solutions, she engages us in the conversations we're not having, channeling educators into productive dialogue about the systems that produce good teaching and learning. She refreshingly balances this systems-level thinking with the lived experiences and voices of actual educators in the trenches of reform, acknowledging the many nuances of leadership and learning. In doing so, she humanizes the realities of reform work, building empathy rather than casting blame. At the same time, her message is clear: All educators, from the boardroom to the classroom, must continually reflect on and expand their thinking about not only the teaching that occurs in the classroom but also the learning that results. Dr. Martin not only builds on the work of leading experts in education, but also draws on her own experiences as an educator and a mother, modeling the same reflection and vulnerability she pushes her readers to engage in. Whether you are a classroom teacher or a district leader, *Learner-Centered Innovation* will energize you—while also giving you practical tools—to take action in your learning community."

—David Trautman,
leadership and professional learning specialist,
Institute for Entrepreneurship in Education, University of San Diego

"*Learner-Centered Innovation* is an inspirational call to action for all educators who dream of a brighter future for our children. Dr. Martin provides incredible perspectives from her personal and professional experiences in tandem with extensive research to convey meaningful insights that are thoughtful, accessible, and actionable."

—Dr. Devin Vodicka,
chief impact officer, AltSchool

"Katie Martin's authentic storytelling capabilities along with real classroom examples set the stage for the reader to question current practices in education. Martin beautifully pens how we, as educators, might navigate the tough topic of designing a systemic culture of learning and innovation. She provides the reader with resources and examples to engage stakeholders in necessary conversations to prepare our learners for the future and shares research to demonstrate how we must place more emphasis on the "why" of what we do. *Learner-Centered Innovation* indeed causes the reader to question conventional wisdom and to unleash the genius not only in those they serve, but also within themselves. I highly recommend this book to any educator, no matter your role."

—Tara Martin, curriculum coordinator, Auburn-Washburn School District

"In *Learner-Centered Innovation*, Katie Martin shows all of us who are concerned about the future of education in the country how to help us 'create experiences that ignite curiosity, develop passion, and unleash genius in your students, your teachers, and ourselves.' Dr. Martin draws on her experience as a successful and inspiring middle school teacher and her work supporting teachers, school and system leaders in creating learner centered experiences—especially for students furthest from opportunity. *Learner-Centered Innovation* provides both research and concrete examples to create a clear path for the reader to take action so that all students can find success in school and life."

—Bob Lenz, executive director, Buck Institute for Education

LEARNER CENTERED INNOVATION

Spark Curiosity
Ignite Passion and
Unleash Genius

Katie Martin

Learner-Centered Innovation
© 2018 by Katie Martin

This book is available at special discounts when purchased in quantity for use as premiums, promotions, fundraisers, or for educational use. For inquiries and details, contact the publisher at books@impressbooks.org.

Published by IMPress,
a division of Dave Burgess Consulting, Inc.

ImpressBooks.org
daveburgessconsulting.com

Editing and Interior Design by My Writers' Connection
Cover Design by Genesis Kohler

Library of Congress Control Number: 2017961689
Paperback ISBN: 978-1-948334-00-6
eBook ISBN: 978-1-948334-01-3
978-1-948334-15-0
First Printing: February 2018

Dedication

For Abby and Zack

May you always know that you are loved
and feel supported to find your
place in this world.

Contents

by George Couros

IN 2015, I HAD THE wonderful opportunity to write and publish the book, *The Innovator's Mindset*. Katie Martin, a dear friend and colleague of mine over the past few years, was crucial in what was written in those pages. Her mind toward where education was and where education needs to go is one of the brightest that I have met in the past few years. When writing my book, after completing each chapter, I gave Katie carte blanche to edit anything that I wrote as she saw fit. To be honest, I can't think of one other person in the world that I would trust so much with a book that would bear my name.

This doesn't mean we agreed on everything, and to this day, we still don't. The push and pull of ideas that Katie has provided me has sharpened my own thinking. It is something I wish were the norm in schools today. Often, we agree on ideas or practices in person, but are we too afraid to have the tough conversations and embrace the meaningful conflict needed to really create the important changes education needs to move forward? If we do not embrace opportunities for challenge, who does that benefit in the long term? Definitely not the educator, and most certainly not the students. We need that balance of "push and pull" if we are going to create effective change, and it is important that we have critical friends in our work as educators. Katie will not only challenge your thinking in this book, but she will also push you to ask more questions. Her approach is about starting and deepening the conversation with you, not telling you what to do. She knows that people who ask questions first are the ones who change the world.

When I met Katie several years ago, we spoke all things education for a significant part of the day. Her ideas challenged me and provided me with inspiration to try new things and question my own assumptions about what I believed I knew on the world of education. As she continued to speak, I stopped her and told her, "you need to blog." My belief was that someone with the vision Katie had for educators and students (learners) should not be limited to a conversation here and there, but her thinking needs to be shared with the world. It would not only help Katie really reflect on her own learning, but more importantly, that thinking would be shared with the world.

Katie eventually took me up on the challenge to blog, and her blog subheading, "Inspired by Research, Refined by Practice," is exemplified through her work. Katie strikes a fine balance between identifying what has worked in the past while keeping an eye on what students need in the future. Too often, books take a stance on one side of the spectrum or the other, but Katie weaves the two intricately together, to help schools create students who ask questions and identify problems in the same way she creates experiences where the adults do the same.

The work of educators is challenging. We must recognize individuals and systems for the gains we have made, and we must create a culture that continuously looks to develop students' strengths and improve in areas of weakness. And just as we expect of the children in our schools, we need to continuously grow as learners. Both elements are crucial for growth that is spurred by validation. Katie provides both in this book. You will end up feeling inspired to push your own learning through stories and examples of practice happening in education right now, and you will feel affirmed by the knowledge that many of your current practices that enhance student learning are putting both schools and individual students on the right path.

Three things I ask you as you read this text:

1. Identify what has challenged you.
2. Identify what has been reaffirmed.
3. Identify what you will do moving forward.

This will give you a path to make your own connections to where you are and where you are going. No idea in education can simply be carbon copied, as each community and learner is at a different place. Katie writes this to provide the ideas, but it is up to the reader(s) to make the actions happen.

I have been blessed to have direct access to the wisdom of Katie Martin for the past several years, and I am glad that her ideas will now reach many more schools through this book. The ideas here will inspire you to challenge your own thinking, ask more questions, and create better schools for our students. What more could you ask?

What If?

IT'S AMAZING HOW TWO VERY small words can make a big impact on our world and have done so throughout history.

What if I say I am not sitting at the back of the bus?

What if I create Hogwarts, a fictional land where young wizards learn and practice magic?

What if we can send people to the moon?

What if I protest with non-violent civil disobedience?

People like Claudette Colvin, Rosa Parks, J.K. Rowling, John F. Kennedy, Malala Yousafzai, and Mahatma Gandhi have changed the course of history by asking, "What if?" These ideas spurred action and more questions while inspiring others to move beyond preexisting norms and perceived barriers and challenging the status quo to seek something better. It's worth noting that not every question changes the world, nor should it be expected to, but we also must consider what we sacrifice when we limit curiosity and ask learners to put the questions aside so that we can focus on the answers or "get through the curriculum."

My children, Abby and Zack, are seven and eight as I am writing this book, and they ask, "What if?" all the time. They are curious about *everything*. They wonder about the world and their place in it. Almost every night, they work on making something, and they ask regularly to do experiments. Whether it is homemade gummy bears, various iterations of slime, a pumpkin to explode with rubber bands, or a few bowls of unidentifiable concoctions, they are always creating, mixing, or taking apart something.

My husband and I see and encourage our children's natural curiosity, driving a constant desire and excitement to learn and discover at home, so we were surprised when we went in for my daughter's parent-teacher conference and learned she was marked "needs improvement" in science. We looked at each other and said in unison, "I thought she loved science!" In reviewing her work, we quickly recognized that she hadn't finished copying the sentences from the board to complete her assignment. Her teacher indicated that her "needs improvement" mark was due to a lack of following directions rather than her actual lack of achievement in science or application of the concepts they were learning. I couldn't help but think about the stark contrast in Abby's interest and motivation for learning when the focus was on compliance rather than creating and the wonder it inspired. I just asked her recently what she thought about science, and although she continues to love to mix and create, she insists that doesn't like science.

Ironically, authentic learning is often at odds with the expectations placed on many teachers to cover, assess, and document achievement based on the standards and accountability systems. The necessity for evidence and a grade for the report card overrides the desire for actual growth and learning. To be clear, I'm not laying the blame for this imbalance on the teachers; we all contribute to this problem. Many parents focus on the grades; school leaders are held accountable for grades and test results, and students learn how to play the game because the larger education system is built for points, grades, and rankings.

We need to ignite curiosity and passions, not extinguish them.

As a middle school teacher, I was certainly guilty at times of creating experiences that were more about the rules of school than learning. I know I could have focused more on how to ask better questions rather than simply finding the answers. At times, I had tightly scheduled classes based on my objectives and not as much as I should have on my students' questions and goals. At times, I know I squashed their "what ifs" to focus on what I, the adult in the room, thought was crucial. When I had these moments, I was often brought back to my experiences as a student. I recalled feeling like my voice rarely mattered and that what I was learning was disconnected from the world and opportunities beyond school. I learned to play the game but felt the potential to do so much more in school. I became a teacher because I wanted students to know that they matter and to empower them to explore their interests and passions, not just complete assignments. This same drive continues to inspire me to ensure that all learners (students, teachers, administrators) are inspired to learn and empowered to build on their strengths and passions to do meaningful and relevant work. Throughout my work as a classroom and graduate course teacher, instructional coach, or in professional learning, my drive continues to be changing how we learn in school to create experiences that I wanted and now, more than ever as a parent, I want for my children and all of our children.

In an article in *Educational Leadership*, Carol Ann Tomlinson describes her viewpoint on learning in schools:

> If we actually believe it doesn't matter whether learners care about what we ask them to learn, we've lost our way. At the university, I teach many bright young adults who intend to learn anything that's put in front of them—as long as all they have to do is commit it to memory and for the purpose of a grade. Sad as that is, they are likely better off than the multitude of K–12 students who halfheartedly poke at the plates full of disconnected and distant information we serve up each day—and the multitude who simply push those plates away. To create real learners, teachers have to reach the hearts, souls, and minds of students. Teaching a list of standards won't get us there.[1]

I completely agree with her that teaching standards will not get us to where we need to be. If we are going to inspire children of any age to be learners, we must all look at how we can, as she says, "reach the hearts, souls, and minds of students, not just teach and assess the standards." If we fail to do so, we will continue to move kids through the system and on to college with the focus on getting good grades and jumping through hoops rather than learning and finding their place in the world. At the same time, we will see even more students (and teachers) disengage from school. When curiosity and exploration are stifled, a child is likely to lose the motivation to study, and his or her work may become less imaginative. But the world demands citizens who are more creative, imaginative, and innovative than ever before, which means we need to ignite curiosity and passions, not extinguish them.

---

1   Carol Ann Tomlinson, "One to Grow On: Lesson Plans Well Served," *Educational Leadership*, 74 (2016): pg. 89-90. Accessed Nov. 30, 2017, http://www.ascd.org/publications/educational-leadership/oct16/vol74/num02/Lesson-Plans-Well-Served.aspx.

Prioritizing Deeper Learning in School

Some days my daughter wants to be a scientist; other days she wants to be a chef. I have no idea what she will end up doing, but I know that she loves to mix and remix and create new things—at least for now. What will we miss out on if her *what if* questions subside and she begins to settle for *what is?* What if her concoctions could someday cure cancer? What if she could open a restaurant where she could happily cook and care for people? What if she stops seeing the value of her creativity and questions and settles for a path that fails to inspire her to lead a fulfilling and successful life as she defines it? Like other children her age, she is developing her self-concept as she interacts with people and ponders her surroundings. She is learning to find her place in this world. The reality of our current system is that grades and academic achievement will increasingly play a role in how she perceives her abilities and trajectory in life. I wonder if she will continue to love learning and exploration as much as she does now if her experience in school is focused on compliance rather than developing skills and knowledge that she can use to be more creative and innovative. I'm pretty sure the answer is no.

If we really value the creation of new ideas, we must model and support this type of learning. We can't say we want creative thinkers and problem solvers while stifling those opportunities in school to ensure that we get through the curriculum or make sure students are prepared for a test. *When we tell learners to complete an assignment, we get compliance. When we empower learners to investigate how to make an impact on the world, we inspire problem solvers and innovators.*

I don't know a teacher or parent who doesn't want to see students thrive and be competitive in both their local and global communities. Even though we say we want kids to excel in today's world, too often the teaching tactics we rely on are stuck in the nostalgia of how we learned. For those who think about students being distracted and needing to learn the way we did, I would ask you to consider what opportunities we might be missing out on. The reality is there are a wealth of amazing opportunities for learners today; for example, students have access to devices that can connect them with the world. How might we use these tools to our advantage? Are we favoring static curriculum because it is truly the best way or because it is comfortable and familiar to us (the adults)? What if there were a better way forward?

Are Traditions Getting in the Way of Innovation in Education?

I sat next to a group of high school students in Starbucks the other day, and I couldn't help but overhear their conversation. The four of them made room on a small table for their laptops and phones while completing a photocopied study packet, which painted such a striking contrast between their lives outside of school and what was required of them in school. Although they were connected and could look up any of these facts within seconds, they were stressed about "cramming for their finals" to show what they knew. They acknowledged that they would never remember all the information, and they begrudgingly worked to complete their packets.

Our traditional experiences in school often reinforce beliefs and expectations about the teacher as the holder of the information who needs to be in control, but this might very well be in conflict with today's learners' needs, opportunities, and skills necessary to thrive in a changing world. Tradition is so deeply ingrained in schools; in fact many educators, having been successful in the traditional model, can't imagine doing it differently. Today, we know a great deal about improving our schools *in theory*, but past experiences and traditional systems can prevent necessary changes in education.

Reluctance to change might feel safe and familiar, but this attitude carries significant risk. We can see this risk played out time and again in the business world. Consider how Kodak, despite its expertise and history of success, suffered because its leaders failed to transition from what they had always done to what the changing industry and technology demanded. As a leader in the photography industry, and the company had tremendous insight into the future but failed to turn that expertise into measurable results. This gap between theory and practice is called the "knowing-doing gap." In *Creative Confidence*, authors Tom and David Kelly highlight what this disconnect meant for Kodak:

> For starters, tradition got in the way of innovation. Kodak's glorious past was just too alluring. Kodak had essentially owned consumer photography for a hundred years, with market share in some segments as high as 90 percent. By contrast, digital ventures all seemed so risky, and Kodak wasn't providing enough "soft landings" for managers willing to take career risks in those new areas. Facing strong global competitors in the digital market, Kodak knew that it would struggle, and fear of failure transfixed the management team. Caught in the knowing-doing gap, Kodak clung too closely to the chemistry-based business that had been so successful for them in the twentieth century, underinvesting in the digital world of the twenty-first century. What we saw at Kodak was not a lack of information but the failure to turn insight into effective action. As a result, one of the most powerful brands in America lost its way.[2]

Fear of failure prevented leaders in Kodak from taking the steps toward a more innovative approach, which ultimately led to the company's demise. In the same way, if we continue to hold on to deep rooted traditions in education rather than turn theory into action to meet the needs of the future, we may well be destined to

---

2   Tom Kelly and David Kelly. *Creative Confidence: Unleashing the Creative Potential within us All* (New York: William Collins, 2015).

fail. To move forward, we too must invest in the world we live in and press toward the future, not focus on the past.

Closing this gap between what we know about learning and the changing world and what we actually do in schools requires that we take action now to impact the trajectory of those we serve. As Kodak's leadership learned, we can't hold on to our traditions just because they were successful in the past; we need to align our learning experiences in schools to meet the needs of learners today. Kodak's failure was due to a singular focus on "what was" rather than "what could be." Past successes do not always ensure future growth when the context in which we live changes—and it always changes.

Teachers Create What They Experience

This change in the world and its impact on education is not to be taken lightly. More is continually required of educators than ever before—and without the proper time and support to learn how to be successful in their changing role. In many cases, teachers have resorted to learning on their own time. Not only is this unfair to them, it's unfair to students. Without a shared understanding of the role of the teacher and how to leverage the powerful tools and resources to create desired learning experiences, many teachers rely on the models of how they have always taught, despite the resources at their fingertips or those of their students.

While meeting with a principal in her school, she explained some of the many priorities and initiatives that teachers were expected to implement in their classrooms. I asked, "If I were a teacher here, how would I learn how to best use all the new resources and strategies to meet the needs of my students?"

Her response was simple and honest: "We have a lot of room for improvement in that area." She acknowledged that they had not made a concerted effort to prioritize goals and align learning experiences for teachers to integrate new ideas, shed outdated practices, and improve teaching and learning. This principal is not alone; she was just very candid about the reality that existed in her school. Her candidness highlights a major challenge that exists in many schools right now. If we want to change how students learn, we must change how teachers learn.

We can continue to create new initiatives and programs, but if teachers are not part of the process, we will miss out on our greatest lever in educational change. Teachers' practices are shaped by their experiences both past and present, and these are mirrored in their classrooms. If we don't prioritize authentic and relevant learning experiences for educators, how can we ensure our students have deeper learning experiences? Making shifts in how we learn, teach, and lead in education requires that we move beyond talking about theory and best practices (or even a really great framework) to ensuring we not only develop new knowledge and expertise but *use it* to change how students learn.

> ## *If we want to change how students learn, we must change how teachers learn.*

What's in Your Sphere of Influence?

It's easy to place blame on others when something doesn't go the way that you want or expect. Think about how many times you might have heard or even said yourself something along the lines of, "If only *they* would have . . . ."

Chances are that you have heard or felt the frustration common to teachers that, "If *they* would have taught them the correct (fill in the blank) skills in (fill in the blank) grade, I wouldn't have to spend time reteaching them." I've heard this statement too many times to believe that the gap in learning is the fault of individual teachers. What it signifies to me is that we have a system to which curriculum, standards, and programs are constantly added, rarely taking anything away, which results in a lot of surface learning. Although teachers might cover a lot of content, the deeper learning required to retain and apply the new knowledge happens far too rarely in classrooms today.

This more-is-better mentality permeates educational institutions. We see it when principals tell teachers about a new initiative, or the district has a training for all teachers to "roll out" the new curriculum, but the new initiative or training never quite takes hold in classrooms and doesn't make the desired impact. Or how about when the district office's new initiative doesn't live up to the hype and is quickly replaced with the next-best thing? New projects and programs are continually added and overlap those already in place. The outcome is more work for everyone and less time for educators to focus on what should be true priorities.

It's devastating when students lack the necessary skills needed to build on year after year. But instead of investigating and addressing the root cause, in most cases the tendency is to reteach the same way that didn't work the first time. Likewise, it's costly and wasteful for expensive programs and resources to go largely unused and then be shelved as ineffective. The cycle continues when the next new program is rolled out in a staff meeting.

If you always do what you've always done, you always get what you've always gotten.

—Jessie Potter

Think about it. The amount of time educators are asked to do something different is woefully disproportionate to the time spent actually doing something different. If we continue to perpetuate the "I taught them but they didn't learn it" mentality prevalent throughout education and place blame on others, we will never see the kind of change our schools require. Someone told me, "If a teacher teaches a student the same way a hundred times and the student doesn't get it, the student is not the slow learner." If we want innovative institutions that will develop the skills students need to be successful now and in the ever-changing future, we need to rethink our traditional systems and structures. This doesn't mean a new program or a new model; it means creating nimble systems from our district office to classrooms to empower learners. Powerful learning will not happen by continuing to create new expectations for others or adding on to what already exists. It *does* happen when we are willing to forsake existing procedures and policies that don't work and take steps to create the change.

What if it starts with you?

The change process has to begin with ourselves. Once we (in all roles) are willing to make changes in our own practices, we can then work together to figure out how we can create better systems to improve learning and positively impact outcomes for our students. We cannot wait for the next great reform; there never has been nor will there ever be a silver bullet. People, not programs or tools, drive change in schools. Small steps in schools across the world have already impacted so many. The power is in the collective movement of educators who begin to make the changes in their classrooms, schools, and districts. The educators who are making these changes and the ones who seek out even greater learning opportunities open classroom doors, work within existing constraints and barriers, and build networks to continuously learn, share, and innovate. To improve our schools to meet the needs of the changing world, it will take all of us.

Just think how you might begin to make the changes and the impact you desire in school if instead of statements like, "If *they* would have, . . ." you started asking, "*How might I . . . ?*" This is what is referred to by psychologists as the *locus of control* or the extent to which people believe they have power to influence events in their lives. A person with an internal locus of control believes that he or she can influence events and outcomes. These individuals might notice that students are not meeting the desired outcomes and decide to take some risks, try new strategies, or design an authentic project to meet the needs of learners. Someone with an external locus of control instead blames outside forces for everything. When these individuals notice that the learners are not meeting desired objectives, they might blame the curriculum or a lack of resources, or they might point out why they *can't* do something rather than thinking about what they *can* influence.

> *Everyone thinks of changing the world,*
> *but no one thinks of changing himself.*
> **—Leo Tolstoy**

Creating an environment where learners are empowered to take risks in pursuit of learning and growth rather than perfection is absolutely foundational to shifting educational practices. To see the changes necessary for equipping our students for their futures, we must empower teachers to make decisions and design learning experiences that meet their students' needs. I have spent the past five years asking teachers and administrators across diverse schools, districts, and states what they feel they need to be successful to make empowering shifts in their practice. Too often the first response is that they have never been asked about their needs or what possibilities they see. I don't see how we can change how students learn in school if we don't involve the educators, especially the teachers who are with the kids every day. These challenges can only be addressed through thoughtful problem-solving and collaboration across the boundaries of teachers and administrators.

I hope this book provides an entry point and examples to ignite conversations between administrators, teachers, students, and the greater community. If we want schools that develop successful students who are prepared for our changing world, we all need to have open and honest conversations about the vision, values, culture, and policies that influence what happens in our districts, schools, and classrooms. As we dive into why there is a need for innovation in education, my goal is to push thinking and provide resources and examples to allow you take steps forward to meet the needs of those you serve and ultimately ask yourself, your colleagues, and your community, "What if?" and then work together to make it happen.

This book is divided into three sections, each designed to help you create experiences that ignite curiosity, develop passion, and unleash genius in your students, your teachers, and yourself. In Part 1, we explore the evolving role of the educator and implications for what the ideal classroom might look like. Ensuring student success today and tomorrow is not about defining one right answer for education but about having conversations to create a shared understanding that helps everyone move forward together. In Part 2, we look at reframing learning as a process rather than an event. Research has consistently concluded that innovation flourishes when teachers collaborate on teaching practices, are provided opportunities to learn and practice new methods, and are guided by a common vision and continuous support. We will explore the context that supports educators to continually evolve their practices based on available resources, new experiences, and the needs of the community. In Part 3, we focus on opening classroom doors physically and metaphorically to connect and share reflections and learning in your buildings and across the world. Educators have been far too isolated, and we are plagued by a culture of closed doors. When given the opportunity (and sometimes a gentle nudge), we all benefit by observing peers and reflecting on our own practice. In addition, creating diverse networks and connecting with others in the education community and beyond is extremely important because when we collaborate and share what we are learning, the students win (and so do we).

Be the Change

I went through most of school thinking and being graded on the assumption that the author's message was a definitive A, B, C, or D and could often be summarized in a sentence that was right or wrong. I was taught the authors or the textbook publishers had all the answers, and my role was to figure it out and prove it to my teachers. I never saw the purpose of this or felt like my ideas were valued or nurtured. Because of this, I didn't choose to read until well into my adult years. It wasn't until I experienced something different in college that I thought, *What if I can teach kids differently? What if I can help students understand that their voice matters and empower them to learn—not because they needed to know information for a test but because it would allow them access to the world, ideas, and opportunities? What if I can inspire my students to read, discover their passions, and share their ideas with the world?*

As you read this book, whether you are a teacher, an instructional coach, district or site administrator, or anyone who cares about how we learn in schools, I hope you consider the power within your sphere of influence to create the change you want to see in your own context. The role of *you*, the reader, is not to just consume and copy my ideas or the ideas of others I will share, but to dive in, question, create new meaning, and ultimately ask

"What if?" and begin to create the change that you wish to see in your context.

At the end of each chapter, "Reflect and Connect Challenges" will hopefully guide and push your thinking about your role and what you can do to make an impact within your sphere of influence. As Dewey said, "We do not learn from experience, we learn from reflecting on experience." So as you read, ask "What if?", try some new things, reflect on your learning, and share your ideas and questions with others. I challenge you to seek to answer these questions for yourself and ask those you serve about their experience, your impact, and how you can collectively learn, improve, and move forward.

I think about my kids and their questions and their passions, and I wonder, what if learners are valued for their diverse talents and not just the traditional model of what's considered smart. What if success can be defined in many ways? What if teachers are supported and empowered to create new and better experiences for the students they serve? This change in education will require more than providing training for administrators and teachers to implement new curriculum or programs and resources. The schools and districts in which I have seen the most movement have focused first on creating a culture of learning and innovation with a shared goal where everyone is encouraged and trusted to try new things to work together toward that goal. In the *Fifth Discipline*,[3] Peter Senge describes how a learning organization encourages and facilitates learning throughout all levels of an organization to enable it to adapt and transform itself to function effectively in a complex and dynamic world.

Change does not require "blowing up" the system. The iPhone changed so much of our world today, some good and some bad,

---

3   Peter Senge, *The Fifth Discipline: The Art and Practice of the Learning Organization* (New York: Doubleday, 1990).

but it was not the first smartphone to exist. Steve Jobs set out to revolutionize the phone, but it was an iteration of things that currently existed, not something brand new. Within the context of where we are today, it will not take a new invention to change the world; many educators are already doing this work by asking "What if?" and working within the constraints of the system to design and iterate experiences that are changing the way we practice and view education. The question "what if?" should not be reserved for our students but is one we all will need to ask if we are to create an educational system that truly inspires this generation to change the world.

If this book provides all of the "what ifs" for you, I have failed. I hope that it will provide some answers but even more questions. What we do in schools most certainly suffers a tremendous loss if we, as educators, squash our students' need to ask "what if?" or stop asking it ourselves. As George Couros states in his book, *The Innovator's Mindset*,[4] "If a student leaves school less curious than when they started, we have failed them." I agree adamantly with this statement, but I would add that if we, as educators, lose our curiosity and ability to ask "what if," we and our students lose out.

If we change the way we learn and how we see our learning, we ultimately change the way our students learn. When we change that, they change the world.

Two simple words can change everything. The first step is asking the question. Many of your students are already asking, "What if?" So fan that flame! Please don't extinguishing their fire with tradition and ineffective and irrelevant practices. Ask that question yourself. What if you could create something better for your students? After all, what *they* do is your legacy.

What if? It's up to you to finish that question.

Two small words can change everything. Let's go!

---

4   George Couros, *The Innovator's Mindset: Empower Learning, Unleash Talent, and Lead a Culture of Creativity* (San Diego, CA: Dave Burgess Consulting, Inc. 2015).

PART 1:
The Innovation Ecosystem

Do the best you can until you know better. Then when you know better, do better.

—Maya Angelou

The Evolving Role of the Educator

I WAS READING A BOOK about giraffes with my kids that sparked questions about how they live and how their babies are born. I didn't have all the answers to their questions, so my son said, "Just Google it, Mom!" I grabbed my phone, and we watched video after video about giraffes and their calves. Each video helped answer their questions and prompted more.

At home, my children are used to easy access to information, which sparks their curiosity. They have learned that the better the questions they dream up, the more interesting the information they discover. This is how my seven- and eight-year-olds like to learn. The truth is, they don't know any different. They have grown up in a world where they can command information and content on demand, where they can pick their favorite TV show on Netflix, or watch videos on YouTube on any topic that piques their interest. They know a vast amount of information exists for their learning, and they can tap into multiple devices to access information, people, and entertainment—whenever they want and wherever they are.

But it's fair to point out that just because we can find the information doesn't mean that a Google search should be our default. Alec Couros, associate professor at the University of Regina, shared in a blog post about how his immediate inclination to look up answers to his son's questions actually curbed their wonder and curiosity. After finding the answer, he realized,

> We no longer had to wonder. I did that entirely wrong. At the very least, I could have asked my boy, "Well, which do you think, son?" perhaps followed by, "So why do you think that?" But I didn't. And because I didn't, I messed up a great learning opportunity. Instead of providing my boy with an extended opportunity to be curious, to imagine deeply, and to think creatively, I reinforced one of the worst habits of our generation. I demonstrated to my boy that you can solve a problem without thinking. And I won't do that again.[5]

Alec's realization has great implications for our work as educators. Learning is messy. Today's technology provides easy access to answers, but if we focus only on the answers and not on thinking, questioning, and solving, we rob students (and ourselves) of great learning experiences. Perhaps more significantly, we fail to develop the critical behaviors that will empower them (and us) to be lifelong learners.

---

5   Alec Couros, "Tips Up or Tips Down," *Open Thinking*, June 22, 2017. http://educationaltechnology.ca/date/2012/11.

As technology advances, the role of educators and parents to model and guide learners to find information *and* to learn to how to ask better questions has become even more crucial in the development of critical thinkers. Our job is not to provide the answers that can be found in a textbook or in a webpage but to create the conditions that inspire learners to continue to wonder and figure out how to learn and solve problems and seek more questions.

The problem is that our current system in education was not set up to foster this type of exploratory, wonder-filled learning. And if we don't change the system, I worry what might happen to my kids and their love of learning as they move through school. A 2016 Gallup poll supports my concerns. Data indicate that as students progress through school, they are increasingly disengaged and lack opportunities to build on their unique strengths, talents, and interests.[6]

Percentage of Students Who Strongly Agree, By Grade (n = 928,888)

○ In the last 7 days, I have learned something interesting at school
○ I have fun at school
○ At this school, I get to do what I do best every day

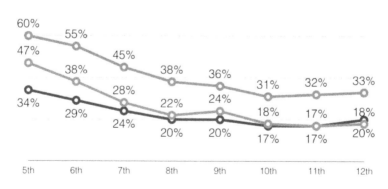

Gallup. (2016). Gallup student poll. Engaged today - Ready for tomorrow. Fall 2015 survey results. Washington. DC. Author.

6   Gallup (2016). Gallup Student Poll. "Engaged Today, Ready for Tomorrow." Fall 2015 survey results, Washington, DC. http://news.gallup.com/reports/189926/student-poll-2015-results.aspx.

When school is characterized by compliance and mandates, opportunities for creation, exploration, and developing connections between people and ideas are limited at best.

How We Live, Learn, and Work

Evolving tools, resources, and access to one another is rapidly changing how we live, work, and learn. David Price describes how access to more information has created a "messy and at times chaotic phenomenon . . . . It has changed how we live and learn, socially."[7] This unprecedented access to one another's ideas and information has also transformed the notion of how we can teach and learn. To harness the power of these advancements, our schools must embrace this sooner rather than later.

In addition to the way this open access is changing education, the way we think about and measure intelligence and real-world readiness is changing. Concern is mounting that doing well in school and maintaining a strong GPA is not enough to fully equip students for their futures. In fact, in many cases, this focus on scholastic success fails to prepare students to be successful beyond school.

In an NPR interview,[8] Todd Rose, author of *The End of Average*, describes the emphasis on standardization and the impact on schools and how students learn:

> You think of things like the lockstep, grade-based organization of kids, and you end up sitting in a class for a fixed amount of time and get a one-dimensional rating in the form of a grade, and a one-dimensional standardized assessment . . . . It feels comforting. But if you take the basic idea of jaggedness, if all kids are multidimensional in their talent, their aptitude,

---

7   David Price, *Open: How We'll Live, Work and Learn in the Future*. (UK: Crux Publishing: 2013).

8   Todd Rose, "The End of Average," *NPR*, Washington, DC. Feb. 16, 2016. http://www.npr.org/sections/ed/2016/02/16/465753501/ standards-grades-and-tests-are-wildly-outdated-argues-end-of-average.

> you can't reduce them to a single score. It gives us a
> false sense of precision and gives up on pretending
> to know anything about these kids.

Anyone who has children of their own or who has worked with children knows children are indeed multidimensional, multifaceted *individuals*. But the measures and methods we use in education continually try to conform to a cohort-based model because of efficiency and tradition. Today's marketplace needs people to think differently, to be innovative, to solve problems that do not have traditional answers. How much more so will our world need innovation as today's children move from the education system and into positions of business and leadership? If we are to prepare students for jobs that don't yet exist, how can we structure schools and education with a set of resources, curriculum, and ideas that are outdated before the kids learn them? Yes, we need to teach foundational skills; knowing how to read and write are critical skills, but they cannot be the end goal. Ultimately, we must ensure students can apply these foundational skills and use their knowledge to communicate, collaborate, and solve meaningful problems.

Caught in the Middle

We are at a turning point in education where we have an opportunity—and I would argue an obligation—to change how all students learn in school. We have the opportunity to align learning experiences to authentic tasks that develop the knowledge, skills, and dispositions students need to be successful in the world we live in now and the world our students will experience in the future. *Disposition* is a key word here. Just like my daughter who earned a "needs improvement" in science because she wasn't engaged (despite the fact that she loves to explore, invent, and experiment), when students feel disconnected or wonder-less, they disengage. Will Richardson's article, "We Feel Lost," showcases the student's point of view. This first-hand perspective he shares on school today and why students don't care is truly heart breaking.

> We are the lost generation. Many teachers think standardized tests, endless worksheets, and piles of homework are the answer. The other half don't believe in homework, think standardized tests are moronic, and believe in activities that make us enjoy the lesson. One year you have a drill sergeant for an English teacher who jams vocabulary down your throat to the point where you can't think anymore and who constantly prepares you (not adequately enough) for the never-ending flow of standardized tests that seem to be as common as the rising tide. The next year you have a teacher who wants to teach, who loves to teach, who's "untraditional." And you want to learn, you really do! But all you can think about when you raise your hand is, "Will this be on the test?" That's all that seems to matter. First period will take your phone on sight if it simply falls out of your backpack while third period encourages the use of all devices.[9]

I have seen the extremes that exist from classroom to classroom in schools across the country. Students in our schools today live in between two worlds; one world is run by adults for whom traditional education methods worked. These educators prefer a linear path to learning that promotes a one-size-fits-all approach to a narrow definition of success. This model has left far too many behind and has produced even more people who, although they successfully navigated school, remain ill prepared to successfully navigate the world in which we live. In this world, the rules and procedures placed on kids (and adults) are more conducive to the game of school than actual learning and can hinder the development of the kind of skilled, innovative, and empowered learners our world needs.

---

9   Will Richardson, "We Feel Lost," WillRichardson.com, January 18, 2016. Accessed December 19, 2017, https://willrichardson.com/we-feel-lost.

The other world is shepherded by those who understand the world is evolving and, as such, are working to align teaching and learning to modern demands and opportunities. This is the world I want my own children to experience. It's a place where innovation—on the side of both the educator and the learner—thrives. Innovation is not for a few; it is critical to create new and better opportunities for all learners. As educational institutions, we can and must do better to create coherent learning experiences for students to explore their passions, understand their strengths, and find their place in the world. Until then, as we vacillate between different philosophies of education, today's students are caught in the middle. We cannot continue to add on twenty-first-century expectations to a twentieth-century model of education.

Leading Change

Life today is driven by change. With this truth in mind, it is impossible to think that anyone could or should have all the answers, although too often educators feel inadequate when they don't. That feeling of inadequacy stems, at least in part, from the idea that the teacher, principal, superintendent, or whoever is in charge should be the expert. This expectation of the leader as the expert not only is unfair (no one can know *everything*), but it also prevents teachers and administrators from being open about what they don't know, which leads to isolation rather than to the kind of collaboration that could solve challenges and make real change possible. This is true at every level of education, but the irony is that although humans crave this authenticity in leaders, we are also hardwired for self-protection. Our egos can actually prevent us from taking risks and admitting that we don't know it all, which creates a disconnect between what we say and what we do.

Nobody is perfect, and at times we don't measure up, but if we can be authentic and open to learning and growing *with* those we serve, we can collectively achieve much more than if we assume we have all the answers. Katie McNamara is a prime example of this kind of willingness to be vulnerable. A superintendent in South Bay Union Elementary School District, she puts herself out there in front of teachers, students, and principals to better understand the perspectives of those she serves. As the district was working with the Teacher's College Reading and Writing Project to shift their literacy instruction, she led the way by diving in and modeling a mini-lesson for teachers. What I love about Katie, though, is she didn't strive to make it perfect; she put in the ten minutes of prep time that she knew teachers would have and openly worked through some struggles with students. She also reflected and shared what she learned with teachers so they saw her not as an expert but as a learner who truly wanted the best for everyone. As a result, Katie gained an appreciation for what teachers were dealing with and was able to authentically connect with them about their challenges and successes in their reading instruction. She led by example, and although many expected her to be the expert, she gained more from being vulnerable and taking a risk. Her authenticity has enabled her to build stronger relationships and lead more effectively.

A true testament to the impact she has is the way her teachers follow her lead and try new things. One of her teachers shared that she was really excited about trying Genius Hour, a designated time in the school day for students to work on passion projects that are learner directed rather than teacher directed. The teacher told the group, "I launched Genius Hour last week, invited parents in, and told them how we could all work together to support the students in their projects." Then she explained how she shared with her students and the parents that this was new to her, and she was learning too. It was awesome to hear how she was taking risks and empowering students while embracing her role as a learner and a leader. Even more impressive (and refreshing) than her willingness to put herself out there was the fact that Katie McNamara, the superintendent, was sitting in on the group meeting, and this teacher felt comfortable enough to admit she didn't have all the answers—and was *celebrated* for trying something new. The example that she set has paved the way for others to take risks and lead by example.

A Tale of Three Classrooms

I often hear people question whether teachers are willing to embrace technology, but if we really want to transform teaching and learning, I think the better question is, "Are we willing to change our expectations for how and what students learn?" If we only focus on the latest programs, makerspaces, or the devices rather than on creating powerful learning experiences that align with the type of skills and character traits we want students to develop, we will continue to perpetuate the same norms in education with more expensive tools.

To explain the difference between adding technology and powerful teaching and learning, I want to share examples of three different types of classrooms I've visited recently.

Classroom 1: In this first classroom, the teacher is calling on her fifth graders one by one to identify each state and its geographic location. When I talked to one of the students, she told me that they were learning the states by copying them from an atlas onto a map packet because "the teacher thought it was important to know them." I asked if she knew a better way to learn about the states. She pointed to the iPad face down on her desk and queried, "The internet?" Looking around the room, I noticed that every student had an iPad, and every iPad was face down on the desk.

Classroom 2: In the second type of classroom, each student had a device to log on to computer adaptive programs that individualize their learning path. Students learn content and practice a variety of basic skills while they move through various levels at their own pace. Although the students have devices, this lesson is basically a digital worksheet.

Some variation of the lessons is still happening in many twenty-first-century classrooms. The emphasis in both of these examples is on compliance and standardization rather than on deep, personal learning. They illustrate the challenge that exists in many classrooms when we add new resources and expectations to an old paradigm of school.

Classroom 3: In the third classroom, Kim Cawkwell co-created the learning experiences based on the learning objectives and students' interests. They called it the Project Ideate. Her fourth-grade students engaged in a project during which they partnered with local businesses to understand their challenges and design solutions to impact their local community. Groups of students planned a pitch to present to a variety of businesses, including the local water board, the Humane Society, and a preschool. They received authentic feedback and made revisions to address the needs of the business partners. While creating prototypes and revising their ideas, they developed and built on their problem-solving and critical-thinking skills. The technology in this class allowed all students access to relevant resources and to connect with people to learn, create, share, and solve problems. Through the design and launch of a website and videos for their business, they learned how to effectively communicate through various mediums to document and share their ideas. Students completed several types of self-assessments, curated their work, and reflected on their learning connected to the desired learning goals to evaluate progress with their teachers and determine next steps. In addition to the standards, Sinqi, one of the students, told me, "I learned to keep persevering with your ideas and don't give up on yourself." This kind of lesson and the learning it provides go way beyond *engagement* to empower students.

The Evolving Role of the Educator

Each of the three classrooms described above have ample technology and might be considered twenty-first-century classrooms—if technology were the only qualification. But the learning experiences designed in each room are developing three very different types of learners, workers, and citizens.

Technology and access to information aren't the most important factors in creating twenty-first-century classrooms; teachers are. The power of the teacher comes not from the information she shares but from the opportunities she creates for students to learn how to learn, solve problems, and apply learning in meaningful ways. Like Kim, teachers around the world inspire their students (and me, for that matter) as they adeptly navigate their evolving role.

THE EVOLVING ROLE OF THE EDUCATOR

CO-DESIGNER OF POWERFUL LEARNING

PARTNER IN LEARNING

COMMUNITY DEVELOPER

CONNECTOR & ACTIVATOR

Katie Martin
@KatieMartinEdu

Co-Designers of Powerful Learning

Teachers who invest the time in learning about their students, their strengths, interests, and goals are best equipped to design authentic and relevant learning experiences based on students and their unique context. The project Kim created didn't come from the mandated curriculum. She designed it with her students and the community, and together they co-constructed experiences to meet the desired learning goals. Kim designed authentic, participatory, and relevant learning experiences for her unique population of students—and no technology can substitute for a teacher who is willing to make that kind of effort to provide optimal learning experiences for students.

As co-designers of learning experiences, teachers must continually evolve to meet the learners' needs with resources, opportunities, and the support of a community, so it makes sense that these kinds of teachers thrive in environments where they are empowered to be co-designers in their own learning as well.

Committed to support his teachers and shift from a program-focused to a learner-centered approach, David Miyashiro, superintendent of Cajon Valley Union School District, convened teachers across the district to develop a shared vision and co-design desired learning experiences. A program provider was scheduled for a three-hour session to help teachers better understand the resources and facilitate the design of the projects. About ten minutes into the workshop, it was clear she was disconnected from the audience and not meeting the needs of the group. He recognized the time would be better spent through the discovery of the resources rather than listening to someone talk about them. He stopped the presenter and redesigned the day to facilitate small groups of teachers to design the projects and explore the resources together. This signaled to teachers he valued their time and expertise. It also showed them that their superintendent knew them and knew that they weren't going to learn about how to create better learning experiences by listening to someone tell them what to do; they had to explore, discuss, and try out some things.

As a result, the teams of teachers dove into the resources, feeling valued and motivated to create something better for their students. Instead of using the prepackaged curriculum, they leveraged the expertise in the room to remix the ideas and build on what was provided to create learning experiences tailored to the students in their community. At the end of the three days together, the team was inspired and felt a deep sense of ownership for the work. They were excited to go back to their schools and share what they had developed with the their teammates and continue to build off what they had started.

Terry Grier, a great leader and retired superintendent, once told me, "Those who create the work support the work." For Dr. Miyashiro and his teachers, this shift was the beginning of empowering teachers to lead, and he has continued to develop the expertise of teachers to develop more leaders in the Cajon Valley Union School District.

Partners in Learning

As Kim Cawkwell's fourth-grade students collaborated with businesses to solve unique challenges, she learned alongside them. The students created novel solutions, and she encouraged them to think through the ideas while allowing them to explore and teach her what they were learning along the way.

When teachers embrace their roles as learners, everyone benefits. With so much information at our fingertips and new content and tools being created each day, our access to information continues to increase. Teachers don't have to know everything, but as partners in learning, they can model lifelong learning and empower students to explore their passions and interests while employing valuable skills. More importantly, they can learn to learn rather than solely consume information.

I love the example Annick Rauch, a first- and second-grade teacher, set for her students as a co-learner with them. She asked her students a question that is probably asked in many classrooms around the world: "What makes a good community?" Instead of taking the first responses and moving on, the question prompted in-depth exploration and opportunities to learn more about their own community. She shares the project in detail on her blog and highlights how she partnered with her students to learn about their community:[10]

> Discussions and research in the form of reading books followed to determine what in fact was a community. We then took several walks, taking pictures of our surroundings while noticing what details were included in our community. During our walks, we also visited three local businesses to learn a bit more about what types of services they provide to our community.

These first graders not only did extensive research but took what they learned and created a 3-D model of their community. This question could have been reduced to a "right" answer but instead became the launching point for questions and discoveries that inspired first graders to want to learn more.

Community Developers

Relationships are foundational to a learning community, and the teacher plays a pivotal role in developing relationships with individual students while also establishing a community where students form relationships with one another. In contrast to the

---

10   Annick Rauch, "Building SO Much More Than a 3D Community," *Annick Rauch blog.* May 31, 2017. http://www.annickrauch.ca/2017/05/31/building-so-much-more-than-a-3d-community.

teacher-directed classroom based on compliance, the structures Kim put in place, such as community guidelines and regular classroom meetings, empowered learners to work together, help students understand diverse perspectives, solve problems, and communicate effectively with one another as well as with others in the school and their local community.

If we want to ensure students have the skills needed to be successful and productive citizens, it is critical that we model and practice them in our classrooms, schools, and communities. Opening lines of communication to listen to and learn from people is an integral part of being an effective learning community rather than creating a vision and sharing it with all stakeholders. As Devin Vodicka, now the Chief Impact Officer for AltSchool, began the journey as the superintendent of Vista Unified School District to create a new model for teaching and learning, he intentionally brought people together to explore the possibilities and collectively define what personalized learning meant in their district. He created multiple avenues for diverse stakeholders to collaborate and learn from each other throughout the process.

In one of their regular personalized learning steering meetings, people shared how they were challenging the status quo—whether it was through creative scheduling, allocating resources, use of space, or what they were using (or not using) for curriculum. As the committee listened and even cheered each other on, nobody got "in trouble," and, as a result of the openness of the group, I noticed that people increasingly shared about their efforts. Students and parents alike spoke up to question ideas, too. In this and subsequent meetings, leaders, teachers, families, and others in the larger community pushed boundaries and supported each other to design learning experiences that meet the needs of their unique population.

Dr. Vodicka has worked to establish a learning community whose members support one another and are willing to challenge ideas to continue to innovate to improve student outcomes. Changing how we learn in school can be a struggle, and there is not always one right way. As one teacher told me, "Some days it seems as if there is nothing that is worth replicating, but I always learn from our challenges." Change is hard, but there are always lessons to be learned. Through collaboration, reflection, and multiple iterations, they look to evidence of impact on learners to inform next steps in powerful ways.

Connector

In her book, *Social LEADia*, Jennifer Casa-Todd highlights many examples of the impact students are making in their local communities and the world through online and face-to-face connections with others. She shared a poignant reflection from two students, Alfred and Catherine, on the power of connection.

> To us, connection is more than just connecting online. We connect at school, in teams, and with teachers. When we connect, we feel that we are using our voices to make a positive impact, and when we connect, we are learning new ideas and perspectives. When we add these up, we are making a difference in our own world and maybe in someone else's.[11]

Understanding the power of students learning from one another as well as experts in the field, Kim Cawkwell designed opportunities for students to connect with one another in the class as well as with people and resources that could provide information and ideas beyond what she knew or could offer herself. She encouraged students to set up meetings with local businesses, and she provided a framework that empowered them to solve relevant problems. This learning experience activated students' questions and required them

---

11 Jennifer Casa-Todd, *Social LEADia* (San Diego, CA: Dave Burgess Consulting, Inc., 2017).

to conduct research, work together, and create a product to meet the needs of their business partners. Through diverse experiences and learning opportunities, students built on their prior knowledge and strengths to design a product for a business. Her role wasn't to provide all the information but to connect students to the community and resources that empowered them to develop the skills, knowledge, and dispositions to solve authentic problems.

Teachers can connect with one another and with experts in various ways. One such opportunity is the Global Read Aloud created by Pernille Ripp, a middle-school language-arts teacher in Wisconsin. Every year, since 2010, she selects a book and invites teachers around the world to read it aloud to their students over a six-week period and to connect with others who are reading the same book to inspire diverse perspectives and connections for teachers and students. Teachers can decide how much or how little they want to be involved based on their goals and students. Some use digital tools such as Skype, Twitter, WriteAbout, or Edmodo, while other educators decide what works best for them. Ultimately, the goal is that "teachers get a community of other educators to do a global project with, hopefully inspiring them to continue these connections through the year."[12] Through these connections, students' worlds can expand as educators inspire learners to make a difference in their lives and in the lives of others.

Activator

Research from John Hattie, author of *Visible Learning*, shows significant impact on student outcomes when teachers guide them on their learning path by providing opportunities for feedback, goal setting, verbalizing, and monitoring their own learning.[13]

---

12   Frequently Asked Questions, *The Global Read Aloud*, accessed January 30, 2018, https://theglobalreadaloud.com/for-participants/frequently-asked-questions.

13   John Hattie, *Visible Learning: A Synthesis of over 800 Meta-Analyses Relating to Achievement* (New York: Routledge Publication, 2010).

Genius Hour or 20% Time (a concept based on Google's model of providing time for workers to explore a project or passion of theirs that could benefit the company) is an excellent example of this kind of learning. A.J. Juliani, co-author of *LAUNCH*, created a 20% Time project in his eleventh-grade classroom because he believes these types of projects give students the chance to learn with purpose and make something for a real audience. The goal for any Genius Hour experience is for students to own the learning and explore their passions and questions. But that doesn't mean teachers take a hands-off approach to teaching during this time. In fact, just because they aren't providing the answers doesn't mean they aren't guiding and supporting the learning process. According to A.J., "The teacher has to be more active in this learning experience than anything else. Because students need coaching. They need to be connected to the right resources, to the right people. They need help on their projects. There are going to be pitfalls and failures, and they need someone there to kind of say that's okay, that's what it's all about."[14]

People commonly say that we need to be facilitators of learning, but I think learner-centered teaching goes beyond simple facilitation. One of the major evolutions of education as related to the role of teachers as activators is that our methods can and should move flexibly from direct teaching to collaborative or facilitative approaches based on the needs of the learners and the desired goals.

This type of self-directed learning should not be reserved just for students; teachers and administrators want to lead their own learning experiences and explore passions and interests that relate to their classrooms too. In collaboration with his staff, Joe Sanfelippo, superintendent in Fall Creek School District, created a professional learning model based on Joseph Campbell's *Hero's*

---

14   Jennifer Gonzales, "What is 20% time?" *Cult of Pedagogy*, Oct. 16, 2014, https://www.cultofpedagogy.com/20-time-ajjuliani.

Journey. In this district, the journey begins with a call to adventure or the development of a goal. As educators begin working on their goals, a heavy emphasis is placed on the importance of a mentor or helper. As they learn and grow, the peak of the journey is the revelation, and with feedback and support, the transformation is when practice changes and goals are reached.

This plan was co-designed by teachers and aims to activate educators to lead their own learning process that includes goal setting, ample opportunities for coaching and feedback, and diverse experiences based on personal goals that are relevant or connected to the district goals. Whether at the administrative or classroom level, an activator creates the context or provides the provocation to spark the learner and provides guidance and support throughout the process.

These examples highlight educators who have embraced change in diverse contexts and evolved to meet the needs of the learners they serve to create experiences that inspire curiosity and unleash talent. In the face of change, there are two ways to react:

1. The primal response: How can I maintain the status quo and protect myself from risk or failure?

2. The evolutionary response: How can I learn from my surroundings and adapt to improve? What do I need to stop doing? What might I start doing?

Focus on Learning and Learners

As expectations for education change, I am often asked about how to deal with resistant teachers and administrators alike. My response to both is always the same: Focus on the students and how to collectively create learning experiences based on a shared understanding of what we want students to know and to be able to do. I rarely meet educators who are against doing what's right for the students they serve. In fact, the opportunity to make an impact drives many people to become educators.

According to the report "Listen to Us: Teacher Views and Voices,"[15] which surveyed more than three thousand public school teachers, 82 percent say that making a difference in students' lives is one of the most rewarding aspects of teaching. In my experience, when teachers are resistant (or perceived as resistant), it is often because their experiences, beliefs, and expertise are not aligned with the desired changes in teaching and learning. The beliefs teachers hold directly impact their actions and decision-making in the classroom and can influence the way in which they design learning experiences. Most educators in today's schools and district offices went through their own education without the access and opportunities that modern technology affords. People don't always know what's possible and can't imagine doing something differently until they experience it. Which is why, as I mentioned earlier, if we want to change how students learn, we have to change how teachers learn.

> ## *When the focus is on learning, and what's best for learners, we look for solutions.*

This truth about the need to experience what's possible with new technologies and teaching methods was made explicitly clear to me when I was working with a team of self-described digital immigrants (a term used to describe people who did not grow up

---

15   Diane Stark Rentner, Nancy Kober, and Matthew Frizzell, "Listen to Us: Teacher Views and Voices," *Center on Education Policy*, Washington, DC, 2016, https://www.cep-dc.org/displayDocument.cfm?DocumentID=1456.

with technology) who were not convinced that the new district initiative to give Chromebooks to each student would benefit their classrooms. They believed their students really needed to focus on basic skills, so integrating technology was not high on their priority list. One teacher told me point blank, "I am not using technology in my class." I listened to their concerns and asked them what challenges they were facing in their classrooms. Writing was a primary area of concern among the group.

Based on their goals, I offered some resources to review, and we agreed to collaborate on a few lessons they would be teaching in the next few weeks. The first step/obstacle was logging into their G Suite. Some complained about accessing the tools years ago with little success; some had felt chastised by others for not knowing about the tools. They were frustrated for many reasons, but we focused on the goal: helping their students. It took twenty minutes for some of them to log in, while others logged in quickly and began creating and sharing Google Docs or helping their peers access their accounts. Once everyone was logged in, I showed them how to create a folder so that they could begin sharing resources for their upcoming units. They quickly began to imagine what their students could do with these tools, and the questions came flying. How do I share with my class? Can the students do *this*? Another teacher experimented with a form and another with slides. The mood shifted as they realized writing and technology are not mutually exclusive learning outcomes. The hands-on practice made them a little less afraid of the technology and more excited to explore the possibilities in their classrooms. Taking the time to meet the teachers where they were and allowing *them* to be learners and immerse themselves in new learning experiences empowered them to imagine the possibilities for students in their own classrooms. Once they saw the benefits, there was no way they were going to keep these powerful learning opportunities from their students.

The problem wasn't really that they were resistant. Rather, they had been told they were receiving Chromebooks and that they were supposed to integrate technology, but they didn't know why or how to do that. They were frustrated and couldn't see how they were going to add one more thing into their day, how they were going to learn to use new tools, or how they were going to figure out how to teach when each of their students had their own device. Their initial frustrations mirror those of educators around the world. Learning more about the tools by using them helped eliminate many of their concerns. When we focus on the tools, we can easily concentrate on the challenges without a clear understanding of the goal or benefit, but when the focus is on learning, we look for solutions. Taking the time to explore the benefits and understand why we need to change can have a dramatic impact on how educators see their roles and the power to improve learning for their students.

A focus on technology further alienates those who are hesitant to experiment with innovative practices. If we as leaders and educators fail to focus on learning without providing a clear understanding of why these new approaches are important, we are just adding to teachers' already crowded plates. We will also continue to waste a lot of time and money on new programs and tools if we don't collectively understand the demand for a paradigm shift in education and the evolving role of educators.

As the role of the educator evolves, the human connection and guidance will become increasingly more— not less—important.

Concluding Thoughts

Learners have more access than ever to information through technology. As such, the role the of educator has and will continue to shift. No longer do students need to access teachers for content, but they desperately need teachers to guide them as they develop the skills, knowledge, and dispositions to be lifelong learners and critical consumers. Students need teachers to help them make sense of information so that they can create new and better ideas that will move us all forward.

As teachers, your greatest power comes from knowing your learners. A personal understanding of your students empowers you to design learning experiences that connect students with their passions and strengths to help them find their place in the world. As the role of the educator evolves, the human connection and guidance will become increasingly more—not less—important.

Reflect and Connect Challenge
Share your thoughts, questions, and ideas using #LCInnovation

O Do you have an evolutionary response to change? Examine your practices and consider the following questions: How can I learn from my surroundings and adapt to improve? What do I need to stop doing? What might I start doing?

O Examine the evolving role of the teacher with your team. What are your areas of strength? What are some next steps? What would you modify or add?

O How do learners in your context feel? Conduct focus groups or meet ups with a variety of students to understand their experiences. Are they caught in the middle? Share what you learn from your students and what you can do differently.

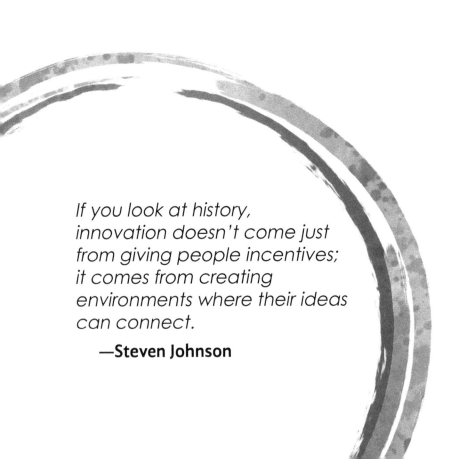

If you look at history, innovation doesn't come just from giving people incentives; it comes from creating environments where their ideas can connect.

—Steven Johnson

The Innovation Ecosystem

EACH YEAR, THE TENTH GRADERS in Matt Martin's chemistry classes improve and expand their knowledge about chemistry as well as how to design, create, and market products for their soap company. When Matt began teaching at High Tech High, he changed as an educator in powerful ways. I know this because Matt is not just a teacher whom I see periodically, he is my husband, and I saw day in and day out the impact that the new environment had on him personally and professionally. Some might think that having students run a soap company is an unconventional approach to teaching chemistry, but he has seen the effect it has had on students and says he would never go back to teaching any other way. Why would he when he hears comments from his students such as this?

"I walked into this class knowing nothing about chemistry; now I feel like I have learned so much and am more interested in chemistry. I even want to do experiments on my own time now that I have been introduced to and shown how to run an experiment."

Matt was featured in Google's It Takes a Teacher campaign, and they highlighted the impact he has had on his students.

Many of Matt's students have also discovered the intersection of their skills and interests. By merging students' various interests—whether in math or English—Matt created a classroom experience like no other. "I've learned so much more than just science or making soap," said another tenth-grader, "I've also learned about the dynamics of entrepreneurship. There was nothing more satisfying than watching people buy and admire something that I made."[16] Students haven't just earned experiences, though; they've earned profits as well.

Over the past few years, Matt has worked with Real World Scholars, a non-profit organization that provides tools and resources to facilitate the process of starting a business for teachers and their students. As a result, students have expanded the Wicked Soap Company (wickedsoapcompany.com) with each new class of tenth graders. While other classes are strapped for resources and asking for donations, these students have learned to make and sell thousands of bars of soap as part of their chemistry class. They are not preparing to make a difference someday; they are making an impact today. They are learning and developing the skills for continued success that they will use and build on throughout their lives. As they have developed their own business, not only have they learned skills that allow them to better interact with the community and their classmates, they are also doing authentic work that

---

16   Melissa Horwitz, "How One Teacher Discovered the Perfect Teaching Tool – A Business," *Center on Education Policy*, June 24, 2016, https://www.blog.google/topics/education/how-one-teacher-discovered-the-perfect-teaching-tool-a-business.

has earned enough money to fund the business, provide supplies for their classroom, and give back to the school community. They decide as a group how to spend and invest their proceeds. As an example, when a community member's house burned down, they made a class decision to donate all their income to support the family. Students have also been able to pay for team activities like attending Padres games with their proceeds. Additionally, they have provided scholarships for fellow students and have donated more than a thousand bars of soap to local homeless shelters.

I highlight Matt and his student's accomplishments not only because they are changing the vision of what's possible in school but because Matt almost left education after his tenth year of teaching due to his frustration with the mandates, bureaucratic systems, and lack of resources and support. He felt unhappy and ineffective as part of a system that pushed groups of uninspired and disconnected kids through school. Thankfully, instead of quitting, he applied to teach at High Tech High, an innovative, project-based learning school in San Diego, and decided to give teaching one last chance. Back then, he would have described himself as a traditional teacher. So when he had the opportunity to teach at such a forward-thinking school, he felt anxious about what he would need to learn and how he would have to change his habits to design authentic and relevant learning experiences. He wondered if he was even capable of doing things differently than he had been accustomed to in all his years of teaching.

In those early years at High Tech High, he worked harder than I have ever seen him work: visiting families of students, asking tons of questions, and seeking feedback on new ideas while collaborating with his colleagues. He was inspired to design projects and connect with students in a way I had never seen. The context of where he was teaching and the culture that allowed for (and even demanded) risk taking and innovation ignited his passion when he saw how his students excelled as they took on authentic projects and challenges.

Five years later, he still loves his job and continues to push his thinking to find new and better ways to teach. Matt's experience elevates how the culture of his school has made a tremendous impact on how he perceives his role as an educator and on how he learns and teaches. The shift in his practice didn't happen by chance. He is a trusted professional and is provided both informal and formal opportunities to learn and empowered to take on leadership roles to develop new programs and opportunities for his students. As a valued member of the High Tech High community, he took on new responsibilities and took it upon himself to learn and try new things. He continues to experiment with his students, and in addition to chemistry and the engineering-design process, they learn things like why black soap is not very marketable or what packaging is most economical and professional. Experimenting and pushing his and his students' thinking are part of what keeps learning fun and relevant.

I know what you are thinking because I have heard it over and over: *Well, that's High Tech High. We can't do that at my school because (list any number of reasons).* While I don't disagree that real, challenging, and seemingly insurmountable factors exist in many schools today, educators in diverse contexts choose to find ways to change how they lead, teach, and learn. And you can too. The leaders at High Tech High have the same regulations and expectations but have designed systems that prioritize learning over compliance.

A simple example of how best intentions and research in education can actually promote compliance rather than learning is the common practice of posting the standard or learning objective on the board. When I was in the classroom, multiple people walked through with the district checklist. The first item was "standards/learning objectives are posted," and so to comply with the mandate,

I posted the learning objectives each day. I even made magnets to organize my board so that it would be easy to fill in the learning objective and aligned activities for the day. I told students our objective for the day, cited the standard(s) and then explained what we were doing so that it made sense to them. This was an act of compliance.

Educators in diverse contexts choose to find ways to change how they lead, teach, and learn. And you can too.

When I visited other classrooms as an instructional coach, I saw objectives posted. I too was expected to mark a box indicating whether the teacher had complied as a measure of their performance. Sometimes it was even mandated that the students be able to repeat the objective. Then one day at a workshop while discussing the purpose of this practice, I had a lightbulb moment. *The reason "they" make teachers put the standards and learning objectives on the board is because when students know what they are supposed to be learning or where they are headed, that knowledge impacts student engagement and achievement.*

While this practice is substantiated by research and makes sense in practice, the roll out of this message and the purpose of putting your objective on the board was buried in the mandate communicated to site leaders and in turn to teachers in the form of a walkthrough checklist. My *aha* moment shifted my conversations with teachers from a compliance stance about ensuring the objective for the lesson was posted to a coaching conversation about how they were helping students understand the desired learning goals, where they are in relationship to the learning goals, and how students could reach their goals. Understanding the purpose (beyond compliance) for posting objectives got teachers excited about finding authentic ways to share and co-create learning goals with students. The lesson here is this: If we don't pay attention to the systems we design and how they impact learning, they can become hurdles to jump over instead of supporting the teaching and learning that they were intended to create.

Creating Better Systems for Learning

As a company, Amazon has repeatedly evolved to meet the needs of customers and to create and nurture an ecosystem that has changed how we buy and sell products. To avoid becoming irrelevant like Kodak as I wrote about earlier in the book, Jeff Bezos, founder and CEO of Amazon, described in his 2016 annual letter to stakeholders the importance of four key practices: 1) customer obsession, 2) a skeptical view of proxies, 3) the eager adoption of external trends, and 4) high-velocity decision making."[17]

High Tech High takes a similar approach in that one of the main differences between the organization and other innovative school districts is how it works with intentionality to remove barriers and give control to those closest to the learners. The constant focus is on evolving to meet the needs of all learners. Schools are not businesses, and I certainly don't think they should be, but Bezos's advice prompted me to think about the implications for complex education systems and what we could learn about innovation and adaptability to evolve beyond the industrial model and ward off a slow death due to irrelevance in our education system.

---

17   Jeff Bezos, "2016 Letter to Stakeholders," *Amazon*, Seattle, 2016, https://www.amazon.com/p/feature/z6o9g6sysxur57t.

Stay Focused on Learners and Learning

Jeff Bezos argues that obsessive customer focus is the key to keeping Amazon innovative. This focus keeps them continually looking to create new and better models to meet the customers' needs. What if we were obsessively learner focused in schools? We can easily focus on test scores, curriculum, programs, or even technology, but when we stay focused on the learners, all of these tools and measurements become secondary—part of what we do but not why we do it. We can have the latest technology or the best curriculum, but if we are not obsessed with who learners are, how to best serve them, and how to partner with them to move forward, we can fail to make the impact that we desire and are working so hard to achieve.

Part of being learner obsessed is ensuing that the teachers have time, support, and trust to do what is best for learners in their classrooms and throughout the school. As a great number of demands are placed on teachers, teacher retention and burnout is increasing, and the revolving door, in many cases, negatively impacts the schools and their students. Not surprisingly, teachers leave schools where they are not supported or valued or feel ill equipped or unable to meet students' needs. We can prevent this by looking for ways to create the conditions that empower all learners and inspire leaders rather than demand followers.

Focus on Why, Not Just What

To operate efficiently and to make sure that we serve those in our classrooms and schools, we often create processes to facilitate work. The problem is that when we stop looking at desired outcomes for learners and focus on implementing curriculum or teaching the standards, we get the process right but don't always achieve the results we want. An example of such a process comes when we focus on report cards and grades rather than on helping the learner understand where they are and how to improve. The reporting becomes the focus along with the completed number of records and assignments rather than the actual experiences and feedback that inform the learner and document and share learning and growth.

"The process is not the thing," Bezos argues. "It's always worth asking, do we own the process or does the process own us?"[18] We must continually refer to the outcomes we want for students, and those outcomes must go beyond test scores and grades if we want to develop learners and improve their trajectory in life. Our question must be, "How do the systems we use serve to develop the skills and mindsets of learners and empower them to find their place in the world?"

In 2016, I had the privilege of seeing Pam Moran, a visionary superintendent of Albemarle County Public Schools, give her TEDx talk, "Hacking School: Getting Ourselves to YES."[19] She talked about supporting her students, teachers, and administrators by removing barriers and overcoming her discomfort by saying, "yes," and taking risks. She acknowledged that she has faced challenges as many of us do moving from the "yeah but" mentality to "what if?" Pam shared an example about students who worked with their teachers to redesign their school's cafeteria. The students and teachers received support from their administrators, who were willing to take some risks. As a result of the district working to get to yes, students were empowered to create new seating options in the cafeteria. Later when they decided to build mobile treehouse structures, Pam acknowledged she had some concerns about using power tools and what students were learning, but when teachers told her that the students were using more complex math than ever before and that students who

---

18   Jeff Bezos, "2016 Letter to Stakeholders."

19   Pam Moran, "Hacking School: Getting Ourselves to YES," TEDx Talk, El Cajon, CA, May 9, 2016, https://www.youtube.com/watch?v=_2MtUegl7YI.

were not typically successful in other classes were leading the project, she realized the risk was worth the reward.

Look Beyond Schools

In a world that is rapidly changing, we are constantly inundated with *more* and *new*. Bezos believes that we are better off adopting new trends than we are if we attempt to ignore or prevent them. "If you fight them, you're probably fighting the future. Embrace them and you have a tailwind," he says. For example, we can embrace how our students use social media and help build their digital leadership skills, or we can fight the use of devices in our schools and leave it to chance that they develop fundamental skills for learning and citizenship. In service of what has always been done, a lot of energy in schools is spent fighting the emerging trends in the world. Even though the intention is to protect students, we might actually be doing them a disservice.

Embracing new trends is not about trying every new app or trying to stay ahead of the curve, which is likely impossible and unsustainable. Our best chances for staying current come when we allow students to teach us and when we embrace what is meaningful to them and for their learning. Does this mean you need to use every form of social media? No, but you can make an effort to connect school to the world we live in, and in doing so, expand the learning environment beyond the classroom. Staying abreast of what trends are and how people are interacting will help create powerful learning experiences in and out of the classroom by bringing experts into the classroom in person and virtually and by sharing learning with others. A big part of embracing new trends is looking beyond schools and partnering with businesses and the community, acknowledging that we don't know it all. As the world evolves, we will need to embrace more, not less. We can no longer dig our heels into the ground because "we have always done it this way."

High-Quality, High-Velocity Decision Making

To make high-quality decisions quickly and create forward movement, Bezos uses a process called "disagree and commit." The practice relies on the assumption that not everyone will always agree, but it's still possible for people who disagree to work toward the same goal. An example he provides is when he disagreed with a plan to move forward on an Amazon Prime show while his team wanted to go ahead. Bezos responded, "I disagree and commit and hope it becomes the most watched thing we've ever made." He's willing to disagree and commit because he believes that waiting for consensus slows the decision-making cycle.

He's right. Waiting for consensus can be a huge barrier to change in schools. Although schools need to develop a shared vision, often the best way to move forward and learn from the process is through action. Vice President of Learning and Development at Discovery Education, Karen Beerer, shares that part of the challenge with waiting for buy-in and consensus is that people don't always see what is possible. She urges leaders to understand that, "while consensus and collaborative decision making is important, it can also be paralyzing to innovation. Understanding the balance between growing buy-in and launching innovation has never been more important than in today's era."[20] Articulating the vision and explicitly defining expectations points everybody in the same direction. Although individuals will fall on different points in the continuum and their paths will vary, everyone should be learning and growing to work toward common goals. As Amber Teamann, principal of Wylie Elementary School, frames it, "You can crawl, you can walk, or you can run, you just can't stand still."[21]

---

20   Karen Beerer, "Greatest Lesson: Teacher Buy in Is Overrated," *eSchool News,* 2017. Accessed Nov. 30, 2017, https://eschoolnews.com/2017/04/12/teacher-buy-overrated.

21   Amber Teamann, "Leading Within the Box, #IMMOOC Week 2", *Love, Learn, Lead,* March 8, 2017. Accessed December 18, 2017, http://technicallyteamann.com/leading-within-box-immooc-week-2.

When one-size-fits-all reform movements and top-down mandates define the expectations for all, it's easy to overlook or altogether miss the needs of some learners. Likewise, these sweeping mandates can have unintended consequences. Consider these examples from Dr. Yong Zhao in his article, "What Works Can Hurt: Side Effects in Education":[22]

> "This program helps improve your students' reading scores, but it may make them hate reading forever." No such information is given to teachers or school principals.
>
> "This practice can help your children become a better student, but it may make her less creative." No parent has been given information about effects and side effects of practices in schools.
>
> "School choice may improve test scores of some students, but it can lead to the collapse of American public education," the public has not received information about the side effects of sweeping education policies.

Research in education has overwhelmingly focused on the benefits of the programs, policies, and practices while too often failing to acknowledge the adverse side effects. As Dr. Zhao argues, side effects we hear about in medicine are just as prominent in education, yet the expectation to study and report them is far less common. To mitigate unintended consequences in classrooms and schools, we cannot continue to make overarching decisions and mandates from afar. High-quality instructional decisions require that we provide time and resources to cultivate educational leaders who have the skills and the mindset to question and problem solve and who continually learn to improve.

---

22   Yong Zhao, "What Works Can Hurt: Side Effects In Education," *Yong Zhao*, Feb. 17, 2017, http://zhaolearning.com/2017/02/17/what-works-can-hurt-side-effects-in-education.

Innovation Ecosystem

The interplay between an individual and his or her environment shapes their development. This means that the past experiences, beliefs, and values we hold influence our perceptions of the world. As educators and learners, we exist within an ecosystem: a complex network or interconnected system that is impacted by national, state, and local contexts. Each district, school, and classroom comprise unique ecosystems that influence opportunities for learning and innovation. To realize desired shifts in teaching and learning in all schools and classrooms, we need to examine the context that exists to support the evolving role of the teacher.

- **Innovation Ecosystem:** the culture, values, vision, and policies that influence the learning context and the development of desired knowledge, skills, and mindsets

- **Learning Experiences:** the models, experiences, and learning opportunities that exist for learners

- **Learner**: the individuals who possess or work to develop the knowledge, skills, and mindsets

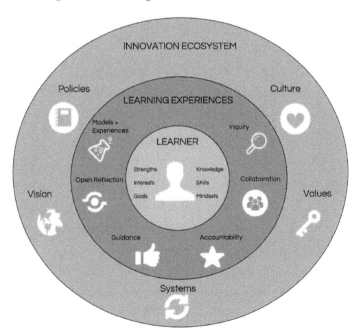

I often ask administrators and teachers this question: Are your systems designed for people to comply and implement your programs and policies, or are your systems designed to empower people to learn, improve, and innovate?

Usually, they give a long reflective pause and an audible acknowledgment that many of the expectations are based on compliance. The truth is that the dominating model of change in education relies on top-down reform programs of practices that have "worked" in another context that teachers are expected to replicate in diverse contexts. This often results in compliance rather than learning, growth, and innovation. A stronger, more effective model for change would empower teachers to learn about new methods and adapt them to their own unique context.

Organizational culture often dictates how people are treated and what we expect of them. These beliefs about people and their inherent motivation drives how we design systems and how we interact with each other. To highlight two contrasting orientations, Douglas McGregor describes these two approaches as Theory X and Theory Y in his book *The Human Side of Enterprise.*[23]

Theory X organizations are driven by the belief that people need to be motivated with carrot-and-stick systems. Theory X assumes that people:

- Dislike their work
- Avoid responsibility and need constant direction
- Need to be controlled and supervised
- Lack ambition and incentives and need to be enticed by rewards to achieve goals

Consider how Theory X might look in schools. A principal is expected to comply with district mandates and, in turn, she expects

---

[23] Douglas McGregor, *The Human Side of Enterprise* (New York: McGraw-Hill Professional, 2008).

the same from her teachers, and her teachers will, most likely, expect the same from their students. Students might comply but will lack engagement and certainly won't be empowered. Students lack opportunities to learn in ways that build on their strengths and interests and become more disengaged. These kinds of schools fail to develop the skills and mindsets needed today, so the schools are labeled as failing; new programs are created to fix the problem, and new compliance-based mandates are handed down to principals, teachers, and students—and then the cycle continues.

Theory Y organizations operate from the belief that people take pride in their work and are motivated when they are encouraged to take ownership of their work. These organizations provide systems for people to take greater responsibility and experience opportunities to grow rather than be controlled.

Theory Y assumes that people:

- Are self-motivated to complete their tasks
- Enjoy being involved in decision-making and taking ownership of their work
- Take responsibility for work and see it as fulfilling and challenging
- Solve problems creatively and imaginatively

Consider how Theory Y might look in schools. A district sets a clear vision and allows principals autonomy to work with the community to make the best decisions for their school to achieve the desired vision. Similarly, she empowers teachers to make decision in their classrooms and teams based on what students need. Everyone works together to learn and improve, and students are part of the decision-making process. All learners have opportunities to build on their strengths and interests and are eager to find and solve problems. In classrooms, teachers develop the skills and mindsets needed today, and in schools, the staff collectively works to improve the trajectory of all learners. In these schools, educators are empowered to make informed decisions that create the best learning experiences for all learners—and the cycle continues.

Of course, neither the Theory X or Theory Y scenarios presented above are as straightforward as they seem. Complex situations exist within our education systems, and you can likely find examples and reasons for both leadership styles. Whatever your position, some external mandates are out of your control, but, within your sphere of influence, you have the power to change how you lead and empower others. You can't expect to develop creative and innovative thinkers when you micromanage every move. If we go back to the example of Matt's classroom, the Wicked Soap company has evolved because the ecosystem has been intentionally designed to create a learner-centered, inclusive approach that supports and challenges each student. The vision is for students to pursue passions through authentic, interdisciplinary projects to engage in work that matters to them and the world. Based on this vision, Matt designs projects that meet the needs of his students. He has time built in to his day to collaborate with colleagues to learn and plan to meet the emerging needs of learners throughout the projects. Matt seeks input from his students to design learning experiences that build off the individual strengths, interests, and passions of his students, and they are empowered to learn, create, and build their business. And they continue to do so because it matters to them and others.

Think about your vision and what you truly want for students when they leave your classroom, your school, or your district. Then think about the alignment between that vision, the dominant beliefs, and accountability systems that govern the procedures and policies in your classrooms, schools, and districts. Do you emphasize high-stakes test scores as sole measures of accountability or do you value measures of growth and outcomes aligned to your vision? What you measure and value influences the type of learners and citizens your systems are designed to create.

Learning Experiences

Learning Experiences, the second layer of the ecosystem, is about how and what people learn. To truly integrate new learning, it is critical to carve out time to allow for trial and error, collaboration, and especially coaching and feedback. The application of the new learning breeds innovative ideas and practices that work for each unique context and begin to make an impact for the learners across schools and classrooms.

In most education systems today, the procedures and policies still convey the message that educators should "sit and get" rather than engage in ongoing activities that foster learning as a part of the work day. An educator commented in a community Facebook group on the irony of professional learning that still exists in many schools.

"One of the most memorable professional learning days in my career was a day when all teachers from the entire district were brought together. We sat in a large gym at tables while two presenters talked to us for an entire day about—wait for it—differentiation. The complete disconnect between the topic and the mode of presentation was mind-blowing to me. I was expected to consume what was presented to not just me, but to hundreds of people in the same way, assuming the same level of understanding for all."

When subjected to or dependent upon a "sit and get" model ourselves, we then, in turn, expect students in the classroom to learn the same way.

The teacher-leader standards highlight that, "An effective teacher is the strongest in-school predictor of student achievement. Teachers teach more effectively when they work in professional cultures where their opinions and input are valued. In such environments, administrators support teachers as they exchange ideas and strategies, problem-solve collaboratively, and consult with expert colleagues."[24] Yet when a random sample of teachers in the United States were asked as part of the Gallup Daily Tracking survey if they believed their opinions counted, teachers scored at the bottom compared with twelve other occupational groups, and only 30 percent of teachers report being "actively engaged" in their jobs. This lack of engagement ties in closely to feeling undervalued and mistrusted as professionals. When those closest to the learners have intimate knowledge of the day-to-day context and the evolving needs of the learners, yet limited decision making power, we miss out on powerful opportunities for learning in our schools.

Accountability systems that are grounded in control and compliance, where teachers and administrators look at data to determine what students learned and what they didn't in order to re-teach specific content and skills or maintain fidelity in a curriculum, might be sufficient if the end goal is passing a test. But if our goal is to develop productive thinkers and learners, as I argue it should be, we have to move beyond collecting and analyzing data to sort kids and penalize the educators. Instead, we need to create structures to gather and make informed decision about learning and learners based on evidence to ensure growth related to desired outcomes. Insights and the learning experiences are so much more powerful and meaningful when they come from the teachers and the learners based on the expectations, goals, and desire to meet the needs of the learners they serve. When teachers and administrators work together to analyze student work samples, assess strengths, and determine next steps, these learning experiences help everyone to continuously improve.

---

24   Gene Wilhoit, "The Vision," *Teacher Leader Model Standards*, May 2011, Accessed Nov. 30, 2017, http://www.teacherleaderstandards.org/the_vision.

The Learner: Developing Knowledge, Skills, and Mindsets

At the core of the ecosystem and the work of educators is the learner. In an effort to leverage the evolving tools to change how students learn in her district, Dr. Candace Singh, superintendent in Fallbrook Union Elementary School District (FUESD), convened site-based leadership teams over the course of the school year to collectively explore diverse models, learn about new tools and resources, and create a shared vision and aligned expectations among teachers and administrators in the district. Based on the shared expectations, each principal worked with their site-based team to create their own plan that reflected the strengths and needs of their school community to meet the desired goals. This approach with clear goals and expectations can provide a structure while still allowing for those closest to the learners to make decisions that foster improvement through reciprocal accountability rather than top-down management.

Consistently, the FUESD leadership team echoed that, "The importance of the shared outcomes is that they inform all of us what our goals are when creating learning experiences with our students. The four shared outcomes keep us focused on the end goals of our assignment or project not only when we're planning, but for our students as well when they are learning." When teachers and administrators have a clear understanding of what they want students to know and do and share collective responsibility for student outcomes, yet have autonomy to get there in a way that makes sense in their context, it improves investment in the process as well as increases personal satisfaction.

A robust, job-embedded culture of professional learning and innovation ensures that educators continually develop and refine practices to meet the needs of the learners they serve. When teachers develop deep expertise and are empowered to influence decisions that impact the school and their classroom, they create environments where students' voices are honored and the learners are empowered. Barnett Barry, the CEO of Center for Teacher Quality, highlights Social Justice Humanities Academy (SJHA),[25] an urban high school in Los Angeles that serves a high-needs population, and illustrates this truth in his paper "Teacher Leadership and Deeper Learning for All Students." Given a voice in the curriculum, instruction, and design of the learning experiences, SJHA teachers embrace these roles, and the impact of teacher leadership is evident in how the students explain their experience. Here is one student's assessment of SJHA:

> At first when I came here, I was a little thrown off by the amount of respect I received . . . I wasn't just treated as a student; I was treated as a person. In middle school, it was always like, "You're the student; I'm the teacher. I have more power over you." And here it's not like that. And I feel like that's what makes students grow. It's transformational . . . you grow to respect other people.[26]

When administrators and teachers work together, everyone wins—especially students. Collaboration between administrators, teachers, and students can help everyone learn, implement, refine, and share ideas that improve learning for adults and students. Teachers like Matt and those at SJHA, who are integral in the decisions around curriculum scheduling, hiring, and student discipline, are more invested in the process and outcomes. Teacher leaders can serve as linchpins that move systems and structures to a culture of learning and make a significant impact for those they serve in their unique context.

---

25   Barnett Berry, "Teacher leadership & deeper learning for all students," *Center for Teaching Quality,* Accessed Nov. 30, 2017, https://www.scribd.com/doc/303397058/CTQCollab-DeeperLearning.

26   Barnett Berry, "Teacher leadership & deeper learning for all students," *Center for Teaching Quality,* Accessed Nov. 30, 2017, https://www.teachingquality.org/deeper-learning.

Working with students every day, teachers can provide great insight into the utility of new strategies, structures, and resources. SJHA teachers teach interdisciplinary courses and co-design the curriculum as a team. Barnett notes that, "When math scores dropped by five percent, teachers worked together to integrate math subjects for students in every grade; thanks to the teacher-powered model, they had the curricular authority to make a quick shift in policy and practice." Involving teachers as decision makers can help ensure that teachers are not only complying and implementing new strategies but that they are improving teaching and learning in the classrooms.

Empowered teachers empower their students.

It's human nature that, the more stressful and the higher stakes, the more we—in whatever role we serve—try to control the situation. Fighting this urge, however, and giving control to those directly impacted by or involved in the situation will have a far more positive effect than delivering mandates. This handing over of control can be done in small steps. For example, one teacher provided her students with a choice of formats for an assignment, such as songs, websites, blogs, videos, or their own format, rather than requiring that everyone write an essay. After taking a risk and trying out some new strategies, she told me that, "Although I had faith that my students would produce quality work for this assignment, what they produced exceeded my expectations. Perhaps I should not have been surprised; for when you give students a sense of ownership and choice over their learning, the creativity this unleashes often leads to great results. The results of this assignment make me want to develop similar projects in the future." More often than not, empowered teachers empower their students. They will challenge themselves to learn more, not because they have to in order to comply with a mandate but because it is necessary for them to learn more in order to create what they have in mind. When we give people control to make decisions that impact their work, they begin to take risks and trust themselves and most often will exceed expectations.

Concluding Thoughts

Scaling innovation requires spreading a mindset, not just a footprint, note Bob Sutton and Huggy Rao, Stanford professors and authors of *Scaling Up Excellence*. They found that across diverse organizations, "scaling depends on believing and living a shared mindset throughout your group, division, or organization . . . spreading and updating a mindset requires relentless vigilance. It requires stating the beliefs and living the behavior, and then doing so again and again."[27] Innovation flourishes when teachers collaborate on best practices; are provided opportunities to question, learn, and explore new methods; and are guided by a common vision and support. Day-to-day interactions within the ecosystem impact what teachers believe, how they learn, and how they design opportunities and experiences for their students. To this end, professional learning is not something that can exist in isolation or be checked off by attending events and team meetings. To create a culture of learning and innovation for all, meaningful experiences for all learners must be situated in an ecosystem that redefines how we measure success, prioritizes learning at all levels, and is always evolving to meet the needs of those we serve. Change in education is about creating better ecosystems for learning and innovation, not just better programs or tools.

---

27   Bob Sutton and Huggy Rao, *Scaling Up Excellence: Getting to More Without Settling for Less* (United Kingdom: Random House Business, 2015).

Reflect and Connect Challenge
Share your thoughts, questions, and ideas using #LCInnovation

O Are people expected to comply, or are they empowered to solve problems and innovate? What type of people is your ecosystem designed to create?

O Examine your Innovation Ecosystem. What are the strengths? Where are there opportunities for growth?

O What is a shift you can make now to foster a culture of learning rather than compliance?

*Culture is not the
most important thing,
it's the only thing.*

—Jim Sinegal

Designing the Culture for Learning and Innovation

IN THE 2013–2014 SCHOOL YEAR, I was on Washington Middle School's campus regularly. I was supervising teacher candidates at a local university, and as the newest member of the team, I ended up being placed at Washington—the most challenging of schools.

I vividly remember walking down the halls marked with yellow caution lines to indicate on which side the kids were expected to walk. I immediately felt anxious about following the rules about where I should be walking, and I could only imagine how the students felt. I watched students navigate the cold halls as teachers yelled at them to stay in line. In the majority of the classrooms, rows of desks and compliance-based structures were the norm. The teachers followed the textbooks that few students had the skills (or desire) to read independently. Staff expressed to me that they were stressed and burned out, which, frankly, was evident from their actions. The kids were well below grade level; most were disengaged, and some acted out as a result. It was heartbreaking, and it is an all-too-common example of under-performing schools.

Toward the end of the school year, I noticed a change in the tone of some of the teachers. The teacher candidates and those on campus had a slightly different level of excitement and energy as they began to share with me about a committee that was working on the magnet-school petition. As I observed classes and debriefed with teachers, I asked about the magnet school and tried to learn more about the change happening at Washington Middle School and the new guy I kept seeing on campus sporting orange sunglasses and Vans. What I uncovered was that under the leadership of the new principal, Dr. Eric Chagala, Washington Middle, a Title 1 school, with 98 percent of its students receiving free or reduced lunches, and about 80 percent of its students in the ESL program, was closing its doors at the end of the year. The following year, Vista Innovation and Design Academy (VIDA) was born.

We can't change who we serve, but we can change how we serve them.

Dr. Chagala and the staff opened VIDA's doors. The facility was the same but with an entirely new approach. All of the teachers were given the choice to leave, but because they had worked collaboratively to develop the new school model and created a shared understanding of the vision, all but one of the teachers opted to stay. (That teacher also eventually asked to return.) Now this rate of retention is rare for schools that aren't going through such a radical change, but for a school experiencing a complete transformation, it is unheard of. But the staff members believed in what they were doing and wanted to come together to create a new culture that valued learning, supported innovation, and met the needs of their community. Remember, these were the same teachers who couldn't reach their students and who were tired and burned out. They chose to stay and be part of a new school with the same students because they believed in the mission that they had helped create.

Redefining the School Culture

As a dynamic leader, Dr. Chagala has worked tirelessly to ensure that VIDA, which translated means *life* in Spanish, is not only a name. His desire and that of his team is to create a campus culture that breathes life into everyone it serves. He will also be the first to tell you that this endeavor isn't a one-man job. He has leveraged community and business partnerships to learn and help shape the culture. The school is rooted in caring and nurturing an environment that utilizes design thinking as a core strategy for learning and improvement. Teachers, parents, students, and community members are all integral members in shaping and upholding the culture.

Their website states:

> We dare to ignite the creative genius in each student by kindling their unique strengths, interests, and values as we utilize the Design Thinking process as a common framework to solve problems across all disciplines.[28]

What makes this school unique is that its mission highlights a focus on individuals finding their passions through an interdisciplinary approach, and its programs align to the mission. To ensure

---

28   Vista Unified School District, "VIDA," *Vista Innovation Design Academy*, Nov. 30, 2017, http://vida.vistausd.org.

teachers have the expertise and mindsets to "ignite creative genius" in their students, they have opportunities to learn and model these same values offered to students. The staff and community learn and solve problems together. The VIDA community of staff and families came together to determine the core values, known as their GILLS, that drive them. (Their mascot is a shark, and the GILLS allow them to breathe and give them life.)

G—Grit to Persevere. *We never give up.*

I—Innovating through Design. *We create solutions.*

L—Learning about Empathy. *We seek to understand the viewpoints of others.*

L—Leading with Integrity. *We make a positive impact.*

S—Sparking Creativity. *We honor imagination.*

I visited VIDA shortly after it opened, and I stay connected to the work it does by following VIDA social media (@vidasharks). The yellow caution lines are gone, and in their place are halls that lead to such inspiring places as design studios where students have opportunities to make and create based on a variety of challenges. Today, students share ideas in their classes, and teachers experiment with a variety of new strategies. Artwork covers the walls, and students meet in classrooms, courtyards, and hallways to work with each other on various projects. When I last toured the school, students gladly shared what they were working on and what they were learning. I couldn't help but smile at the dramatic change I saw on campus as Dr. Chagala, who has since become a dear friend, proudly shared what his staff and students were doing.

In the first months of school, their attendance was up compared with previous years; referrals were down, and smiles permeated the building. During the summer, the teachers had partnered with community members to paint the building, resulting in a learning environment that matched VIDA's newfound philosophy and culture. The teachers didn't change everything overnight or even over the course of the full year. They freely admit it is a work in progress, but they continue to work together and focus on learning new approaches and improving to meet the needs of their unique population. Four years after VIDA opened, attendance is still up, scores continue to increase, and, more importantly, the people (students, staff, and community) know they matter. It's a place where learners are fighting to get in rather than out. The example and the work happening at VIDA highlights that, although we can't change who we serve, we can change how we serve them.

If our schools aren't working for those we serve, we can no longer accept that *they* need to change. We must consider how we can change to best serve them. Professors Bill Lucas and Guy Claxton[29] explain that intelligence is made up of a number of complex attributes that are shaped by how and what we learn. Teachers who actively cultivate broader definitions of *smart* and strive for better opportunities to learn for both themselves and their students have demonstrated dramatic successes with teaching the diversity of students they have responsibility for educating. The staff at VIDA learned and continues to learn how to better meet the needs of those they serve because their principal believes in them and has worked to create an environment where they feel valued and are empowered to do better for their students. This team has created a culture of learning for everyone that is not just about a shared purpose, but one that is truly owned and moved forward by everyone.

---

29 Bill Lucas and Guy Claxton, "School as a Foundation for Lifelong Learning: The Implications of a Lifelong Learning Perspective for the Re-imagining of School-Age Education," *IFLL: Inquiry into the Future for Lifelong Learning,* University of Winchester, 2009, http://citeseerx.ist.psu.edu/viewdoc/download;jsessionid=B6971BA924D6CE00B46DCFE4E8F04DC6?doi=10.1.1.539.8759&rep=rep1&type=pdf.

As Shelley Burgess and Beth Houf share in their book, *Lead Like a PIRATE*, "People are less likely to tear down what they have helped build."[30]

Culture Is Everything in Schools

Nothing is more inspiring than working toward a common goal with people who share your passion and commitment. This collaboration creates a contagious vibe. Working with such a team motivates us to be better and makes us want to provide similar passion-filled experiences for others. In short, our behaviors are impacted by the cultures where we work. When schools or districts focus on compliance and mandates to implement programs and procedures, voice and choice are limited, which squashes creativity and innovation. On the flipside, an environment that honors the expertise of the educators can empower those in our schools who are working with the students every day so that they make informed decisions based on the needs of the learners.

In many conversations about curriculum and instruction in schools, I still hear the focus on implementing programs with "fidelity" to cover the curriculum. At the district level, however, the vision is about developing critical and creative thinkers and problem solvers. If you have policies about fidelity and expect compliance in your classroom, school, or district, I would challenge you to consider whether fidelity and compliance are really the goal. Do you expect everyone to be on the same page at the same time? Or do you want to create authentic learning experiences? It's hard to do both. This doesn't mean that the standards and the curriculum are irrelevant; it means they are used to meet the needs of the learner and in service of meaningful learning outcomes rather than expecting the learner to adapt to the curriculum. Personal

---

30   Shelley Burgess and Beth Houf, *Lead Like a PIRATE: Make School Amazing for Your Students and Staff*, (San Diego, CA: Dave Burgess Consulting, Inc., 2017).

and authentic learning experiences require knowing the learners in the classroom.

We can change policies and implement new programs, but if we don't empower teachers and create school cultures where people feel valued and free to take risks, we will miss out on our greatest opportunity to change how students learn. Creating an environment where teachers are supported and empowered to take risks in pursuit of learning and growth rather than perfection is absolutely foundational to shifting practices. To see the changes that we know are necessary in education, we must trust teachers—and they must also trust themselves—to make decisions and design learning experiences in ways that meet the needs of those in their classrooms.

> *We can change policies and implement new programs, but if we don't empower teachers and create school cultures where people feel valued and free to take risks, we will miss out on our greatest opportunity to change how students learn.*

We know that kids and adults learn better when learning has an authentic purpose, subjects are integrated, and the learner has agency and choice in the process. Because of this, many approaches like project-based learning and personalized learning are all methods that educators are trying in schools. You might wonder, *Is there professional learning to support these new approaches? Are there programs that provide resources? Are there models that teachers can see and use?* The answer to all of these questions is yes. Yes, you can provide these things *and* support teachers in the process to develop great projects, and you should, but these steps are not enough.

I have seen some amazing examples where educators embrace integrated, authentic ways of learning in school for diverse groups of students. I have also seen these ideal methods tacked on to traditional methods or used as a project at the end of the unit that rarely changes how kids learn. Too often in education we tend to focus on the programs, procedures, and policies. In reality, the culture that values relationships and what is best for the learners they serve is what is foundational to making a meaningful impact on student outcomes.

As schools and districts move toward a new vision, it is critical to examine the culture: What is valued, celebrated, and expected? How do the systems and expectations align to support the vision? In your own school or district, look at your goals and question your practices and expectations of others. Are they in service of your vision or impeding it?

Developing Academic Mindsets That Foster Belonging, Growth, and Innovation

Why do some students willingly engage in academic tasks? What makes learners persist in challenging tasks? What compels learners to want to learn more and improve? These questions are on the tops of minds for researchers and practitioners alike.

Camille Farrington, who has done extensive research and made the case for creating a culture that develops academic mindsets for deeper learning, found that students with positive academic mindsets work harder, engage in more productive academic behaviors, and persevere to overcome obstacles to success. Conversely, students with negative mindsets about school or about themselves as learners are likely to withdraw from the behaviors essential for academic success and to give up easily when they encounter setbacks or difficulty.

According to her research, the following mindsets have been identified as critical to student motivation and willingness to persist in academically challenging work.

- I belong in this community
- I can succeed at this
- My ability and competence grow with effort
- My work has value to me

These mindsets can be seen as both motivators and outcomes of engaging in authentic learning experiences. I would also argue that although Farrington's findings here are focused on students, the mindsets apply to all of us as learners. As learners, teachers, and leaders, we must cultivate and model these mindsets too. Here are some examples and ideas for how to cultivate these four key academic mindsets for a culture that supports learner-centered innovation.

I belong in this academic community.

As a first-year teacher, I was handed a book of policies and procedures to cover each day for the first week of school, but I knew in my heart that no significant learning was possible without first developing relationships. Even though I was a new teacher, I made the decision to minimize the policies and maximize the time I spent building relationships, and I am so glad I did. I was reminded recently of how powerful that choice was when I received a message from a former student on Facebook. She wrote to tell me I was "one of the few teachers that genuinely cared about students." It was an amazing compliment, but I know it isn't true. I worked with many great people in that school who truly care about the students. I suppose the difference is perception: The kids must *feel* like you care about them. As educators, we work to help learners develop knowledge and skills and to reach their goals. Foundational to this, however, is creating a community where people feel valued and that they belong. No matter the curriculum, my priorities in the first few weeks of school and throughout the year were to learn names, get to know students as individuals, co-create community guidelines, and encourage a community of learners.

Learn and use names right away—Throughout my life, I have made it a point to remember people's names because I appreciate it when people remember mine. It makes me feel like they care and helps to establish a connection. In my teacher-education program, this practice was reaffirmed as essential. So I challenged myself to learn names on the first day. As a middle-school teacher, learning almost 150 names presented quite a challenge, but I was committed because I knew that knowing my students' names would be a step toward building relationships with them. I took pictures of each student and wrote out their names and studied them a lot. The next day, I knew and used my students' names when greeting them or calling on them in class. This one practice proved to be foundational to building relationships that have lasted to this day.

Get to know your students' interests and strengths— While I was taking pictures, I had the students write to me so I could get to know who they were. I asked about their family and their interests, and I asked questions about how they like to learn, what they enjoyed doing, what they were good at, and what their goals were for the year and beyond. I created cards for each student that included the picture I had taken and put each class on a ring that I used all year to create groups and reflect on how to best support them. The interest inventory helped students share who they were and allowed me to gain a better understanding of them as individuals. As the year went on and things changed and I learned more, I added notes to the cards.

Co-create community guidelines—From day one, I wanted my students to feel that the classroom was ours, not mine. The process of co-creating the community guidelines was modeled in my teacher-education program, so it was only natural to do the same for my students. I asked them to think about how they wanted to be treated and how they wanted to treat others in our community. Students first independently reflected, then they shared in small groups, and finally, we condensed the big ideas into four to six community guidelines. Each class made a poster with the final guidelines. Just like the kids, they varied across the five classes, but ultimately, these co-created guidelines helped establish the culture for each group. We all signed the class poster and hung it up on the wall to remind us of our agreements to one another.

Establish classroom jobs—Within the first week or two of school, I created a list of classroom jobs and had students apply for the ones that appealed to them. The jobs consisted of roles, such as classroom photographer, greeter (for guests), birthday celebrator, historian, and others. I tried to match the kids and the jobs, so they typically got one of their top three choices. These jobs created a sense of ownership for the students and empowered them to take on responsibilities to help make the classroom community function.

Greet them at the door—No matter how much I needed to get done in that five-minute break between classes, I prioritized greeting my students at the door. Creating jobs for the students allowed me to do this because they could take care of the logistics of setting up class while I focused on the learners and their disposition as they walked in the door. This investment helped me connect with my students and see who was having a particularly good or bad day. I believe that greeting them each day made our time together more productive because they knew they were cared about and therefore were mostly willing to try their best and work to meet our learning goals.

Although what happens in the rest of the school, district, and world impacts our classrooms, teachers have the power and obligation to create an environment that ensures their students have a place in the world where they feel safe, valued, and cared about. If we truly want to see different outcomes for learners in our education system and develop the whole child, we need to prioritize meaningful relationships for significant learning to occur.

When learners feel they belong, they are more likely to see challenges or failures as part of the process and not indicative of their own self-worth and value in the group. Creating a sense of belonging and sharing the learning process, not just the product, can help all learners see that they are not alone in their struggles and can grow as part of the learning community.

I can succeed at this.

Every year, we have gone on a family trip to the mountains, bundled up our kids, rented skis, and put them on the mountain. When Zack, my son, was six years old, he was content skiing the bunny hill. He had been pretty successful, so we decided to take the gondola up the mountain for lunch and take him on a more challenging run. But it was quite a bit more challenging than we anticipated. He fell a few times and lost his skis once, but overall I thought he did pretty well. Yet when we got to the bottom of the run, he said, "I didn't like that at all!" He told me that there were too many "bumps," and he didn't want to do it again. I tried to encourage him, but he was frustrated and wanted to go back to where he was successful and wouldn't fall. Against my wishes, we skied a few more times down the bunny hill and called it a day.

On day two after a few easy runs, we convinced him to go back on the gondola to the Big Mountain. Our family split up, and, after we all finished our respective runs, we met at the bottom with my brother. He said, "I accomplished my goal." He had attempted a back flip and *almost* landed it. Zack watched the video my dad had taken and saw my brother's attempted back flip, saw him fall and also saw that he was excited about it because he was pushing himself to try something new. Zack didn't say much about the video, but his attitude toward falling and interest in getting up and trying again changed after hearing his respected uncle talk about falling and getting back up, not failing and quitting. At the end of each run, he started to update me on his progress and how many times he fell, except he was more excited to go back up and keep trying. After about the fourth run, we arrived at the bottom, and I leaned down to tell him how proud I was of him. Before I could say anything, he said, "I accomplished my goal—I made it down the hill without falling!" I couldn't have been more proud of him, not because he hadn't fallen but because he was setting his goals and working to achieve them. He knew what he wanted to do to feel successful and worked to get there.

As I think of how Zack's view of failing changed because of a model of an older and more capable individual, it changed how he thought about success and what he needed to do to accomplish his goal. I see how he was inspired by a mentor and support systems to help him when he was frustrated and how he pushed through to accomplish his goal. I can't help but think about the parallels in our classrooms and the importance of empowering learners of all ages to set their own learning goals and support them in working toward them. When learners know where they are going and when they have agency to determine their paths, there is no limit to what they can achieve. You know the age-old wisdom attributed to Henry Ford, "If you think you can or can't, you're right." Research and practice support this too. When students believe in their ability to succeed in tasks even when those tasks are challenging, that belief impacts their ability to persist. Creating opportunities for students to set goals, receive feedback, and reflect on their progress can impact their beliefs about and their expectations for success. This self-awareness enables people to make better decisions, collaborate effectively with a diverse group, and accept areas of weakness in oneself and in others. Creating authentic learning experiences that empower learners to develop the skills and talents to manage themselves and build on their talents rather than focus on deficits maximizes the motivation and impact of all learners.

My ability and confidence grow with effort.

In *Creativity, Inc.*, Ed Catmull, Pixar's co-founder and president, describes how their movies are always bad to begin with. He acknowledges, "First drafts always suck." Yes, this is the same company that has produced *Toy Story, Up, Monsters, Inc.,* and so many more number one movies. He shares that instead of creating systems that prevent errors and striving for perfection, he understands that the creative process takes time, and their approach is to create systems for feedback and support to take initial ideas for movies and move from "suck to unsuck." He urges, "Don't wait for things to be perfect before you share them with others. Show early and show often. It'll be pretty when we get there, but it won't be pretty along the way."[31] At Pixar, their movies go through multiple drafts and revisions, and teams receive candid feedback from others to make sure the ideas are the best they can be. This resonated with

---

31   Ed Catmull and Amy Wallace, *Creativity, Inc.* (New York: Random House, 2014).

me because I think this is exactly opposite of how we too often expect learners to perform and to be perfect in school. Here's a scenario that I commonly see:

- Student receives an assignment
- Student maybe receives a rubric on how the assignment is graded
- Student is expected to do the assignment on their own in class or for homework
- Student is expected to turn in a perfect product
- Grade is given based on the expectations of completing the assignment
- Repeat

This is *not* teaching. This is evaluating.

Don't get me wrong; there is a place for evaluation, and it needs to happen sometimes, but it shouldn't be confused with or substituted for the learning process. We have this notion in education that "work" needs to be perfect when it's turned in. Sometimes it's the first time that the student has seen it with no opportunity for feedback or revision, but the assignment is graded and recorded, and we move on. When we organize classrooms and learning experiences this way, we communicate that intelligence is fixed and that you either know something or you don't, not that we can improve with effort.

My work has value to me.

I used to start the year with blank walls and have the students fill them as we learned and grew together as a community. I love it when I walk into a classroom or school, and I see pictures of students, their artwork, and evidence of their learning process. Honoring the unique talents and interests of the individuals you serve can help them see that they belong in the community and have value. When we only focus on the end result, we fail to communicate to learners the importance of sharing ideas early, receiving feedback, and revising to improve. If we don't honor the learning process, we communicate that we either get it or we don't, and learners often fail to see how the work has value to them personally. And as a result, we are negatively impacting learners' confidence, creativity, and investment in their own learning and growth with an increasing focus on failure in the learning process. This is certainly part of learning, but the bigger picture to me is acknowledging that success isn't black and white. Learning is a process that takes time, effort, and growth to achieve success even when we don't see it. I have been thinking about how they approach their work at Pixar to ensure that the work that individuals do has value to them. They embody the Innovator's Mindset, a concept that George Couros defines as the belief in one's ability to develop talents and skills to create something new and better. What would it mean for classrooms if we acknowledged that ideas are often not perfect when they are first conceived; that first drafts aren't usually very good, and that we learn through the process of creating new and better ideas?

So if we go back to the initial scenario that I presented and apply the Innovator's Mindset, it might look something like this:

- Student chooses a problem to solve or investigate based on learning goals
- Student receives a rubric on how the assignment is graded or even better—it is co-created
- Student generates some ideas
- Student shares ideas with diverse people and receives feedback (kind, specific, and helpful)
- Student revises ideas and creates something new and better, repeating as necessary

- Student conferences with teacher for feedback based on learning goals and to determine next steps

- Student is expected to turn in a perfect product that demonstrates learning and growth based on learning goals

- Student receives feedback based on the expectations of learning goals

- Lessons learned are applied to new problems and ideas, and growth is documented along the way

In either scenario, you can replace student for a teacher, administrator, or any learner. If we are honest, anything that is worth doing and learning takes time, feedback, critique, and multiple revisions to improve. To maximize learning opportunities, not only do we need to allow room for mistakes, but we need to create a culture that relies on learning from others and build in opportunities to reflect, revise, and improve.

I don't teach it that way.

In a conversation with some teachers, we brainstormed ways to improve learning experiences in their classrooms. Although excited, they dismissed the new ideas as they were brought up because of having to keep up with the pacing guides and the fear of not meeting expectations of their colleagues or their administrator. Yet they were frustrated because they knew that their students needed something different. Boldly, another teacher countered, "I *don't* teach it that way." All eyes quickly moved to her as she shared that instead of assuming that she wasn't allowed to do something in her classroom, she proactively approached her principal to share her ideas and described why she wanted to do something else.

Whether you realize it or not, both of these approaches require making a choice: to comply or to challenge the status quo. You might think that following the rules is the easiest course of action, but it's not always as fulfilling or the best option for kids. As one teacher acknowledged in this conversation, "There is nothing worse than teaching something in the pacing guide when you know that there is a better way to teach it." I would argue that there is something worse: not doing it. If you know that there is a better way to meet the needs of learners, you owe it to them and yourself to try it.

What choice are you making?

For this to work, however, teachers have to trust themselves as the professionals they are and be willing to take risks. If you are doing something to truly make school better for kids, don't hide it. If you want to try something new, make your goals and your learning transparent—share your idea with your colleagues, communicate with your principal, talk to your students, ask for feedback, use it, and then share what you are learning.

What's Holding You Back?

How many times have you heard, "This is the way we have always done it"? These words plague education and prevent us from moving beyond the status quo. Seth Godin points out, "The status quo is safe, it's here, it's now, it's known, and it won't hurt us, not as much as the unknown future might hurt us." The fear of being wrong, not being enough, making mistakes, and sometimes even the fear of doing something great, prevents us from taking risks and putting our ideas out into the world. Every time someone holds back on a new idea or fails to try something new, ask for feedback, or offer ideas to improve an idea or product, we miss out on the opportunity to create something better for individuals, communities, and possibly the world. On the contrary, when learners are nurtured and their ideas are heard, they demonstrate a greater willingness to accept and solicit feedback.

If we don't have the right conditions and are afraid of the ramifications, we avoid trying new things, which means growth and development can be stunted. With the foundation of solid relationships, creating a culture that allows for risk-taking is foundational to innovation. Kaleb Rashad, an incredible person, leader, and Director of High Tech High, is intentional about creating a culture where teachers and students can take risks to be creative and innovative with what he calls the 3Ps: Permission, Protection, and reduction of Policies.

- **Permission**—Give people permission openly and remind them often that they have your permission to try new things in the best interests of the learners.

- **Protection**—Assure people that you will protect them when things go wrong. When you are trying something new, they will fail, and that has to be honored in the process.

- reduction of **Policies**—Remove barriers and policies that encumber people from putting innovative ideas into practice. Empower them to make choices within reasonable boundaries rather than creating hoops to jump through.

Permission, protection, and reduction of policies are important to create the conditions for those you serve to take risks, but changing these habits and behaviors that are deeply ingrained in a culture takes time. I have seen visionary leaders tell teachers that they have freedom to teach what they feel is best for their students and they are free from pacing guides only to be frustrated that many still cling to the pacing guides for fear of not doing it right or not being sure of the new way. It's hard to blame them. Many have been trained to do it this way and rewarded for being compliant in many cases. The same thing happens when teachers tell their students that their projects are open ended and that they can explore topics of interest. Instead, students beg for the worksheet or the formula to just get it right rather than have to think and learn in a more ambiguous, unknown space. You can't tell people to do something different or simply give them permission without showing them that they are protected and actively work to remove the barriers. You have to intentionally create the culture of learning and innovation every day.

I would also add a fourth *P* to Kaleb's list that all of us need to embrace, which is to eliminate **Perfectionism,** an unattainable goal. If we expect perfection (or more accurately, the illusion of perfection) of ourselves or others, we are setting ourselves up for failure. Brené Brown describes it like this: "Perfectionism is not about striving for excellence. Perfectionism is not about healthy achievement and growth. *Perfectionism is a defensive move.* It is the belief that if we do things perfectly, and look perfect we can minimize or avoid the pain of blame, judgment, and shame."[32] I had never thought about perfectionism as a defensive move, but it makes complete sense if you think about it. If you follow the pacing guide and teach by the book, you can't be blamed if your students don't succeed because you did what you were told to do. If students follow the formula and memorize all the answers for the test, they are safe because they did exactly what you told them. When we do things to please others and receive positive feedback for doing it right, it can be frightening to try something that is not tried and true with a clear recipe for pleasing others or being seen as perfect. This fear of the unknown can be crippling if you are used to operating in this perform, please, perfect cycle as Brené describes it. The risk can seem far greater than the reward.

Focusing on continuous growth over perfection in our schools will require deviating from the notion of best practices. The safe

---

32   Brené Brown, *Braving the Wilderness* (New York: Random House, 2017).

and perfected lessons that might have worked in the past might not be the best for the learners now. Consider some of the best practices that have shifted over time. It was once a best practice to put babies to sleep on their bellies, which we now know can be dangerous, so practices were updated with recommendations that babies sleep on their backs. When students misbehaved, best practices used to include paddling them. This is no longer looked upon favorably and is even against the law in many places. At one time, and in some places still might be, a best practice was giving ten minutes of homework per grade level, yet a great deal of research shows that this has little to no impact on student achievement. Will we continue to do this because it is a cultural norm, or will we push back to create better practices that meet the needs of learners today? Learner-centered innovation requires understanding the context, learning to improve, and assessing the impact of our practices on the learners we serve to determine what is working and what might be next.

The world is not linear, and the path to success is not a fixed trajectory. Our students will need to learn to navigate diverse and unfamiliar pathways for which no roadmaps exist, so our best bet is to start equipping them with the tools and dispositions to begin exploring with us by their sides. We would all be better off if we eliminated the notion of perfection and instead strove for continuous growth and improvement, not just for our own emotional well-being but to actually create better ideas and products. To illustrate this, a study shared in the book *Creative Confidence* by Tom and David Kelley[33] details that how we design learning experiences can impact how learners see their work and their ability to improve over time. In one class, half of the students were told they would be evaluated on the quality of a single clay pot due at the end of the

---

33   Tom Kelley and David Kelley, *Creative Confidence: Unleashing the Creative Potential within Us All* (New York William Collins, 2015).

class, and the other half of the class was told they'd be evaluated by how many pots they created. The first group attended to creating the best clay pot possible. The second group generated as many as they could. In the end, the group focused on creating more pieces had better pots than the group focused on creating the one, perfect piece. The group who made more pots actually spent more time iterating and improving their craft with each piece rather than just working on perfecting one piece. Continuous improvement is about seeking to learn and improve, whereas perfection is about pleasing others to earn approval. Does your culture empower learners and value growth and improvement over perfection?

What Kind of Culture Have You Created?

My hunch is that this teacher I described earlier who asked her principal to do something differently is probably a great teacher, but I also believe that she likely became that way, like so many great teachers I know, by trying new things and adapting to meet the needs of the learners in her class. How do you respond when you don't have all the answers? How often do we hold students back from doing great things and exploring their passions because we aren't sure of the outcome or it doesn't fit in the day's plan? Often in school, when we focus on answers and dismiss learners' unique ideas, we squelch creativity. Instead, encouraging learners to ask more questions, empathize with others, and seek problems to solve can kindle their creative spark. Culture is made up of the collective attitudes, beliefs, and behaviors of the group, and everyone contributes to this. If we want to create learning experiences that unleash the talent in all students, teachers, and administrators, we have to work together to push back against existing norms and traditions and intentionally design a culture that serves the larger goals. At the beginning of a meeting or on the first day of class, the leader commonly defines expectations and sets norms for how the group will work together. This is an important step in setting up the culture, but it's more important to attend to how people act. Is everyone's voice honored? Are correct answers sought, or are questions encouraged?

You can't just do a lesson on growth mindset and expect it to change the culture. You have to align your words, expectations, and actions and live it every day. For example, I walked into one classroom where a whiteboard had a space for classroom wonderings. Some people responded or added more questions and ideas. You could tell questions were valued and actively encouraged. While in another classroom, students were asked to hold questions until the end of the lesson. I am fairly certain that both teachers want their students to believe their ideas matter and desire to foster excitement about learning, but this is much more likely to occur when the culture supports that type of learning. If people are afraid to try something new and are holding back ideas because it's not in the curriculum or wasn't part of the assignment, think of all of the opportunities for new and better learning that are squashed. If we create cultures where teachers don't feel like they have to ask for permission to deviate from the curriculum map but are empowered and held accountable to meet the shared goals in a way that meets the needs of the learners in their classrooms, imagine what is possible. If we really want creative, inspired learners in our classrooms, we have to design a culture to nurture this type of learning. Learning and innovation must be encouraged and supported for all learners, not just a few.

Concluding Thoughts

Examples abound of educators, who, like my husband, Matt, are frustrated by mandates, bureaucratic systems, and a lack of resources and support. You too might be frustrated with an ineffective system that moves uninspired and disconnected kids through school. But education doesn't have to be this way! The example of VIDA highlights the reality that a school's culture, which *everyone* helps to create, contributes to how teachers see their role and the impact they have on students. We all thrive when we feel valued and have positive relationships with colleagues at work. These relationships are also the most predictive of teachers' job satisfaction and intentions to stay in the teaching profession. If you think that relationships don't matter or that they will just happen, your culture will suffer. The shift at VIDA didn't happen by chance. They created a culture, a shared way of doing things, that valued people first and created the conditions for everyone to learn, develop, and grow. The following factors are critical to the culture of learning and innovation that facilitated change in VIDA's practices:

- Emphasis on relationships to meet the needs of the learners and align school with the world in which they live
- High expectations with support and inspiration from colleagues and administration
- Autonomy to take risks and create amazing opportunities for learners

If you see your role as learning, teaching, and leading to create opportunities for students above focusing on test scores or managing programs, you too can create the kind of environment where people feel valued, cared for, and empowered to learn and make an impact. And the ultimate result is improved student outcomes.

Reflect and Connect Challenge
Share your thoughts, questions, and ideas using #LCInnovation

O How would people describe the culture of your school? Are you okay with that message?

O Does your culture support the type of learning that you value? What steps might you take to shift the culture?

O Do the 4Ps, permission, protection, and reduction of policies, and elimination of perfection, exist in your culture? How can you support and model these practices?

O Does your culture value and promote growth and development for all learners?

Leadership requires two things: a vision of the world that does not yet exist and the ability to communicate it.

—Simon Sinek

What Does Your Ideal Classroom Look Like?

I ASKED A DISTRICT LEADER what his ideal classroom looked like, and he responded, "It's hard to put my finger on it, but I know it when I see it."

His response is common but also problematic.

Think about it for a minute: If you were a teacher in the school and your administrator couldn't articulate what desired teaching and learning looks like, how would you ever know if you knew how to or if you even could meet the expectations?

As I talk to district and school leaders, I hear another common refrain of "transforming teaching and learning." But when I talk to teachers, they rarely have a clear understanding of what that means or what their role in that change is. In order to realize the type of teaching and learning necessary in classrooms today, we (from administrators, to teachers, to parents) need to have open discussions about what we want learners to know and do. And we also need to admit that no one person has all the answers. We need to be willing to have conversations, seek out research, and explore approaches together without punishment or fear but in service of learners in each of our classrooms and schools.

In the article, "How Does Professional Development Improve Teaching," Mary Kennedy describes the conflicting messages that many teachers receive regarding expectations for their classrooms. "[A]s a society we expect teachers to treat all children equally, yet respond to each child's unique needs; to be strict yet forgiving; and to be intellectually demanding yet leave no child behind."[34]

District leaders, principals, and teachers have different experiences and beliefs about what equality, personalization, and innovation mean in each classroom and what policies and procedures need to be in place to reach our desired goals. The problem is often a lack of common understanding about what this actually looks like in diverse classrooms. What might sound good in the district office or make sense on paper might not work as intended or imagined in the classrooms. Or what works in one classroom with one population might not apply to another classroom with a completely different dynamic. On the other hand, many teachers have ideas or know a better way to meet the needs of learners in their classrooms but don't share their ideas or try something new because they assume they aren't allowed, it's not in the district framework, or unclear expectations raise too many questions. The lack of discussion about the type of teaching and learning that we want to see in classrooms has resulted in classrooms centered on programs and subject areas rather than on deep, meaningful learning.

---

34   Mary M. Kennedy, "How Does Professional Development Improve Teaching?" *Review of Educational Research*, Volume 86, Issue 4, (2016): pp. 945-980.

What's Your Message?

Frustration and miscommunication stem from an absence of vision or a vision that is disconnected from professional learning and day-to-day practices. Perceptions of priorities can vary widely across team members if those in leadership do not intentionally develop a common understanding and consistently message and support a common vision. In *The Fifth Discipline*, Peter Senge describes this confusion as wasted energy. It leads to individuals working very hard, but due to the lack of alignment, their efforts fail to efficiently or effectively move the team toward a common goal. Without coherence, people often move in fragmented directions or even worse, fail to move at all.

Most districts have a vision statement, but few know what it is or use it to guide their work. When I ask people at all levels of a district about their vision, I hear a few common themes that hold districts back from living out that vision:

No Buy-In—The first is that people don't know the vision because it's way too long, and they have no buy-in or connection to it. Some committee developed it a long time ago, and it lives on the website or on a plaque on the wall, but nobody ever pays attention to what it actually says, let alone uses it to drive decision making.

Multiple Visions—Another common challenge is multiple and competing vision statements. When I ask teachers about the school's or district's vision, I know there's a problem if they respond, "Which one? The one for technology? For literacy? For the school?" A system should have one unifying vision to ensure a common focus. Each school, team, and department should take time to define what the vision means for them and how their work is guided by it rather than create multiple and or competing vision statements.

Accountability Focused—One of the most common responses I hear from teachers in regard to their district's vision is, "I'm not sure what our vision is but our focus is the standards and college and career readiness." In other words, they know what the school measures them on even if they aren't sure of the vision that *should* serve to help them achieve those goals. The message regarding what is important and what is valued within a district is constantly being communicated by what we ask people to spend time on, what learners are evaluated on, and what is recognized. Are the messages you are sending and priorities aligned with your vision?

What it seems that we are lacking in education is what renowned educators and authors Michael Fullan and Joann Quinn[35] define as coherence or the "[s]hared depth of understanding about the purpose and nature of the work." When systems struggle to meet desired goals, it is often a result of a misalignment between the vision, assessment, and practices. Most educators go into the profession to make a difference, but a stark contrast exists in systems where the goal is to improve test scores versus one where people aspire to develop the individual talents and skills of the learners. Many district vision statements indicate the latter, but what they *do* does not always serve this goal. The messages you send in professional learning for teachers, expectations in the classrooms, how principals lead schools, and how educators talk to kids say more about what is important and more clearly communicate what your district is about than any vision statement. Here are a few contradictions in messaging that have stood out to me as I visit schools:

---

35   Michael Fullan and Joann Quinn, *Coherence: The Right Drivers in Action for Schools, Districts, and Systems* (Thousand Oaks, CA: Corwin Press and the Ontario Principals' Council, 2015).

Message	Contradicting Reality
Students are provided with their own laptops.	Cell phones are banned.
Open access to digital resources is provided.	Classes use and print static "digital textbooks."
Google can be used to find any fact.	Students are required to memorize facts.
We want students to be global citizens.	The school blocks access to YouTube and social media.
We believe no two students are alike.	Standardized assessment practices are used to measure performance and success.
We want students and teachers to be motivated.	Opportunities for autonomy, purpose, and mastery are removed.
We believe that when students share their learning, they experience more meaningful education experiences.	All grades are based on assignments turned in to the teacher.

It's a little ironic, don't ya think?

What We Say and What We Do

Schools commonly use strategic plans or vision statements that describe the desire to develop life-long learners, global citizens, critical thinkers, and the like, yet a misalignment often occurs between the vision, policies, and practices. Bill Ferriter, a sixth-grade teacher in North Carolina, shares how that impacts learning and teaching:

> There's a constant tension between what we SAY we want our students to know and be able to do and what we LIST as priorities in our mandated pacing guides. Almost twenty years into the twenty-first century, we continue to give lip service to the importance of things like creativity, communication, collaboration, and critical thinking, but we create no real space for that kind of content in our school, district, and/or state curricula guides. Worse yet, we do nothing to assess those skills. Instead, we are still holding students and schools accountable for nothing more than the mastery of settled facts. That has to change. Plain and simple.

So going back to the opening thought of this chapter, if we want to better align our schools with the world we live in and develop the type of learners and people that will be productive citizens, administrators, teachers, families, and the greater community must work together to develop a shared understanding of the desired outcomes for students and align the vision, policies, and practices. I hope that we engage in more conversations in our communities and seek to better understand answers to the following questions:

1. What type of learners do we want to develop?
2. How might we develop the desired knowledge, skills, and mindsets?
3. How might we assess the desired outcomes?
4. What is the role of the teacher?
5. What is the role of technology?
6. How can we all work together to achieve our desired outcomes?

I don't believe that there are any right answers to these questions as they will differ based on context, but we can't assume the answers are the same as they have always been. To ensure schools evolve to meet the needs of learners in our schools today, it is incumbent on leaders to convene the greater community to examine beliefs about learning and teaching and consider how schools can best serve the learners.

Doing well on a test is not an end goal.

The Future of Jobs Report describes the urgency to prepare people for the not-so-distant future.[36] "The talent to manage, shape and lead the changes underway will be in short supply unless we take action today to develop it. For a talent revolution to take place, governments and businesses will need to profoundly change their approach to education, skills, and employment, and their approach to working with each other."

According to the report, the skills that will be in high demand by 2020 are:

- Complex Problem Solving
- Critical Thinking
- Creativity
- People Management
- Coordinating with Others
- Emotional Intelligence
- Judgment and Decision Making
- Service Orientation
- Negotiation
- Cognitive Flexibility

---

36 "The Future of Jobs Report," *World Economic Forum*, 2016, http://reports.weforum.org/future-of-jobs-2016.

Doing well on a test is not an end goal.

As 2020 is quickly approaching, we must look beyond. The world of work demands individuals who embody these skills, but many schools still rely on antiquated systems and testing practices. We must rethink why, what, and how we learn in schools for students to thrive in the information economy of today and tomorrow, not yesterday.

Create your future from your future, not your past.

—Werner Erhard

What Is Your Desired Graduate Profile?

Great leaders at all levels cultivate a shared vision and create the conditions that inspire and support others to achieve that vision of the future. One effective strategy for communicating this vision is to create a profile that defines the skills, knowledge, and mindsets that students should develop by the time they graduate. To support the development of a graduate profile, our team at the University of San Diego's Institute for Entrepreneurship in Education developed the following Student Competencies and accompanying graphic. It is based on research and defines the critical knowledge, skills, and mindsets necessary to be successful in personal, academic, and professional environments.[37]

---

37 "Innovative Teaching and Learning," *University of San Diego: Institute for Entrepreneurship in Education*, 2016, http://www.sandiego.edu/iee/itl.

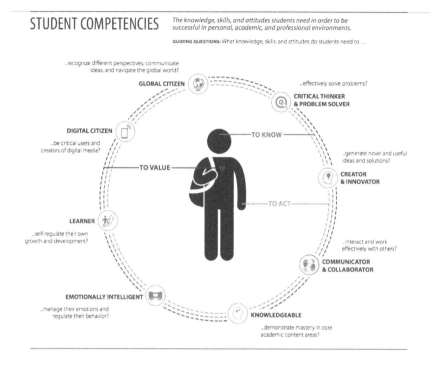

STUDENT COMPETENCIES — The knowledge, skills, and attitudes students need in order to be successful in personal, academic, and professional environments.

GUIDING QUESTIONS: What knowledge, skills, and attitudes do students need to …

...recognize different perspectives, communicate ideas, and navigate the global world?
GLOBAL CITIZEN

...effectively solve problems?
CRITICAL THINKER & PROBLEM SOLVER

DIGITAL CITIZEN
...be critical users and creators of digital media?

TO KNOW

...generate novel and useful ideas and solutions?
CREATOR & INNOVATOR

TO VALUE

TO ACT

LEARNER
...self-regulate their own growth and development?

...interact and work effectively with others?
COMMUNICATOR & COLLABORATOR

EMOTIONALLY INTELLIGENT
...manage their emotions and regulate their behavior?

KNOWLEDGEABLE
...demonstrate mastery in core academic content areas?

A graduate profile can serve as the north star to align the initiatives and resources to develop the desired "graduate." It is not meant to be something that is copied or adapted as a whole, but it is used to spark conversation about the goals in your context. The power of creating a graduate profile is not just the final product but in the conversations and the alignment that comes as a result. A shared vision and clarity about what you want students to know and do should guide all decisions, not the minutes that a publisher says you should spend on a program or the sequence of a textbook. Instead, use a graduate profile to define what you want students to be able to know and do and then backwards map from there what it will take to design authentic learning experiences that will facilitate the development of the desired competencies (knowledge, skills, and dispositions) in learners. I believe we would then see a greater shift in our classrooms.

Creating a Shared Vision

Peter Senge points out that the only vision people ever commit to is their own. Without ongoing conversations about the vision and what it means in your unique context, it's impossible to build a shared vision across a community. One of my favorite strategies to begin this conversation is called *Significant Learning*. This strategy not only builds community but helps foster purposeful conversations about past experiences and beliefs and allows a team to co-create a vision for what is possible in our classrooms.

Here's how it works:

1) Reflect on a significant learning experience where you learned something new that has stuck with you and made an impact. This doesn't have to be in school. Think riding a bike, learning to snowboard, driving a car. Anything.

2) Take a minute or two and independently jot down some thoughts about a significant learning experience. Think not only about what you learned but how you learned.

- What was the context?
- Who was involved?
- How did you feel?

3) In small groups of three to five people, have each person take three minutes to share their experience.

4) After each person has shared, the group should come up with some common themes from each of the learning experiences.

5) Share the themes as a whole group and capture them on a shared document. (Note: This can serve as a great tool for conversations about teaching and learning.)

6) As a group, reflect on the following prompts:

- How often are these types of experiences the core of our learning in classrooms?
- What might be areas of strength that you are seeing? Areas for growth?
- How might you collectively close the gap to create the significant learning experiences?

No matter how often I do this activity or how diverse the crowd, the themes that surface in Significant Learning experiences remain consistent. People discuss learning in ways that are purposeful and for an authentic audience. Typically, these experiences involve a variety of opportunities to explore models, receive feedback, and reflect. Most often, the learning and growth required productive struggle, risk, guidance, and mentorship.

I love watching people engaged in these Significant Learning conversations because they can't keep from smiling as they conjure up memories of experiences that impacted them. The power in this strategy is that it provides space for teams to connect and creates a shared understanding of what Significant Learning means to the community. Reflecting on our own learning experiences and how we traditionally learn in schools connects a community around what matters and drives conversations about the type of learning you want to see in classrooms and the conditions necessary to make it happen.

Create a Common Understanding of Desired Teaching and Learning

So what *does* good teaching and learning look like? Sound like? Feel like? Can you define this without any buzzwords? I often hear educators say, "We are 'doing' personalized learning, blended learning, or inquiry or project-based learning," but a great deal of variation still occurs in how people perceive these types of learning or what they actually look like in classrooms. In today's rapidly changing world, teachers are bombarded with a multitude of resources and often conflicting messages about what they need to prepare students to be successful (or what success actually is).

Education Reimagined defines the paradigm shift from teacher-centered to learner-centered as shifting how we see learners and their critical role in their own learning now and throughout their lives. The critical focus is that "learners are seen and known as wondrous, curious individuals with vast capabilities and limitless potential. This paradigm recognizes that learning is a lifelong pursuit and that our natural excitement and eagerness to discover and learn should be fostered throughout our lives, particularly in our earliest years." When we focus on learners and connect to their interests, needs, and goals, we can create experiences that spark curiosity, ignite passion, and unleash genius. As I work with diverse educators and talk with students, common characteristics always surface when people share powerful learning experiences. They often share significant learning experiences:

- Are personal
- Allow learners to exert agency
- Have goals and accountability
- Are inquiry-based
- Are collaborative
- Are authentic
- Allow for productive struggle
- Provide and use models
- Ensure time for critique and revision as well as reflection

As I think about some of the most impactful learning experiences in my own life, they align with the same characteristics that I hear from others. One of the most recent and definitely impactful learning experiences was the opportunity to participate in a TEDx event and do a talk along with some amazing friends and educators. My experience encompassed diverse opportunities for growth and empowered me to grow and learn significantly. Reflecting on my own learning and what others share with me regularly makes me think about how we learn in schools and how critical it is to create the conditions that support learner-centered experiences in diverse classrooms.

The following examples expand on these ten characteristics of learner-centered experiences.

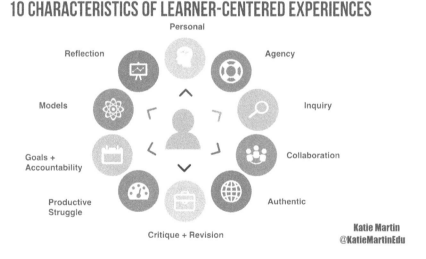

10 CHARACTERISTICS OF LEARNER-CENTERED EXPERIENCES

Reflection · Personal · Agency · Inquiry · Collaboration · Authentic · Critique + Revision · Productive Struggle · Goals + Accountability · Models

Katie Martin
@KatieMartinEdu

Personal

In an effort to create more purpose and autonomy in schools, educators have moved to an increased focus on personalized learning. This is positive, but it can also be overwhelming for those who are responsible for the outcomes to allow learners (educators and students) to learn in ways that meet their needs. Too often, for the sake of convenience, we standardize learning experiences that rarely meet the needs for all. Instead, personal learning connects to learner's beliefs, strengths, experiences, and passions to start from where the learner is and move forward toward the desired learning goals.

As I reflected on this and connected it to the TEDx experience, I realized that what made it personal is that I got to choose the content and had the autonomy to organize the talk in a way that made sense to me. What is also important to note is that nobody else spent time making this a personalized learning experience for me. The goals were the same for all of us: eight minutes to share your idea worth spreading. The difference was in the flexibility and resources to learn in ways that met our unique goals and needs. I had access to resources on public speaking to watch at my own pace and set milestones to reach along the way that directly related to developing and delivering the talk.

Agency

To support my learning, I had access to an online course with a variety of modules. If I wasn't interested in a course or if it was not helpful at the moment, I skipped it and found additional resources that best helped me to meet my overall goal. I was not micromanaged to complete each and every task. Everything I learned was purposeful and related to growing my own expertise and confidence to be at my personal best, and I was held accountable by an authentic task.

What these experiences have continuously taught me is that we can't control the learners and simultaneously expect them to be motivated without opportunities to exert agency in the learning process. Agency comes from the power to act and requires learners to have the ability to make decisions and take ownership of their own behaviors in the process. To close this gap in how we want to learn in schools will require changing how we design learning experiences for educators.

Goals + Accountability

From the time we finalized the speaker list to the event date, we had four weeks to prepare our talks, and it was intense! We backwards mapped our plan from the date of the event and created a plan and strategic goals to be ready in time. I had weekly check-ins with coaches and assignments each week that were directly related to crafting the speech. At the end of the four weeks, I was accountable for delivering an eight-minute talk, and my own level of accountability to bring my personal best to the TEDx talk far exceeded any external measures that anyone else could have placed on me.

We often prioritize what we are held accountable for, and for this very reason, accountability systems are set in place to check homework, take attendance, and make sure that you teach the curriculum. This is where accountability gets a bad rap. Because it is often easier to measure, we hold people accountable for standardized tests, grades, and other data that are easy to capture yet often fail to set goals and hold others accountable for developing the skills that we say we actually care about, like creative thinking, complex thinking, problem solving, communication, and innovation.

Inquiry-Based

Inevitably, when learners are posing questions and seeking answers, they are more invested than if they are being told what to think or do. In my case, I asked, "What makes a great talk?" and "How can I best organize and share my ideas?" I was motivated to read, watch, and listen to a lot of different speakers to organize my ideas and develop the talk and the slides. When challenges are presented or learners can find their own to solve, they are often more intrinsically motivated to seek answers to questions that they are genuinely interested in figuring out.

Collaboration

Although I was the only one on stage, this was far from an individual endeavor. I had to work with many people along the way who were critical to the process and called on different individuals based on their strengths. And at times when I wasn't ready, I had a team that pulled me along and made sure that I was pushed to do my best. The face-to-face collaboration was important, but I wasn't limited by that as I could reach out to others in my network and learn from diverse individuals. Creating opportunities for learners to build on the strengths of others and work together allows for new and better ideas to emerge. When we are exposed to diverse ideas and perspectives, we grow in our own practice and impact others as well.

Authentic

My excitement and anxiety about the event was fueled by the public accountability of my performance in front of people I really admire. The fact that it was being recorded for anyone to see took it up a notch too. Having this experience reinforced the importance of creating opportunities for students to share their work beyond the classroom. Connecting students with experts, peers, and other learners allows for a different level of accountability and authentic feedback than one receives from simply handing something in to a teacher for a grade. Experiences, where learners solve a challenge that is meaningful and relevant to their context, can empower learners to take action and do something that matters to them and others.

Critique + Revision

Over course of the four weeks, I had many, many iterations of my talk. The first ones were bad. Really bad. Thankfully, nobody was grading my first drafts, and I had multiple opportunities for critique and revision. I had to push myself to practice in front of my peers, knowing it was far from perfect. Feedback, by nature, will unearth what needs to improve and is not always easy to hear. But if we don't create conditions where feedback is part of the process, how can we expect real growth in our learning?

Each version that I shared with my friends, family, and coaches became better (never perfect). Instead of expecting the first draft to be the best, we need to realize that with time, clarity, critique, and revision, we are capable of much more than we realize. When we raise our expectations and create the conditions to achieve those expectations, people will often go above and beyond. It is important to deliberately create the conditions where learners feel valued and can openly share challenges to grow and improve as a critical part of the learning process.

Productive Struggle

Creating an environment where learners are encouraged to take risks in pursuit of learning and growth rather than perfection is absolutely foundational to shifting practices. I know a lot of people have done these talks or some version of them, and it's not a big deal. I also had people tell me that it would be their worst nightmare. It definitely was a step out of my comfort zone but within reach, and I am thankful for the opportunity to push myself. This reminded me of one of my students in seventh grade who had just moved from the Philippines, and his English was not very strong yet. I had assigned each student to give a presentation, and he wouldn't do it. I could have tried to force him, or I could have failed him, but instead I asked if he would be willing to share his presentation with me and a friend. He thought about it and agreed. This was the right amount of struggle for him and a safe learning environment, whereas he felt overwhelmed at the thought of speaking in front of the class. The learning task has to be within the right range of discomfort and allow for a productive struggle, or some learners will shut down if they feel it is too far out of reach—even if you threaten them with a failing grade. This also means that the right task or product will likely be different based on the learners in the class.

Models

While I was preparing for my talk, I watched a lot of TED Talks. They helped me see how great speakers put their stories together, how to craft their slide deck, and how they connect with their audience. Each time I watched, I had a different focus, depending on where I was as a learner. Models are very powerful in the learning process, but so often in school, we have this fear of copying or cheating. We hear a lot of talk about creating rather than consuming, but to create something better, I relied on models to inspire new ideas and build off and stimulate my own thinking and creativity. No matter how much I loved Brené Brown's or Simon Sinek's talk, I couldn't copy them, but they did inspire me in a lot of ways. If an assignment has only one right answer or final product, maybe there are some opportunities for it to be revised.

Reflection

Reflection is often the forgotten part of the learning process. In a fast-moving world, taking time to pause and reflect can easily be cut when we lack time, but it is often the most valuable part of the learning process. I videotaped myself, and although this was painful and I hated every minute of watching it, it helped me see what I looked and sounded like so that I could reflect on where I could improve. Taking in what I had learned from others and the feedback I received and figuring out how to make the changes in my own way was critical to my growth.

—

These ten characteristics can help identify what we want to see in classrooms and ignite conversations about the current reality. I was working with a group of school leaders, including administrators and teachers, to dig deeper into what each of these characteristics would look like in their classrooms. Each team picked a different characteristic and dove into what it meant to them, brainstormed what success would look like if they saw these characteristics in the classroom, defined the behaviors that they would expect, and designed something that they could do to bring it to life the next day to make this shift. One group created a list of challenges designed to stimulate ideas for learners to explore. Their list included open-ended questions such as, What problems would you like to solve? What is the job of an engineer? Where did your lunch come from today? Another group focused on connected learning and created a form for parents and community members to sign up based on topics that they would be willing to advise the class on based on their expertise. These were just a few of the ideas the teams came up with that were way more interesting than those I could have imagined, and they were much more likely to take them back and implement them because they were their ideas.

When educators have opportunities to talk about how we learn best and what that looks like in the classroom rather than what curriculum or program we are using, it can help create a shared understanding and allow for opportunities for learner-centered innovation to create the desired experiences that we are striving for in schools. Too often without bringing teachers into the conversation, decisions are made based on assumptions as well as our own beliefs and perspectives rather than what is currently happening in classrooms. What if you spent time with your staff talking about what to look for, adding your own ideas, or creating your own list and examples that resonate in your context?

Build the Foundation, Not the Ceiling

The best teachers do not use a single approach or follow one curriculum; they create the context and experiences for diverse students to learn and grow. To meet the needs of the kids in our classroom, we need to use a variety of approaches depending on the learners and the learning objectives. A culture that empowers teachers to take risks can allow for better practices to emerge as teachers learn, iterate, and invent new practices based on the needs of the learners. To do this well, once you've established within your learning community what the students need to be able to know and do and what learning should look like, the next step is to find resources that empower learners at every level to excel. High-quality resources and frameworks allow for creativity and innovation when they provide the foundation—not the ceiling—for what teachers can build on and adapt.

Based on the context, the resources, and the desired learning goals, teachers can vary designs across the following continuum to meet the needs of the learners:

Replicate—Uses externally designed curriculum and resource in existing sequence and format as designed

Adapt—Uses externally designed curriculum and modifies existing sequences and format based on the learning goals

Integrate—Curates resources from a variety of sources to meet the needs of the learners and learning goals

Innovate—Creates new and better learning experiences based on the context, learning goals, and needs of the learners.

Teacher as Designer Continuum

Replicate
Uses externally designed curriculum and resources in existing sequence and format.

Adapt
Uses externally designed curriculum and adapts existing sequence and format based on learners and learning goals

Integrate
Curates a variety of externally designed resources to meet the learners and the learning goals.

Innovate
Creates new and better learning experiences to meet the needs of the learners based on the needs, learning goals, and context.

In *Scaling up Excellence,* Bob Sutton and Huggy Rao describe what they call the Catholic-to-Buddhist continuum that plays a critical role in scaling efforts in diverse organizations.[38] On one end, expectations allow for local, customized decisions (Buddhism). On the other end, expectations lean toward increased standardization and replication (Catholicism). The authors describe the role of leaders: "managing the tension between replicating tried-and-true practices and modifying them (or inventing new ones) to fit local conditions weighs on decision makers, shapes key events, and leads to success or failure." This continuum could be powerful to discuss as a staff or a district to define what you value and what practices you believe need to be standardized and which need to be customized to scale up best practices or create new ones.

Here are some examples of this Catholic-Buddhist continuum in schools:

Catholicism—Student art projects are hanging neatly in a well-organized fashion on the back wall. Every project looks exactly the same and is differentiated only by the student's name. Each part of the art project was done step by step, with a correct way to complete the picture. Each student

---

38   Bob Sutton and Huggy Rao, *Scaling Up Excellence: Getting to More Without Settling for Less* (United Kingdom: Random House Business, 2015).

had been given the same sentence starters and followed the same format to describe his or her picture. Students in this school read through the textbook/curriculum, staying on the same page at the same time to ensure all learners have access to the same content. These lessons will likely ensure that students complete the desired assignment with access to the same content but leave little room for the creation of new ideas or knowledge.

Buddhism—Students in this school stay busy working on their Genius Hour or inquiry projects. They can pick anything they are interested in to explore and learn more. Customization and personal control are key parts of learning. Students make decisions about the resources they want to use and the learning path they will take. They enjoy a great deal of autonomy and choice, and students often create new knowledge and ideas. Not every student learns or masters the exact same set of skills or knowledge.

Somewhere in between these two ends of the continuum might be a reading workshop model with defined skills and strategies that students need to learn, yet teachers are able to use resources based on the learners in their classrooms. Another example is when students have learning objectives they have to master but can choose the content or the format to learn. This allows for standardization of the skills to be learned but customization by the leader and learner on how to get there.

Students definitely need key foundational skills to be successful in school and in life. As such, we (educators and students) benefit from standardized systems when replication is the goal, but we also need room for flexibility to meet the needs of unique individuals. Many school systems struggle to find this balance and align the right approach to meet their goals. Although completing a worksheet with the main idea of a passage might help students decipher the so-called right answer, I have yet to see how this practice has developed passionate lifelong readers. The work of leaders is defining and navigating this balance based on the goals of the system. Being clear about your end goal will help you clarify and align your beliefs and practices (standardization or customization) when designing learning experiences.

The Impact of Leadership on Desired Teaching and Learning

Aligning schools with the world we live in is not about replacing existing curriculum and instructional practices with technology. It is about seeking to understand how students learn best. It is about creating better experiences to help drive desired outcomes for all students. The expectations, support, and models teachers experience all impact the culture in schools, which results in diverse approaches to teaching and learning. As I have visited classrooms and worked with diverse leaders, I have identified three types of change in schools: 1) pockets of innovation, 2) device-centered innovation, and 3) learner-centered innovation.

Pockets of Innovation

Isolated pockets of innovation exist in schools when individual teachers have a desire to change while the staff as a whole lacks a clear understanding of the goals or why change is necessary. There is no shared vision of the desired teaching and learning. In these schools, teachers often work in isolation and teach in their comfort zones without collaborating regularly with their peers. They are neither supported nor pushed to change pedagogical practices.

A lack of structured time to engage in rich professional learning is the norm in these schools. It's rare for teachers or administrators in these schools to analyze the impact of teaching on student learning as part of their schoolwide expectations. Without time and opportunities to discuss new thinking with their peers, innovative teachers in these situations remain isolated, and their ideas fail to spread beyond their classrooms to impact the rest of the school community. This climate can create frustration for teachers who are pushing boundaries as well as for those who are comfortable with the status quo. In addition to creating tension among colleagues, these pockets of innovation often result in inequitable learning opportunities for students.

Device-Centered Innovation

As technology becomes increasingly common in schools, technology-focused innovations begin with the digital applications of programs and often replace paper worksheets or textbooks. The majority of technology integration and professional learning becomes focused on the device rather than on learner-centered pedagogy. Technology is often piled onto what teachers have always done or replaced it with little to no functional change in how students learn.

Adding devices to a classroom can overwhelm some and be new and exciting for others. It is tempting to see devices as the key to engagement, but device-centered approaches rarely change how students learn. Without clear goals for desired learning and teaching and systems for examining evidence to ensure the new programs and resources achieve the desired learning outcomes, devices alone cannot transform schools. It's the people who do it—always has been and always will be.

Learner-Centered Innovation

Widespread learner-centered innovation is most often observed in schools with a shared understanding of the vision, diverse opportunities and support for growth, development and innovation, and systems that foster a culture of collective efficacy to improve outcomes for all students. The school leaders do not necessarily see themselves as the experts, yet they lead with the belief that excellent teaching can be accelerated by technology to create learner-centered experiences. These leaders ensure that the staff works collectively toward desired outcomes through multiple measures and evidence. In Part 2 of this book, we will explore learning experiences to make shifts that support learner-centered innovation.

Does Your *What* Achieve Your *Why?*

The misalignment between what we say we believe and what we do creates tension for people and impacts motivation. Author Simon Sinek aptly points out in his TED Talk,[39] *How Great Leaders Inspire Action*, that most organizations can tell you what they do but not why they do it. This is true of many school systems. When we are unclear as organizations about why we do what we do, it is easy to let the systems of efficiency and standardization take over. A hyper focus on improving standardized test scores can prevent us from the larger goals of developing learners who can think, communicate, and be contributing members of society. I understand that we have to focus on test scores because they are the measurements and how we are held accountable. I also know that if we continue to do things the way they have always been done, we will get the same results. If we truly value learners as individuals and want students to be able to find and solve problems, communicate effectively, and learn to learn, we can no longer simply prepare kids for a test or for the next grade. We have to rethink how and what we teach in schools to ensure we are creating space to model, guide, and practice the skills that students need to be successful in life, in work, and as contributing citizens.

---

39 Simon Sinek, "How Great Leaders Inspire Innovation," Sept. 28, 2009, https://www.youtube.com/watch?v=u4ZoJKF_VuA.

Concluding Thoughts

Empowering and inspiring those you serve to achieve great success requires leading with a unified vision, confidence, and sense of purpose. To better align schools with the world in which we live, it is critical to engage in conversations among diverse stakeholders to develop a shared vision. Teachers need to not just be part of these conversations; they need to lead them.

Reflect and Connect Challenge
Share your thoughts, questions, and ideas using #LCInnovation

O Engage your team in the Significant Learning activity. What are your most common themes? How might you use them to create a shared vision for desired teaching and learning?

O How might you use an existing Graduate Profile or create one to move toward a shared vision?

O How do you create learner-centered experiences? What might you add or revise in the characteristics shared in this chapter?

O How do your professional learning experiences create opportunities to develop and sustain a shared vision?

PART 2:
Learning to Improve

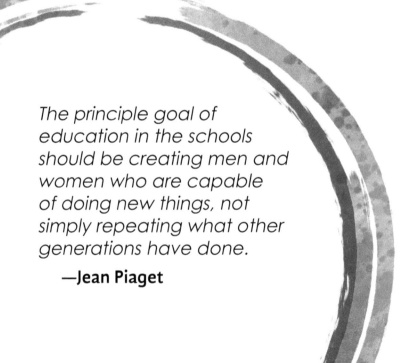

The principle goal of education in the schools should be creating men and women who are capable of doing new things, not simply repeating what other generations have done.

—Jean Piaget

Learning in a Changing World

WITH LITTLE MONEY, RESOURCES, OR experience, a single mom and her four children from Arkansas managed to pour concrete, frame the walls, and lay bricks to build a five-bedroom, 3,500-square-foot home. While some people turn to YouTube to make minor home improvements or learn how to sew, improve their golf swing, or just be entertained, Cara Brookins bought the land and supplies and learned how to build a house by watching videos.

In an interview with CBS News, she recalls how she became inspired as she drove by a tornado-hit home, "You don't often get the opportunity to see the interior workings of a house, but looking at those [boards] and these nails, it just looked so simple," After seeing the inside of the house she thought, "I could put this wall back up if I really tried. Maybe I should just start from scratch."[40] Cara Brookins epitomizes what Daniel Pink[41] defines as the foundation of motivation:

- **Autonomy**—the desire to direct our own lives
- **Mastery**—the urge to become better and better at something that matters
- **Purpose**—the yearning to do what we do in the service of something larger than ourselves.

Cara demonstrated that she had both the desire and the drive to master a process and achieve her purpose of building a house. YouTube provided the ongoing support she needed as she accomplished each step.

Autonomy, mastery, and purpose are essential to motivation in the real world, which makes those characteristics essential in our classrooms. We know that when learners have a clear purpose, voice, and choice in their learning, they are empowered and can exceed our expectations. Creating environments where learners are supported to develop their ideas and questions and turn the smallest ideas or biggest dreams into their reality is possible and increasingly becoming a goal for many educators. To make this a reality in schools, educators must first be learners themselves and learn how to learn in a changing world.

Learning to Learn in a Changing World

As we think of the possibilities in schools and the access to information available at our fingertips, we quite commonly assume

---

40   Christina Capatides, "Mother of Four Builds Home from Scratch after Watching YouTube Tutorials," *CBS News* (New York City, New York), Jan. 12, 2017, http://www.cbsnews.com/news/mother-of-four-cara-brookins-builds-her-family-a-house-by-watching-youtube-tutorials.

41   Daniel Pink, *Drive: The Surprising Truth About What Motivates Us,* (New York: Riverhead Books, 2011).

that we are all constantly learning; however, according to research from the Bureau of Labor Statistics,[42] only 3 percent of adults in the United States spend time learning during their day. As an avid learner, this shocked me, and if you are reading this, that statistic probably shocks you as well. Despite access to new ideas and resources, the majority of people do not *independently* choose to learn or develop new skills or knowledge. Seth Godin makes the comment below about why people might not choose to pursue learning:

> The current era of on-demand, widespread looking things up offers a whole new level of insight for those that care enough to take advantage of it. Unfortunately, most people don't.
>
> Most organizations, most leaders, most scientists, most doctors... hesitate to look it up. We're not sure exactly what to look up, not sure of what we don't know, not sure of what might be out there. It still takes talent and time to find the right thing in the right place at the right time.[43]

What the Labor Bureau's research and Seth Godin both highlight is that we need to *learn how to learn* in the information age. There is no way to know everything. What is more valuable than retaining and being able to regurgitate information is knowing how to find and make sense of the right information.

A study published out of the Stanford Education History Group found that middle and high school students showed an inability to evaluate information online. They had a hard time distinguishing between advertisements and news articles to determine the validity of the information or identify the information's source. The

---

42   Bureau of Labor Statistics, "American Time Use Surveys—2015 Results," June 24, 2016, https://www.bls.gov/news.release/archives/atus_06242016.pdf.

43   Seth Godin, "You can look it up," *Seth Godin*, Jan. 21, 2017. http://sethgodin.typepad.com/seths_blog/2017/01/you-can-look-it-up.html.

challenge is that many adults who are guiding young learners don't always know how to make sense of the information themselves and, therefore, are not teaching students in school how to learn and evaluate information online. The authors of the Stanford study point out the urgency for learning these skills: "Never have we had so much information at our fingertips. Whether this bounty will make us smarter and better informed or more ignorant and narrow-minded will depend on our awareness of this problem and our educational response to it."[44]

If people like Cara Brookins can learn to build a house from scratch because of the information, online tutorials, and other resources available, shouldn't we all be able to make something amazing? Shouldn't we emphasize with our students that learning is for *life, not just for schools?* I certainly believe so.

Educate for Life, Not School

While talking recently with executives from a large corporation about intersections between learning in K–12 schools, universities, and the corporate world, we couldn't help but acknowledge that *everyone* brings a mobile device to work. In fact, we use multiple devices to work, learn, and communicate throughout the day. The same is true for most learners in college. With this future ahead of our K–12 students, how are we preparing learners for this world of work and opportunities for learning if we are still banning cell phones and blocking access to websites and resources? The short answer is, we aren't. At least not in every relevant way.

I don't know a teacher or parent who doesn't want to see students thrive in their current setting and be prepared to be competitive in both their local and global communities. But many educators

---

44   Sam Wineburg, Sarah McGrew, Joel Breakstone, and Teresa Ortega, "Evaluating Information: The Cornerstone of Civic Online Reasoning," *Stanford Digital Repository*, 2016. http://purl.stanford.edu/fv751yt5934.

and parents advocate that devices be checked in, powered off, or taken away during school hours. How many adults could function without their handheld devices throughout the day? The paradox is that even though we want students to excel in our modern world, we can easily stay stuck in the way we learned rather than focusing on the amazing opportunities that learners have today and, instead of banning devices, teaching learners how to effectively manage their attention and resources. For those who think about the distractions students face and that they need to learn the way we did, I would ask you to consider what opportunities we might be missing out on. If students have access to mobile devices that can connect them with the world, how might we use this to our advantage?

New standards that promote more complex thinking and new curriculum with more challenging questions will not take us where we need to go if we continue to use standardized teaching methods. As discussed in the previous chapter, engaging students in authentic tasks that are driven by *their* questions and ideas can help develop the skills for life, work, and citizenship. That sense of autonomy and ownership of learning is a powerful aspect of intrinsic motivation.

Autonomy is just the beginning in providing educational opportunities that prepare students to thrive today and in tomorrow's marketplace. The world is not static and neatly packaged. It is exciting, complex, and continually changing. To meet the needs of the learners and the demands of society, our schools must embrace this truth sooner rather than later. Thomas Friedman argues, "The notion that we can go to college for four years and then spend that knowledge for the next thirty is over. If you want to be a lifelong employee anywhere today, you have to be a lifelong learner. And that means: *More is now on you.* And that means self-motivation to learn and keep learning becomes the most important life skill."[45]

---

45   Thomas Friedman, "Owning Your Future," *New York Times,* May 10, 2017. https://www.nytimes.com/2017/05/10/opinion/owning-your-own-future.html.

With the pressure on to instill learning skills, not just knowledge, the response I hear from educators is, "but today's kids aren't motivated to learn!" You might be thinking, as others have expressed to me on occasion, "my students don't even know how to read or aren't even fluent in their basic math facts; shouldn't we focus on those skills first?" These are real concerns, but I would argue that students' lack of motivation is largely due to how learning experiences are structured in schools. We shouldn't make learners wait until they master the basics to engage in authentic learning, nor should we ignore foundational skills. Clearly, focusing on the basic skills without a greater purpose does not solve the motivation challenge.

Here's what I see too often in schools:

- Kids are held back from reading books they are interested in because the book isn't at "their level."

- Students are forced to practice their letters over and over before they can create their own stories.

- In math, learners work on basic facts and rote computation before they can try solving complex problems.

When students are behind in a subject or lack skills, what they need is more context. They need to understand the purpose for what they are learning. Instead we reduce their education to drill and kill and never-ending worksheets, and then we wonder why they hate reading or think math is boring. Foundational skills are absolutely necessary, but students won't master them without the motivation to practice and guidance to improve. If we want learners to be motivated, we need to provide opportunities that allow them to engage in authentic tasks that foster autonomy, invite the pursuit of mastery, and intrigue them with sense of purpose.

If you're wondering how to bring these experiences into your classroom—how to empower students to effectively and *ethically* use their devices to access information—I promise, it can be done. I'm not advocating that kids text and play games on their cell phones all day when they are bored in class or need a break. Those kinds of distractions will not improve anything. What I am advocating is that you consider how to leverage technology in ways that allow learners to engage with content, experts, and their peers in class, next door, and around the world.

A Sense of Purpose

In his 2017 commencement speech at Harvard, Mark Zuckerberg shared this with the new graduates:

> As I've traveled around, I've sat with children in juvenile detention and opioid addicts, who told me their lives could have turned out differently if they just had something to do—an afterschool program or somewhere to go. I've met factory workers who know their old jobs aren't coming back and are trying to find their place.
>
> To keep our society moving forward, we have a generational challenge—to not only create new jobs but also create a renewed sense of purpose.

Getting back to our *why*—the reason we choose to be educators—is critical to defining a sense of purpose in our work as educators. If you're feeling stressed or burned out, maybe you're wondering *why **did** I get into this?* Check out #whyiteach for some inspiration, and take a minute to reflect on what you believe the purpose of school is and why you teach and lead.

For me, my *why* is tied to a desire to unleash the power that exists within each individual. At the core of that desire lies my purpose: building on the strengths, interests, and experiences that learners bring to the classroom. I love to connect with students and hear about their experiences in school as often as I can. I vividly remember one group of elementary students who shared with me what their typical day was like and what subjects they were learning. I asked, "Do you ever get to choose what you learn?"

In unison, they responded with a resounding, *"No. Never!"*

When I asked what they would like to learn, Brandon, a spunky fourth-grader, shared without hesitation, "There is a garden out back with plants that need to be taken care of, and I'd like to learn how."

Another student shared that he just wanted to learn about different people and read books about kids like him. A few others wanted to learn about chemistry and physics because "science is cool."

The possibilities for authentic learning are endless with so many important, student-driven topics and ideas to delve into that could help kids learn about how to change the world. Instead, the students shared, "We take a lot of tests." They weren't complaining; they were just stating a fact. Tests and teacher-driven learning had become their reality; that's what they knew school to be. These students are conscientious and willing to comply with the rules to earn good grades; they are learning to play the game of school. Remember the Gallup poll that highlighted how decreased opportunities to do something fun and something they are good at leads to less student engagement? It's only a matter of time before these same students—who were so vibrant and excited to share that they were literally jumping out of their seats—become less interested in learning or in making an impact on the world as they move through content that seems irrelevant and "take a lot of tests." If we aren't providing opportunities to engage in personal and meaningful learning, what are we doing? Are we educating for life or school?

Personal Learning

In recent years, we have seen a push to create more purpose and autonomy in schools by placing an increased focus on "personalized learning programs."

Personalized learning and technology sometimes seem synonymous in some educators' minds. While technology definitely makes personalized learning more feasible, technology alone is not enough. Sitting kids at a computer and having them click through personalized software might allow for individualized practice of skills, but if those skills aren't connected to a larger purpose, students won't be engaged, much less feel empowered to solve problems, connect to their passions, and learn more than rote facts and skills. When the technology is the focus rather than the learner, students have little buy-in because it feels purposeless. Adding technology doesn't change how we learn in schools. Change comes with the design of the questions we ask and the expectations we set. And sometimes, that means going off script because much of the existing curricula in schools was either created before the arrival of the internet or has been repackaged to offer the same one-size-fits-all content in digital format. In either case, these curricula don't give students agency or teach them how to use the resources at their disposal.

I facilitated a professional learning day with a group of educators who were describing to me their successes and challenges as they led efforts in their district to create more personalized learning experiences for their students. A fourth-grade teacher noted that not all of her students knew how to personalize their learning. She had to teach and guide them. She acknowledged that it was definitely a work in progress. Then a high-school teacher shared a similar story about his students having devices and resources but being timid and unclear about how to go about personalizing their own learning. Throughout the conversation, we talked about their learning goals as educators and the support they needed. Many of the teachers finally admitted that they didn't have experience and frankly were unclear about how to chart their own professional learning, let alone how to set up and guide the personalized learning of others.

Empowerment is critical to personal learning, and, as a result, many have resorted to providing options for teachers to attend and choose what they want to learn. This sounds great, doesn't it? We know learners respond well when we have voice and choice in our learning. As I talked to a friend who was contemplating next steps for his staff, he shared that, on the surface, providing choice in professional learning was working. Not many teachers were complaining, but when I asked about the change in practice that he wanted to see, he acknowledged that not everyone was making the choice to learn and try new things and actually creating more pockets of innovation then moving toward the desired learning in their classrooms. A select few were seeking new learning opportunities while the majority remained doing what they had always done and staying where they were comfortable.

Empowering people is not to be confused with doing whatever you want—this rarely helps people move forward toward shared goals just as too much control and compliance restricts creativity and innovation. Instead of providing free choice, which sounded great in theory, he met with each teacher and helped them select a specific inquiry or area of focus connected to the larger school goals. This goal was co-constructed and allowed for more focused coaching and support. The teachers collected evidence of what they were learning and the impact on what their students were learning and had buy-in because they selected their focus. Navigating the individual and system goals is a delicate balance that great leaders are always attending to based on the needs of those they serve.

When Teachers Become the Learners

One morning on the baseball field, I was asked to be the dugout mom and line up a team of seven-year-olds and ready them to bat while they would rather wrestle with one another and climb the chain-link fence in the dugout. The coach instructed me to hold the clipboard and tell the kids their lineup and position each inning. I did as I was told, constantly reminding and rearranging them. The next inning, I did the same thing without thinking about it, and most paid little attention to their spots and just waited for me to tell them to get ready. I ended up exhausting myself lining them up. During the next inning, I decided to try a new approach. All I said was, "You have thirty seconds to line up, and I will come and check to see if you are all in the right spot." Turns out, they knew the lineup and lined up more efficiently than with me guiding them every step of the way. There were clear goals, and they needed to be in line, but it didn't matter how they did it. This little bit of agency to line up motivated them to do it well and take ownership of the process.

Too many kids put in little effort and just wait to be guided, which is also known as "learned helplessness." When learners have clear goals and ownership over the process, they are forced to rely on one another and employ strategies to figure out how to get it done and learn in the process. This is as true in Little League as it is in classrooms—for children *and* adults. I used the same approach in a class assignment for a Masters of Education class that I was teaching for the third time. The first and second times I taught the class, I modeled how to create a blog and took the class members through the steps of making their blog, and then they all ended up looking just like mine. They all watched my mini lesson, and then, for homework, they were expected to create their own blog by following my model and directions. They did as they were asked and wrote a weekly blog post, completing each assignment, but I am pretty sure that when the class ended, not one of them continued to write, reflect, and share their learning on their blog. Blogging was just an assignment for class.

The next time I taught the class, I wanted to do better, so I tried a new approach. I had students read some blogs on the power of social media and professional learning networks in hopes that they would develop their own learning network based on their goals and needs. Then I shared some of my experiences and why openly reflecting and sharing on our blogs was a central component of the course. I talked about the foundational elements of the blog that needed to be included and provided some alternatives for how they might add on if they were so inclined. Instead of my step-by-step, how-to lesson that was too fast for some, too slow for others, and just right for a very few, I provided time for the students to go for it and start creating on their own—after all, that's how I learned to create my own blog. To guide the process, I created a tiered list of expectations: 1) must include, 2) highly recommended, and 3) optional extensions. These clear expectations allowed individuals to check their progress and find some areas in which to challenge themselves. They tracked their progress openly so that they could ask each other for help if they couldn't figure out something that one of their classmates had already mastered. They could look up any specific questions, and they had access to a variety of experts to answer their questions at their own pace and level.

I wanted the teachers to begin using this space to learn and connect with others. I also wanted them to feel ownership over their learning and work. When I checked out their blogs, every person had met the criteria, but even better, they had each created their own unique sites. Unlike the blogs from the first two classes, these didn't look just like mine. They had been created using a variety of platforms, designs, and formats. They were personal. For class, they had to post their weekly posts tied to the learning objectives to the #EDCS480 hashtag on Twitter. But when they started sharing other articles and resources, I knew they were owning the process and going above and beyond the established expectations.

Similarly, when I was teaching language arts in middle school, I wanted students to read and write for an authentic audience. I had my students each create a blog, much like the assignment for the teachers. One of my students created a blog that reported on his favorite football teams and players. Because he was passionate about the topic in school and on his own time, he read a variety of articles on football. He also began to seek out information on how to gain more followers and build his network of blog readers. He then taught the rest of us what he learned. Another student was interested in fashion and began scouring blogs and magazines to showcase on her own site. The students eagerly researched a variety of topics. They read and commented on each other's blogs, simultaneously improving their reading and writing skills. An unintended benefit was that students developed better relationships because of their blogs. As each one became an expert in certain topics, they happily shared and learned from each other in our class and from people around the world.

What these experiences have taught me is that we can't control learners and simultaneously expect them to be motivated. Motivation comes when learners have opportunities to exert agency in the learning process. Agency comes from the power to act, which requires learners to have the ability to make decisions and take ownership of their own behaviors in the process.

These experiences also offer one more bit of proof that if we want to close the gap between how we say we want learning to look in schools and how it actually looks, we must change how we design learning experiences for students and educators. Leaders from the district, to the school, to the classroom levels often feel pressed for time and try to fit it all in. Shortcuts might ensure that all the boxes are ticked, but they don't allow learners at any level to engage in deep learning or take ownership of their learning. When educators have not truly experienced personal, agency-driven learning in their formal education, they can struggle to imagine how to create new and better experiences that rely on purpose and agency for their students. And without new models, people tend to revert back to what they experienced as learners as creatures of habit.

The Learning Project

Dean Shareski, who teaches preservice teachers at the University of Regina, wanted to shift the thinking of his students who had mostly experienced a system he refers to as "mind-your-own-business learning," in which they were rarely expected or given opportunities to be self-directed learners. He explains in his blog that he wanted these young educators to experience a different type of learning. His goal was for them to understand not only how to learn but how to articulate the process and express their learning. With this goal in mind, he created the "Learning Project,"[46] which required his students to choose something to learn, reflect on how they learn, and then share their process over a given period of time.

I often do a modified version of the Learning Project in my own classes with teachers. I call it the Personal Learning Challenge, and it is always one of my favorite professional learning experiences because of the impact it has on one's thinking and practice. Based on clearly stated learning goals, I give some guiding prompts and ask that students use a variety of face-to-face and online networks and resources to learn and make their reflections public.

The basic prompt is this: Identify a skill, talent, or activity that you would like to learn. You could learn a new hobby (e.g., play chess, bake a cake), adopt a new sport (e.g., surfing, golf), or cultivate new skills within an existing practice (e.g., learn to meditate or sew).

---

46   Dean Shareski, "Ideas and Thoughts," *The Learning Project*, Accessed Nov. 30, 2017, http://ideasandthoughts.org/2011/09/13/the-learning-project.

The guidelines are as follows:

- Set a goal for your target learning. How will you know when you've achieved success (e.g., I can stand up on my surfboard without falling)?
- Identify resources to support your learning process. Resources can include people, organizations, websites, books, etc.
- Begin learning your target activity or skill. As you learn, monitor your progress through a minimum of weekly blog posts for the next four weeks.
- Use social media such as Facebook, Instagram, and Twitter to connect with your network, share progress, and get both feedback and support from your friends and colleagues.

One teacher's reflection on our Personal Learning Challenge highlighted the impact of publishing her work and the power of an audience. "I was skeptical about this project and how it would impact my learning if all I was talking about was running. Then I posted my blog to Twitter and Facebook, and I started to receive a lot of feedback. I realized that publishing work brings a different level of accountability that I had never expected. You know you have a wider audience to critique but also to support."

Another teacher noted that, throughout this process, she was most struck by the support network that helped her achieve her goal. "Whether they came up to me with advice, posted articles on my timeline, or commented on my blog, I had a support group that would not have existed without social media. I also felt motivated to succeed because I had so many people checking on my progress. If I can use these resources and have my students publish their work, it will have a huge impact on their learning."

Creating structured opportunities to be metacognitive about how and what you are learning can inspire the creation of new learning experiences for students. Throughout the Personal Learning Challenge, teachers began to see the value of the vast resources online as well as the variety of opportunities that exist for learning. Beyond the resources, they also experienced the power of connecting across diverse networks. Most importantly, they see the possibilities for their own students and are able to imagine ways to bring those learner-centered experiences to their classrooms.

Voice, Choice, and Agency

As a result of completing the Personal Learning Challenge, Rhiannon Graves, a graduate student in my class and a middle-school teacher, was inspired by what she was learning while practicing yoga. She became aware of how much she gained from pushing herself beyond her comfort zone, from the connections with others, and from the willingness to try something new even if it meant her results weren't perfect. During her reflection, she thought about how her students would react if she asked them what they wonder about and wanted to learn instead of teaching them about the Civil War in chronological order. Within two days, she ditched her beloved Civil War packet and created project iWonder, which she organized similarly to the Personal Learning Challenge that she experienced. Students selected a topic of interest to delve into more deeply, found resources, and decided how to present what they learned with their peers and others beyond their classroom.

Rhiannon was amazed to see her students arrange themselves into groups based on common interests so that they could use one another as resources, sounding boards, and editors. She left it up to her students to determine how they wanted to demonstrate their understanding to their peers. For example, two boys decided to code an app to teach others about ironclads. Leaving the options open to the learners allowed students to invest in the content and develop their own ideas that went far beyond what Rhiannon could have ever imagined as the teacher. She reflected on what she learned in the process. "A's and F's are no longer as important and certainly should not be the driving force of our learning. My students and I are better partners now, and they navigate the unchartered waters with me because their voice is just as important as mine. We co-construct our direction and discuss together what ultimately makes our plan successful."[47] This shift from teaching the content and assessing what they retained to sparking curiosity and empowering learners to question, curate, and teach one another created a sense of agency that took the learning to an entirely new level for Rhiannon and her students.

When we focus narrowly on assigning and grading, we can miss out on the learning. Learning that comes through exploration of new tools and resources is an inherently different experience than what results from following a strict lesson plan or planning how to integrate technology. When educators become the learners, reflect on their experiences, and consider implications for their own practices, it can translate to more robust learning experiences for their students. In these moments, teachers gain personal insights about how circumstances, connections, and motivation impacted their learning. By building in time and structure to understand the existing opportunities and challenges, their beliefs about what is possible are impacted, and, in turn, those beliefs shape significant changes in practice.

It's highly likely that if Rhiannon had been told she needed to replace the packet she had been using for years with a new

---

47   Rianne Graves Grantham, "Final Thoughts on EDCS 480: Not Just 'Computers in Education,'" *Rianne Graves Grantham*, Dec. 6, 2016, https://riannegravesgrantham.wordpress.com/2016/12/06/final-thoughts-on-edcs-480-not-just-computers-in-education.

curriculum or resources, she might have done so begrudgingly—or just used the new materials in a similar way that focused on compliance over agency. What was powerful about Rhiannon's shift is that the changes she made were meaningful to her and her students based on the context.

Creating the Space to Explore and Learn How to Learn

Personal learning is much less about learning to implement something and much more about establishing choice and ownership in the process that drives the learner. Likewise, the opportunity to engage in a worthy challenge can illuminate what one is capable of and expand one's horizons and dreams.

> *The opportunity to engage in a worthy challenge can expand one's horizons and dreams.*

Educators commonly talk about science, technology, engineering, and math and the need for students to develop skills in these fields. Schools today are focusing even more on these subjects, often bound together by the acronym STEM, because of the increasing need for these integrated skillsets in the world of work. Based on this goal, a lab was created at Qualcomm's headquarters in San Diego to provide an opportunity for students to explore the practical applications of these disciplines, to see why these skills matter, and how they connect to their present and future career aspirations. Students spend the day at the Thinkabit lab, created by a visionary friend of mine, Ed Hidalgo, to ensure that students have a place to learn about the highest priority careers in the San Diego region and the kind of education and salary associated with these careers. With no prior experience, students are given an engineering challenge to code and program *arduinos,* an open-source electronic prototyping platform that allows users to create interactive electronic objects and design something that moves by the end of the day. This experience that thousands of students have attended for free exposes middle schoolers to new possibilities and allows them to ask, "What if?" as they explore their strengths, challenge themselves to create something new, and open their minds to different possibilities. I always love the reflections, like the one that follows, that students leave on the tables at the end:

> I enjoyed learning about new and different careers that interest me. It has made me think more about what I want to do when I am older. I also really loved crafting our invention themes, and the food was great.

Seeing the experience through the reflections of the students reinforces the fact that optimal learning environments facilitate intrinsic motivation in learners by establishing contexts where students can engage in challenges and work toward interest-driven problems based on the larger learning goals. The ideal learning space is one of encouragement and mentorship that empowers self-guided learning rather than a place where the focus is on the teacher managing and monitoring student compliance.

Over and over again, students exceed their own expectations at Thinkabit lab, but an unintended benefit of the experience is that it demystifies the engineering process and shows teachers and administrators just how capable their students are. Too often, our own inhibitions and lack of experience are projected on the learners we serve. If our goal is for students to create better opportunities for themselves and others, we have to step back and allow them the space to explore and learn how to learn.

*Too often, our own
inhibitions and lack
of experience are projected
on the learners we serve.*

Rethinking Traditions

Some traditions are great; they can bring people together and create a sense of unity. But not all traditions in school serve learners. If you are still doing something simply because "it has always been done this way," you might want to rethink your reasoning. As artificial intelligence becomes increasingly capable of doing things that humans once did, jobs that require pattern recognition, following instructions, or recalling content are likely to be taken over by a machine. Yet these kinds of skills are the basis of what is taught in many schools today. Instead of setting up our students to compete with machines, we also need to focus on helping them develop the aspects that make humans unique. We need to help them learn how to drive the technology so that they can thrive in an age of acceleration. In an article in the *Harvard Business Review*, "In the AI (Artificial Intelligence) Age, 'Being Smart' Will Mean Something Completely Different," the author, Ed Hess, makes the point that intelligence must be redefined:

> What is needed is a new definition of being smart, one that promotes higher levels of human thinking and emotional engagement. The new smart will be determined not by what or how you know but by the quality of your thinking, listening, relating, collaborating, and learning. Quantity is replaced by quality. And that shift will enable us to focus on the hard work of taking our cognitive and emotional skills to a much higher level. Technology cannot replace

the human connection, the relationship and the guidance and support that we are meant to provide one another.[48]

As we think about what it means to be smart and what we value, we have to acknowledge that information is abundant. Rather than memorizing and regurgitating content, we need students and educators who can learn, think, and act in ways that create new and better opportunities for everyone. This need requires that we examine traditions in education and eliminate those that get in the way of learning and innovation. Cramming all night for a test is not a badge of honor; more homework does not make your class more rigorous; and good grades don't guarantee a student will make a difference in the world. Innovation in education is not just about adding; it's also about subtracting. Prioritizing what matters most can help us go deeper and create better learning experiences that meet today's and tomorrow's desired outcomes.

> *Innovation in education is not just about adding; it's also about subtracting.*

Eight Questions to Create Personal Learning Experiences

Personalization is increasingly part of our daily lives. For example, when I go to a workout or take a barre class, I'm in a room with twenty women, but my teacher provides opportunities to work at my level and then pushes me further, simultaneously

---

48   Ed Hess, "In the AI Age, 'Being Smart' Will Mean Something Completely Different," *Harvard Business Review*, June 2017, https://hbr.org/2017/06/in-the-ai-age-being-smart-will-mean-something-completely-different.

providing individual feedback and corrections to make sure I am getting the best workout. I leave tired, sweaty, and prepared to be sore just like all the other people in class. The teacher, on the other hand, doesn't sweat a bit and is ready to teach the next class. Similarly, I have noticed on flights that the entertainment choices have become much more personalized. Rather than showing the same movie to everyone, travelers can plug in their headphones and connect to a variety of entertainment options that suit their personal preferences. And at home, my kids have no idea what it means to wait for their favorite show to come on; Netflix shows them what they want anytime. I love Netflix too because I can set the parameters for what they can watch and when.

Personalization is an expectation in our food and entertainment today. So why shouldn't our students expect personalized learning in schools? It's true that allowing for personalization would require drastic changes in school systems that have been hyper-standardized to meet the demands of high-stakes testing. But isn't it time to admit that flawed accountability measures have failed to deliver on the promise of meeting the needs of all learners? To see the change that is necessary in our schools, we *must* provide learning experiences that offer personal learning paths that include learner voice and choice. The access to individual devices and online resources affords learners countless opportunities to learn and grow at their own time, place, and path. Teachers can and should set up the parameters aligned with clear learning objectives and allow for flexibility and choice—just like you can on Netflix. For the teacher to facilitate powerful learning experiences, they must utilize their expertise and time with students to coach and provide feedback so that, like my barre teacher, students are working hard and being pushed to their limits. The learners, not the teacher, should leave class exhausted.

Today we have an abundance of resources and access to experts to learn in ways that extend beyond the individual teacher and their expertise, but I believe that our traditional expectations around lesson planning hold us back from creating more personal learning experiences. Use these eight guiding questions, divided into four categories, to design personalized lessons that will help you guide and support the development of diverse learners with whom you work.

Who Are We?

- *Who are the learners?*—Too often we start with the learning goals rather than the learner, but to learn anything, the individual must be involved in setting those goals. As educators, we have to honor who our learners are and build on what they bring to the table. As my colleague and dear friend Ed Hidalgo frames it, "Honor the individual's strengths, interests, and values." Ask yourself: "How can I move from recognizing students as individuals to empowering learners to understand and act upon their unique strengths and talents?"

- *How does our community foster risk-taking and innovation?*—The community and the norms of how people interact make a huge impact on learners. How are relationships developed and sustained to ensure meaningful connections? How do they support one another? How do you model and encourage risk taking? How do you share the learning process to foster a culture of learning and innovation?

What Do We Want to Achieve?

- *What are the learning goals?*—In the standards-based paradigm, our learning goals are primarily the standards or subsets of standards. This is a good start but as many employers, vision statements, and solid common sense allude to, there is more to developing productive and empowered citizens than simply having them master isolated standards. How might we design learning goals that not only develop knowledge but also attend to the skills, interactions, and mindsets we know are critical for students to develop so that they can be successful in our evolving world?

- *What might be the value or impact of what we are learning?*—Connecting the learning to a greater purpose helps learners take ownership of their learning. Whether it is to build and improve skills or to make an impact and solve a challenge, ensuring the learners have purpose in their learning is critical.

- *What does success look like?*—Models are instrumental in helping learners visualize what success looks like and move toward the desired learning goals. How might we use models to spur new ideas and help learners understand the desired criteria without limiting them to what currently exists? How might success also be defined by the individuals rather than only external evaluators (i.e., the teacher)? How might success differ based on the learners?

How Will We Learn to Improve?

- *What resources exist to support learners?*—We all have a finite amount of resources and are accountable to meeting specific objectives within a given period. Knowledge and skills are foundational to authentic application, and we need to make sure learners have the support to achieve specific learning goals. But we also need to balance the basics with personal voice and choice. How can we move beyond the static textbooks or worksheets to provide opportunities for students to access resources and create new knowledge and ideas at their own pace, place, and path?

- *How will students understand where they are in relationship to the learning goals?*—We have become obsessed with grades; they serve as the "feedback" to learners about their performance, which is too often the end instead of the beginning of learning. Instead of teachers bearing the sole burden of assessing and grading, how might we empower the learners to understand their progress in relationship to the learning goals? What processes will you include for students to receive feedback on their work in order to revise their ideas and products or conduct further inquiry?

How Will We Make Learning Visible?

- *How will learners reflect and share the learning process with an authentic audience?*—Learning accelerates when students have an audience beyond the teacher or their classmates. How can thinking be visible? How can learners share their process and receive feedback from peers and experts in and out of the classroom? What are the major products of the project (or unit or lesson), and how will they be made public or shared with an authentic audience? How will this be connected to the learning goals and learners' strengths and interests?

When I think about what holds us back from offering personalized learning that moves individuals from their point A to their Point B, I don't think the reasons are that teachers and leaders don't believe this kind of learning is best for kids or that they don't know how to make learning personal. I think the reason we don't see more schools devoted to meeting the unique needs of each learner is that we are still operating in systems where standardization is deeply ingrained in our procedures and policies.

The reality is that we can't ensure all students go through every unit in a book if we aspire to personalize. These two don't fit together. We have to omit some existing practices to make room for new ways of learning. Just as United got rid of most of the overhead TVs in their new planes to provide access to more personalized digital content, teachers should be allowed to omit some or all of the lessons in textbooks or prescriptive pacing guides.

Educators who are providing learner-centered experiences have prioritized the learners' and aligned learning experiences to meet and develop the desires, knowledge, skills, and mindsets. This alignment requires keeping some practices, refining some, and eliminating others to make room for new practices that allow for more personal and authentic learning.

Concluding Thoughts

As I walked into an elementary school, I saw a sign prominently displayed that reads, "Prepare today to be successful tomorrow." This narrow view of educating for school rather than life will no longer suffice if we are going to develop learners who can navigate an uncertain world. I think that we can do better to help all learners be successful today *and* tomorrow. Traditional professional learning is often structured and facilitated for people to attend, learn, and implement. But what if professional learning were driven by teacher goals, student needs, and personal learning opportunities? I believe, and best practices have proven, that when teachers have structured opportunities to learn and reflect openly about their process, they become more cognizant of how it feels to be a learner. They learn about and explore some of the many available resources and are able to imagine the possibilities for their students to use them.

Reflect and Connect Challenge
Share your thoughts, questions, and ideas using #LCInnovation

O How do you model your process as a learner? How do those you serve know what you are learning?

O How might you make time to engage in a Personal Learning Challenge and blog about it?

O What traditions do you need to rethink? What can you start doing? What can you stop doing?

O How can you create more personal learning experiences for those you serve?

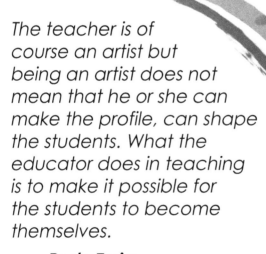

The teacher is of course an artist but being an artist does not mean that he or she can make the profile, can shape the students. What the educator does in teaching is to make it possible for the students to become themselves.

—Paolo Freire

Designing
to Empower

STEPHANIE BUELOW, ONE OF MY best friends and an amazing teacher, went back to the classroom after three years as her school's literacy coach in Ewa Beach, Hawai'i. She knew the expectations and the curriculum well and could have taught it with fidelity and maintained the practices that students had come to expect in school, but she chose not to. With clear goals in mind and an understanding of the expectations, she made the conscious decision to teach the students—not the curriculum—in her classroom. With an understanding of the learning goals, she learned the passions, strengths, and interests of her students and designed learning experiences that they connected with and that empowered them as learners and leaders.

From Expert Teacher to Expert Learner (and Vice Versa)

In an article titled "Popular Culture and Academic Literacies Situated in a Pedagogical Third Space," Stephanie details how she redesigned the classroom learning environment to create space for student interests and popular culture to be a central part of the curriculum. She also acknowledges that the redesign required her to shift out of the role of expert to allow students to share their expertise. She describes the breakthrough she had in her own teaching when she realized the power of co-constructing the learning:

> I didn't teach them how to do these things [create an iMovie, edit the movie, download music from other sources to add background music, etc.]. I just gave them the resources [CDs, cameras, computers] and the foundation of the literary elements and standards I was addressing. They figured the rest out on their own. They were in their element. I went into this unsure of how we would arrive to the final product but they proved to know more about these digital literacies than me. I learned a lot from them! Now I know that they can run with it and figure things out.[49]

Stephanie could have easily avoided bringing new technology and resources into the classroom and stuck with the tools she felt comfortable using, but doing so would have limited her students to what she knew. Instead, she took a risk and allowed herself to be a learner; she let her students lead and teach her. Everyone benefitted in the process. "After our experiences in the poetry unit, I felt empowered to create more opportunities for students to serve as experts and for me to serve as the novice," she writes.

---

49   Stephanie Buelow, "Popular Culture and Academic Literacies Situated in a Pedagogical Third Space," Volume 56 (2017) *Reading Horizons*, Accessed Nov. 30, 2017, http://scholarworks.wmich.edu/reading_horizons/vol56/iss1/1.

Stephanie found collaboration and communication to be key components of empowerment for her sixth graders. They democratized the classroom by discussing and voting on matters as simple as the classroom schedule, choosing books to read, and options for presenting and assessing projects. Roles between teachers and learner shifted based on the task and expertise. One of her students commented that, "As the people in my group talked about our assignments, everybody would share their ideas and what they were learning. We had time to talk about what we were learning, and it made learning more fun to learn from each other."

In addition to involving students in the decision making in their classroom, Steph sought feedback from her students in surveys, focus groups, and one-on-one conversations throughout the year. She often asked a variety of open-ended questions to find out students' interests and what motivated them. As she learned more about her students and the out-of-school experiences, she learned they "were frequently engaging in the literacy practices involved in online social networking and online games outside of school." She reflected about the role of this in the classroom and their learning. "As students engaged in these out-of-school literacy practices, I realized how they were extending their learning beyond the school day through collaborative online discussions. I decided to incorporate online social networking as a tool for literature circle discussions in response to their out-of-school literacy practices."

Stephanie didn't focus on test scores because her focus was (is) on how much she learned about being a better teacher and how connected she felt to her students. However, when the test scores came back, 91 percent of her sixth-graders had met or exceeded proficiency in reading. Even more impressive is that the scores show an extraordinary gain of 34 percent over the student's fifth-grade level of 57 percent proficiency. Especially noteworthy is that 87 percent of her students who are classified as economically disadvantaged met or exceeded proficiency. Her students outperformed students in her school, as well as in the entire state, by about 30 percent on the standardized test results.

The test at the end of the year was a high priority for her administration, as it is in many schools. The rest of the school was engaging in what had become common practice to prepare for the test by reviewing the questions aligned to standards with kids who were not yet proficient or providing extra test prep for groups of kids who were teetering between proficient and approaching. But Stephanie maintained her focus on the learners and their needs. She taught specific skills and empowered students to understand the importance of the skills they were developing in their own lives. She offered choice and encouraged their voices. They co-created projects based on areas of strength and growth and designed lessons that piqued students' interests with pop culture, including fashion and video games, all while developing and using the foundational skills. The lessons were fun and engaging but were specifically designed to target the skills and achieve the learning outcomes that sixth graders were supposed to master—and they did. Her reflection on her experiences highlights how she came to understand how to design powerful learning experiences once she really got to know her students:

> I reflected on ways that I could have better supported the learners in my classroom. However, I feel confident that the year I spent learning with this group of students has forever changed me. While we both tried something out of our comfort zone, I am left to wonder: What if we were not successful in doing so? What if student test scores were below expectations? What if creating websites and multimodal texts was a distraction from producing high-quality writing? The complexity and uncertainty of these questions can only lead me to report on what I know. I know that I learned to let students take the lead, that powerful learning experiences will

produce academic results, and that being mindful of the larger purpose will give you focus and clarity as you learn to embrace, expect, and dwell in the struggle of learning.

High-stakes standardized tests and the accountability connected to them are a reality. No matter how much we want to say that the test scores don't matter, the reality is that in our current system, they do. The irony, however, is that we will never achieve the results we want by focusing on performing well on a test.

Do You Focus on Testing or Learning?

In an article titled, "I Can't Answer These Texas Standardized Test Questions about My Own Poems,"[50] poet Sara Holbrook shares how she came across test questions on a standardized test that were designed to analyze *her own poems*—and she couldn't figure out the answers. Here is an example of an actual test question:

Dividing the poem into two stanzas allows the poet to:

A) compare the speaker's schedule with the train's schedule.

B) ask questions to keep the reader guessing about what will happen.

C) contrast the speaker's feelings about weekends and Mondays.

D) incorporate reminders for the reader about where the action takes place.

As she read the options, even though she wrote the poem, none of the choices resonated. She shared, "I just put that stanza break in there because when I read it aloud (I'm a performance poet), I pause there. Note: That is not an option among the answers because no one ever asked me why I did it."

---

50   Sara Holbrook, "I Can't Answer These Texas Standardized Test Questions about My Own Poems," *Huff Post*, Jan. 5, 2017, http://www.huffingtonpost.com/entry/standardized-tests-are-so-bad-i-cant-answer-these_us_586d5517e4b0c3539e80c341.

Reading the poet's comments brought me back to being in school when we had to answer questions about the main idea or the author's purpose. I remember being frustrated that there was only one "right" answer. I kept thinking, *How does my teacher know? Did she call the author?* Well, it turns out that, in this case and likely in many others, they were just guessing. Just in case you are curious, the (made-up) answer to the stanza question is C.

When I read the article, I initially felt validated, but my feelings quickly turned to frustration. As Sarah Holbrook uncovers, "These test questions were just made up, and tragically, incomprehensibly, kids' futures and the evaluations of their teachers will be based on their ability to guess the so-called correct answer to made-up questions."

I have worked in schools where support programs or "response to intervention" programs, designed with the very best of intentions, pull kids out of class to provide extra time to ensure that students have the skills to be successful. The problem is that success was defined by the test scores, and, in some cases, this focus resulted in limiting (or eliminating) authentic learning experiences to make room for repeated exposure and practice on drill-and-kill test-prep questions. The primary goal wasn't learning, rather it was to ensure students were well versed in the test genre and able to select the appropriate answers. In my experience, this test-centric approach rarely leads to significant gains in test scores, nor does it increase motivation for learning (or test taking) by students or their teachers. Reading this article from Sarah Holbrook makes me question: Have we created a system that is so caught up in preparing students for a test that we spend valuable time analyzing test data and reteaching narrow "skills" that are based on answering made-up questions and, even worse, fail to measure the scope of what we say we value?

In an era where test scores and test prep dominates conversations, educators feel compelled to stick to the curriculum and cover it all, and we work to convince ourselves that we have "prepared" students by teaching them how to take tests. Most educators know in their hearts, however, that there is far more to teaching than success on a test, which puts them at odds with what is measured and how they are held accountable.

I get it. We focus on test scores because it is what is measured and how we are held accountable. It's safe to stay within the comfort zone of compliance—to cover the curriculum and stay in line with colleagues. The students who do well in school similarly follow suit. But is this the best approach for authentic learning?

Jeff Duncan-Andrade, founder of Roses in Concrete Charter School in Oakland, argues the virtues of test-focused teaching:[51]

> You have to create pathways for kids to get to college and that includes tests. We need to stop seeing it as binary and you can't be talking out of both sides of your mouth. You have all of these degrees hanging on a wall, but you are not giving kids a route to those degrees.

I understand what he is saying and acknowledge that we can't ignore the high-stakes tests because this is the system that exists; tests and grades are how kids get into college and earn degrees that are important to accessing many jobs. The standards and curriculum will likely always play a role in schools and classrooms. That isn't negative unless we mindlessly move through the prescribed content without focusing on desired learning and the impact on the learners. If we are going to change how students learn in school, we will need to work within these constraints and think about how we can meet (and go beyond) the standards. The standards, pacing guides, and curriculum can serve as tools for educators to

51 Emmanuel Felton, "Should an urban school serving black and Hispanic students look like schools for affluent white kids?" *The Hechinger Report*, Dec. 1, 2016, http://hechingerreport.org/should-an-urban-school-serving-black-and-hispanic-students-look-like-schools-for-affluent-white-kids.

design the authentic learning experiences that empower learners to develop the skills addressed in the standards, but they should not be a checklist of content to cover.

Standards should serve as guides, not checklists.

Here's an example of what I mean: Convection, a topic that appears throughout the science content standards, is relevant to our daily lives in many ways: weather, cooking, and heating your house. I was taught this concept at various times throughout school, and you probably were too. Just in case you need a refresher, convection is the movement that occurs when hotter and therefore less dense material rises, and colder, denser material sinks. It results in a transfer of heat. I always earned As and Bs in school, living up to my parents' expectations, so I know I must have answered questions about convection with some level of proficiency. But when I was assigned this concept to teach my peers in a science class in college, I had no idea how to explain it or why it was important. My motivation for truly understanding this concept suddenly changed when I had an authentic purpose and audience beyond my teacher or a test. I spent time researching, watching videos, taking notes, and looking for real-world examples that helped me learn. As a result of that purpose-driven learning, I developed a deep understanding of convection and was able to create an experience that helped my classmates understand it too. I'll never forget teaching my peers about convection, and, more importantly, that hot air rises, and cool air sinks.

If we truly value learners as individuals and want students to be able to find and solve problems, communicate effectively, and develop other necessary skills, we can no longer simply prepare kids for a test or the next grade, we need to empower them to learn how to learn, not just memorize. We need to equip them with skills that they can use to solve real problems—not just made-up test problems—to be successful in life and work and as contributing citizens. To do those things, we must rethink how and what we teach in schools.

Rethinking the Lesson Plan

When I was in my teacher-preparation program, my professors taught me to complete extensive lesson plans to ensure I was prepared to engage students in learning the specified content. They expected me to know how to differentiate for the diverse needs of students, so I thoughtfully planned modifications for students with special needs and for English language learners. I differentiated for those who needed remediation, those who met the standard, and those who needed extension activities. Sometimes my plans for forty-five-minute lessons were up to five pages long; I planned what I was going to say—and what they were going to do and say.

Now some of you might be thinking, *That sounds great*! In a lot of respects, this kind of detailed, differentiated lesson planning is considered a best practice; it's what many teachers are still trained to do. The problem with this approach is that students are treated like participants; they are expected to "do school." (Some learn that lesson better than others). In my early efforts to teach the supposedly necessary content based on pacing guides and standards, I left little space in my tightly crafted lessons plans for their questions, their interests, or for learning and exploring beyond what I knew.

I have been thinking a lot about the lesson plans and "best practices" and how those translate (or don't) to learner-centered innovation. I wonder, to make learning more personal and meaningful, *What if teachers did less, not more*? I am not arguing that we should wing it and just see what happens; that rarely goes well. I am suggesting, however, that instead of teachers doing all the work to plan overly structured lessons and deliver the content, we might be better off if we spent more time understanding the learners and helping them understand the learning goal. In fact, I know we would all be better off if our students understood where they are in relation to the desired learning target and how they can close the gap. That is the essence of personalized learning.

We are conditioned to create perfectly structured learning experiences, but we must consider what we are taking away from the learners by doing this. William Yeats said that "Education is not the filling of a pail, but the lighting of a fire." When we can connect learners to ideas and questions that they are passionate about and motivated to solve, they amaze us with their capabilities and imaginations. Too often, however, universities prepare, and schools perpetuate the expectations of teachers to fill the pail rather than light the fire. When you as the teacher do all the work, you also do all the learning. What if the key practices that we learn in teacher preparation programs, reinforced in our evaluations and professional learning that characterize "good teaching," are preventing us from the type of learning possible in classrooms today? Before you move into the next section, take a moment to consider your answer to a question that John Spencer and A.J. Juliani ask in their book, *Empower*, specifically as it relates to designing learning experiences: "What decisions am I making for students that they could make for themselves?"[52]

Move from Engagement to Empowerment

Many teachers are taught to measure student engagement by the number of students who actively participate in class. Administrators evaluate student engagement by looking around

---

52   John Spencer and A.J. Juliani, *Empower: What Happens When Students Own Their Learning*, (San Diego, CA: Dave Burgess Consulting, Inc., 2017).

the room to see if everyone's eyes are on the teacher and all the students are listening intently; the expectation from both teacher and administrators is for students to raise their hands and wait to be called on. As teachers, we learn to create and deliver lessons that engage students with hooks and fun activities to connect them with the content we want them to learn. This is not necessarily a bad thing, but in *The Innovator's Mindset,* George Couros pushed me to think beyond engagement to empowerment:

> If engagement is the ceiling—the highest bar—then we may be missing the point. Think about it: Would you rather hear about changing the world, or do you want the opportunity to do so? A story about a world changer might engage us, but becoming world-changers changes us. So the question for you as a professional educator is: If you had to choose between compliant, engaged, or empowered, which word would you choose to define your students?[53]

When I hear educators in professional learning ask questions like, "Did I do this activity right? Is this what you wanted me to do?" it's a clear indicator that I have missed the mark in designing the learning experience. These questions are not usually a sign of someone owning their learning and are generally a function of a performance orientation—doing the task to get the grade or the accolade—rather than an orientation to learn something and improve. It's like when kids in the classroom ask, "How many pages is this supposed to be? Did I get the right answer? What do I have to do for an A?" These questions rarely signify intrinsic motivation. I understand that, at times, we all definitely need to do things a certain way and that not everything we learn is intrinsically motivating, but if these types of learning experiences consume the majority of learning time in schools, what are we really teaching?

---

53   George Couros, *The Innovator's Mindset: Empower Learning, Unleash Talent, and Lead a Culture of Creativity* (San Diego, CA: Dave Burgess Consulting, Inc. 2015).

I recently heard a teacher acknowledge that grammar lessons don't work because students can't recognize mistakes and fix them in their own writing. She noted that, while they might receive 100 percent on a quiz, they often fail miserably at writing a few grammatically correct sentences. (Just ask eighth-grade or high-school teachers how many of their students have perfect grammar and spelling despite the amount of time spent on the subject throughout school.) But when you ask students to publish real work and share ideas that matter to them, they have a reason to fix the grammar mistakes and are motivated to write their ideas in a thoughtful, coherent way. This teacher's comment addresses the point of the real issue: Is our ultimate goal as educators for students to get the answers right on the test, *or* is it to help them understand the process of developing and improving their ideas so they can communicate and share with the world?

When learners are empowered and embrace the work because it's meaningful to them, they ask questions like: How can I make this better? Did I accurately communicate my ideas? Is there another way to solve this problem? What is the impact that my work has on others? Not, did I do this right? When people have an opportunity to solve important problems that make their life or work more meaningful and impactful, it's not about compliance, it's about doing work that matters.

What Questions are Learners asking?

Performance-Orientated Questions

Learning-Orientated Questions

- How many pages is this supposed to be?
- Did I do this right?
- What do I have to do for an A?
- Is there extra credit?

- How can I make this better?
- Did I accurately communicate my ideas?
- Is there another way to solve this problem?
- What is the impact that my work has on others?

Move from Standardization to Personalization

While talking with a teacher recently about the changes he wanted to make in his classroom, he told me he couldn't imagine *how* to create more authentic learning experiences given the current expectations of him. He wondered how he could possibly plan to "personalize" for every student. Maybe you have similar questions or concerns.

If you think about lesson plans in a traditional sense, yes, it is overwhelming, if not completely impossible for a teacher to plan personalized learning experiences for each student. In spite of our understanding that no two people are the same, we have set up a system that prioritizes and demands overly structured lessons for every student to meet the same objective at the same time in the year, regardless of the individual's unique strengths, interests, or questions.

A conversation I had with a first grader highlighted this challenge. He asked, "Why do I have to learn about butterflies?"

I asked what his class was learning about and after a little probing, he told me they had glued some parts of the butterfly on paper and colored a picture. A display on the back wall of the classroom presented twenty-seven similar butterflies.

Curiously, I asked, "What do you want to learn about?"

"Chickens," he said. "I already know about butterflies."

His comments stuck with me the following week and were starkly contrasted with students in another first-grade classroom I visited where they were recording videos in pairs to narrate their informational writing. I asked a student what she was writing about, and she informed me that she was learning about turtles and that some of her friends were writing about Helen Keller. Still others were writing about owls, and she went on to list a variety of other topics. The content was based on what the students wanted to learn, but the student, regardless of their chosen topic, was learning and practicing the skills to be better writers, communicators, and collaborators. The teachers had taught them the skills they needed to research their topic on their iPads, organize information, and share what they were learning. The students were in different stages of the writing process. They taught and learned from one another, and they were beyond excited to share what they were writing. They made videos to communicate what they had learned about their topic of choice and excitedly shared them with their teacher *and* with friends, parents, and anyone else who wanted to learn from them.

The point is, we can teach necessary skills while creating experiences that allow for learners to take personalized learning pathways. We and our students have access to an abundance of resources and experts that enable us all to learn in ways that extend beyond the expertise of one teacher. By tapping into those resources, we can create more personal learning experiences that can allow students to apply their newly learned skill in ways that are meaningful and relevant *to them*.

Move from Scaffolds to Agency

I was once told that for every class, you should spend two hours planning. As the saying goes, if you fail to plan, you plan to fail.

(No wonder that teachers are exhausted at the end of the day, and students have energy! Teachers are doing the bulk of the work of learning.) Now I believe it's important to plan and necessary to scaffold sometimes, but I also wonder if we guide learners every step of the way, how might the structures and scaffolds we put in place actually inhibit the learning process? When the teacher bears the cognitive load and is the one who finds the resources and plans the sequence, the learners are coaxed along in the process to move down a prescribed path. Are we taking away meaningful learning from them in that process?

Learner agency is about moving students from passively responding to acting with purpose to reach a desired goal or outcome.

Consider the example above of the butterfly unit. In that classroom, the teacher was the one who picked out the books, created the worksheets for students to fill in, and planned to scaffold for different achievement levels; the students passively responded to the activities. In the second class, the teacher set up the process for students to learn and taught them the necessary skills, but they owned the learning and had autonomy and purpose throughout the process, even in first grade. The skills (and the learning) will stick with the students because they owned them. Ten years from now, will all the students in the first class remember the correct names for the stages a butterfly goes through? Probably not, but they have Google for that if they need to know. The skill of researching and using the information they find is what is important. The important thing here is that choice and purpose naturally empowers learners to move at their own pace and path and to seek support based on their needs from peers, online resources, and the teacher. *Learner agency is about moving students from passively responding to acting with purpose to reach a desired goal or outcome.*

Move from Skills to Application

A common approach to curriculum, instruction, and assessment is often referred to as "standards based." According to the *Glossary for Education Reform,* standards-based grading is defined as:

> Systems of instruction, assessment, grading, and academic reporting that are based on students demonstrating understanding or mastery of the knowledge and skills they are expected to learn as they progress through their education. In a school that uses standards-based approaches to educating students, learning standards—i.e., concise, written descriptions of what students are expected to know and be able to do at a specific stage of their education—determine the goals of a lesson or course, and teachers then determine how and what to teach students so they achieve the learning expectations described in the standards.

We all have a finite amount of resources and are accountable to meet specific objectives within a given period. Foundational knowledge and skills need to be taught, but we also need to balance these foundational skills we want all students to attain while allowing for authentic application of those skills. In the standards-based paradigm, our learning goals are primarily the standards or subsets of standards. While this is a good start, many employers, vision statements, and basic common sense allude to developing productive and empowered citizens instead of mastering isolated standards. We need to prioritize learning experiences that not only develop knowledge but also attend to the skills, interactions, and mindsets we know are critical for students to develop to be successful in our evolving world.

A collaboration with Tanya Weida, my friend and team teacher at Ilima Intermediate, demonstrates this balance. She was the special-education teacher and I was the general education teacher, but instead of teaching a different version of my lesson, we combined our classes. Like many classrooms, our seventh-grade classroom had a range of reading levels from first grade to postsecondary. According to our pacing guide, we were supposed to be teaching narrative writing and focusing on literary devices. Rather than having students read sections from the basal reader and answer the questions on literary devices at the end of each lesson, we had students write their own book with a narrative story structure, including a variety of literary devices. With a date set to read our books to the elementary students next door, we set off to read and learn as much as we could to become authors.

Over the course of a month, we read and analyzed so many amazing children's books—the messages, the tone, the art, and the structures of narrative writing. We curated lists of hooks, literary devices, dialogue, and all the things we loved and wanted to use in our own books. Some students created an entirely novel story; some adapted versions of existing stories, and two students who had just joined our class from the Philippines and spoke very little English learned new words and phrases as they captioned a wordless book. All of our students met and exceeded the standards to identify the literary devices and write a narrative story with descriptive language and conventions. More importantly, they saw themselves as authors. They had an authentic purpose to apply the skills we were learning; they sought feedback, revised their work, and, as a result, they built their confidence and excitement for reading, writing, and sharing their ideas.

From Classroom Management to Classroom Community

Classroom management is a staple of any teacher education and/or induction program; it is seen as a foundation of good teaching. Training in this area for pre-service teachers typically means preparing them to use a multitude of strategies to ensure they know how to maintain classroom control. For example, a common practice is to use public-management displays to identify who is following the rules as a way to motivate students to choose the appropriate behavior. Alfie Kohn shares that,

> Threats and bribes can buy a short-term change in behavior, but they can never help kids develop a commitment to positive values. In a consequence-based classroom, students are led to ask, 'What does she want me to do, and what happens to me if I don't do it?" In a reward-based classroom, they're led to ask, "What does she want me to do, and what do I get for doing it?"
>
> I believe that we need to have rules and procedures that facilitate productive learning environments but to create learning environments where students feel valued and a sense of ownership, we must move beyond management to creating learning environments that foster a community of empowered learners.[54]

As Steven Covey notes, we manage things but lead people.[55] Instead of spending time managing students, what if we engage students in thinking for themselves? We demand student obedience and the following of our morning procedures with little to no buy-in or reason other than compliance to follow. Instead, Alfie

---

54   Alfie Kohn, "Discipline Is the Problem, Not the Solution," *International Chiropractic Pediatric Association,* http://icpa4kids.org/Wellness-Articles/discipline-is-the-problem-not-the-solution.html.

55   Steven R. Covey, *The 8th Habit: From Effectiveness to Greatness* (New York: Free Press, 2004).

Kohn suggests we ask questions such as, "How long is it taking us to get settled? Why? What can we do about that? This questioning approach saves time in the long run, reduces the number of problems, and ultimately gets kids started thinking their way through their problems."

I love the way that Alicia Gelaro, Abby's third-grade teacher, reframed her classroom management as a classroom leadership approach to parents at back-to-school night. "I don't have a lot of rules and consequences. I respect students, and I hope they respect me." When you take this approach, you don't need a bunch of other rules and consequences.

Experimenting or Evolving?

I know, for many, it can be daunting to think about redesigning classroom experiences based on student and teacher interests rather than a set curriculum that ensures everyone gets the same material. One experienced teacher told me it wasn't fair to kids to experiment on students and that we needed to make sure the curriculum was vetted prior to rolling it out in classrooms to avoid messing it up or "failing students." This fear is prevalent in education, and too often we end up sticking with what we have always done because it is safe—and, if we are honest, because managing the status quo rarely gets us in trouble. The reality is, our current approach is leaving many students behind, and if we are really focused on what's best for kids and if our goal is to ensure success in work, life, and citizenship, we need to be nimble and create learning experiences that reflect the context and the resources to best meet the needs of all learners. This is not experimenting just for the sake of doing something new but intentionally creating better experiences to ensure that schools continually evolve to meet the demands of learners in our changing world.

Pedagogy Trumps Curriculum

Experiences that change how kids learn in schools today rarely come straight from a textbook. They come from teachers who know their learners and design experiences to meet their needs based on the desired learning objectives. As Dylan Wiliam, professor emeritus and formative assessment guru, so beautifully articulates, "A bad curriculum well taught is invariably a better experience for students than a good curriculum badly taught: Pedagogy trumps curriculum. Or more precisely, pedagogy is curriculum, because what matters is how things are taught, rather than what is taught." This is precisely why teachers matter and why teachers will always matter. Great teachers teach the learner rather than teaching a curriculum and trying to make the learners adapt.

Will Richardson, co-founder of Modern Leaders, wrote a blog post titled "9 Elephants in the Classroom That Should 'Unsettle' Us" highlights many things we do in education because we have always done them—not because those things are best for kids. One thing he lists stands out to me as I think about curriculum and how it can hold us back from teaching kids in really powerful ways:

> We know that curriculum is just a guess. The way we talk about "The Curriculum" you would think that it was something delivered on a gold platter from on high…. But we know that much of what every student in 1894 was supposed to learn isn't really what every student in 2015 needs to learn.[56]

Think about how learning might change in schools if we would have more conversations focused on a deeper and shared understanding of desired learning goals and effective pedagogy rather than the programs or curriculum that are to be implemented.

---

56   Will Richardson, "9 Elephants in the (Class)Room That Should 'Unsettle' Us," *Will Richardson*, April 9, 2016, http://willrichardson.com/9-elephants-classroom-unsettle-us.

Prioritize the Learners

The best educators do not use just one approach or follow the curriculum to the letter; they get to know the learners and create the context and experiences to meet their needs. We can become fixated on labels such as blended learning, project-based learning, or personalized learning, but the reality is that, to meet the needs of the learners in our classrooms, we need to utilize a variety of approaches depending on the learners and the learning objectives.

For my first year of teaching, I moved across the Pacific Ocean from San Diego to Oahu, Hawai'i, to teach seventh graders. Many thought I was crazy, and maybe I was. To this day, I will never forget meeting a local boy who was running one of the activity booths at a *luau* I attended on one of my first few days on the island. (So cliché, I know!) He asked where I was from and when I told him I had just moved to the island to teach, he looked at me and said, "*You* are going to teach at Ilima? They are going to kill you!" Based on my expression, he quickly retracted and said, "You know, as long as they know you care, they will be good to you." Whether or not he was just backtracking or he really meant it, he could not have been more accurate.

As described earlier, I made the decision to focus on building relationships first. Relationships will always be foundational to developing the culture. Although what happens in the rest of the school, district, and world impacts our schools and classrooms, so many educators create an environment, in spite of it all, to ensure their students have a place in the world where they feel safe, valued, and cared about. If we truly want to see different outcomes for learners in our education system and develop the whole child, we need to prioritize relationships with individuals and invite learners to show up as who they are and be seen. This is why I placed so much emphasis on creating the right kind of culture from the first day of school. They had to trust me enough to learn with me; they had to know I cared.

Let's go back to my friend Stephanie's classroom. Her students showed tremendous growth in one year because she created an environment that honored students based on their interests and empowered them to be learners and teachers. Together, they co-constructed the learning experiences to meet the learning objectives. Given that success, she could have taken all the lessons she taught that year and recreated the same lessons year after year, but she probably would not get the same results. Neither could the teacher next door get the same results with her lessons. What made the difference was how she leveraged student interests and expertise to co-design the learning experiences that allowed her students to be both teachers and learners. What was current and relevant in her class five years ago would not suffice to meet the needs of sixth-grade students today. In just the past five years, cell phones have advanced, new social media has emerged, and we all have ever-increasing access to information. Not to mention that she would have a totally different group of students with different interests, talents, and questions. To stay current, she needs to continually evolve based on her own learning, the identities of her learners, and the context.

Supporting versus Supplanting the Role of Teachers

Our world needs people who can think differently, solve problems, and thrive in a constantly changing and unpredictable society. So how can we structure learning experiences with a fixed curriculum that is outdated before learners access it? We can't! That said, endless possibilities exist to structure learning experiences for students to discover problems to solve, to develop and test ideas, and to receive feedback on the value of their ideas and products. You never know who will start a business, invent a cure for cancer, or change the world, but if we don't provide students with opportunities to develop skills and their own interests, we will miss out on the existing potential in so many of our creative and innovative thinkers. When learners are deeply engaged in creating better experiences and products, they are willing to do the daily work to bring new and better ideas to life. As Sir Ken Robinson says, "Thinking of education as a preparation for something that happens later can overlook the fact that the first sixteen or eighteen years of a person's life are not a rehearsal. Young people are living their lives now."[57] We must rethink why, what, and how we learn in schools for students to thrive in the information economy of today and tomorrow, not yesterday.

> *You can't mandate learning,*
> *but you can create*
> *the conditions in which*
> *people are inspired*
> *and empowered to learn.*

Many educators are beginning to challenge the notion that the textbook or the scope and sequence are the "right" ways to teach. In many districts today, schools are opting not to purchase new textbooks because of the constantly changing standards and learning expectations. Happily, I have seen an increased focus on personalized, competency-based learning, and project-based learning supported by open educational resources (OER) as well as learning environments that are shifting to support these resources and teaching methods. As we move away from traditional textbooks, teachers need access to high-quality models and digital content. But if we simply repackage content in digital

---

57   Ken Robinson, *Out of Our Minds: Learning to be Creative*, (West Sussex, Capstone, 2011).

textbooks and limit access to what we know when we compile them, how have we improved opportunities for students to engage with dynamic resources to learn in powerful ways? An article from *The Atlantic*, "The Deconstruction of the K–12 Teacher," highlights the significance of a teacher as a designer. "There is a profound difference between a local, expert teacher using the Internet and all its resources to supplement and improve his or her lessons, and a teacher facilitating the educational plans of massive organizations."[58]

My point is that prescribed lessons and programs, in digital format or in print, will never be sufficient. As educators, we need to leverage resources to create opportunities and connect students with one another and resources to develop lifelong learners. If we want to inspire innovation rather than compliance, teachers and students need time to experiment with new ideas, openly reflect, connect, and revise to ensure authentic learning and growth.

A great video, "Help with Bowdrill Set," shows just how easy it is for anyone today to access help and resources. In the video, a young kid, Nelson Smith, films his attempt to use his bowdrill set, although he knows he is doing it wrong, to solicit advice and tips from others who are more experienced and skilled. His video has over 30,000 hits and more than eighty comments from people sharing both support and expertise to help him. Here is one of the many examples of people willing to help: "Hey buddy, did you ever get anything figured out with this? If not, shoot me a message and I'll make a video for you on what works well to use and how to use it. Good try though! We never learn unless we try! Good on ya!" I love that Nelson put himself out there to seek help and that so many mentors are willing to support him. With this mindset and

---

58   Michael Godsey, "The Destruction of the K-12 Teacher," *The Atlantic*, March 25, 2015, https://www.theatlantic.com/education/archive/2015/03/the-deconstruction-of-the-k-12-teacher/388631.

networked approach to soliciting feedback, is there anything that Nelson (or any of us, for that matter) couldn't learn?

Who could your students access to help them learn? How might your students reach out to learn something new? What could your students learn? What could they teach others? The possibilities are endless if you are open to them. Ultimately, the best educators understand that you can't mandate learning, but you can create the conditions in which people are inspired and empowered to learn.

Concluding Thoughts

Traditionally, curriculum has been organized in a linear path that promotes a one-size-fits-all approach to success. When we simply follow the curriculum map or implement programs, we fail to take in the context and uniqueness of individuals into consideration. When the focus is on compliance and testing, it drives shallow learning in which we simply cover content rather than make deep connections to the content. This curriculum, standards-based model has left far too many behind, and even those who have successfully navigated school remain ill prepared for the world in which we live. Let's remedy this by taking some advice from middle-school educator and advocate, Rick Wormeli:

> Let's admit to students that we aren't really sure what the author meant symbolically, what really happened during a particular moment in history, whether or not a politician is misleading us, what an object is made of, or if our teaching strategy is the best way to teach.
>
> Let's get out of our students' way and not limit them to our imagination. If we're doing it right, every subsequent generation will be superior to the current one. If students only learned what we teachers know, society would grind to a halt. The goal is always that students will write a better paragraph, conduct a scientific experiment more wisely, compose more

> efficient computer code, and sing more beautifully than we can. Are we committed enough to let them? Let's ask questions of students to which we don't already know the answer.[59]

Eliminating the facade that we know it all or that we have the right answers requires being vulnerable and opening ourselves up to learn with and from our students. If we are serious about authentic learning, we must be willing, as Rick says, to ask questions to which we don't know the answers. Of course, we don't want to leave children behind or provide experiences in school that don't prepare them to be successful in life, college, and careers, but the reality is that schools today *are* leaving kids behind, offering experiences that are irrelevant to their lives, and failing to equip them with the skills they need to be learners and creators. Designing for learning and empowerment is about knowing the learners and the learning goals and being willing to co-create the path to get there.

---

59   Rick Wormeli, "The Courage It Takes. Middle Ground," *Virginia Commonwealth University*, Virginia, 2007, http://wp.vcu.edu/hhughesdecatur/files/2012/08/Rick-Wormeli_Courage-to-teach.doc.

Reflect and Connect Challenge
Share your thoughts, questions, and ideas using #LCInnovation

O   How might you better understand the strengths and passions of those you serve? How can you use these to design authentic and meaningful learning experiences?

O   How might you co-create learning experiences with those you serve?

O   How effective is your model in meeting the unique needs of learners? What might you do to change this? Do your learning experiences foster compliance or empowerment?

If we create a culture where every teacher believes they need to improve, not because they are not good enough but because they can be even better, there is no limit to what we can achieve.

—Dylan Wiliam

Learning Is a Process, Not an Event

WHEN MY DAUGHTER, ABBY, WAS in second grade, I volunteered as a guest to teach a variety of character education lessons in her class. As I taught the last lesson of the school year, I couldn't help but notice how respectfully the students spoke to one another and how engaged they were in conversations about the content. They were actually listening and responding to one another. I know many adults are still working on these skills, so I stopped the lesson to tell them how impressed I was with their communication skills. They all smiled and looked back at their teacher, who was beaming too.

This shift in how students were communicating and how they were working together was the result of a yearlong inquiry project guided by the school-wide focus: How can we improve meaningful student engagement? Liz Sloan, the principal, had asked each grade-level team to identify a specific focus or problem of practice. The second-grade team initially identified that students were having trouble listening. (I am sure other teachers can relate to this problem.) Based on this assessment, the team posed the question, "What strategies can we use to improve our students' listening skills?" The collective inquiry provided both structure and accountability for the teams while allowing the teachers to determine their focus (based on schoolwide and district goals) and exert their own agency to determine what to read, explore, and implement in order to achieve the goal of helping students learn to listen.

During collaboration time, the team members researched and learned about new strategies. They went back to their classrooms to try them out and later came back together to share their successes, challenges, and new ideas. As a result of this collaboration, Christine Kazerian, Abby's amazing teacher, taught them strategies for engaging in productive dialogue and how to listen and respond respectfully. They practiced and received feedback on how they were progressing. Because they had a shared goal, they worked to improve as a class and took pride in their growth. Christine shared her biggest takeaways from that year with me:

1) **Explicitly teach communication skills.**
   She taught lessons on effective feedback, showed videos, and gave examples of effective communication. She described the behaviors that she wanted to see, observed them in action, and used the evidence to plan for the next lessons.

2) **Hold students accountable for what they are learning and putting into practice**.
   She videotaped them, gave feedback, and allowed them to reflect on their behaviors.

3) **Have students lead the work.**
   She called this having "students lift the weights."
   Allowing students to determine their own level of
   engagement and how to increase it provided
   them with the agency to make changes in
   their behaviors.

The first two takeaways are foundational for teaching, but what I think is critical for learning and improving is the third: agency. In this process, the teachers were empowered to lead their professional learning and, in turn, empowered their students in their own learning process. As the second-grade team of teachers explored how to encourage students to be better listeners, they learned to teach their students to be better communicators and learners. Through the year of inquiry and learning, a series of small tweaks led by a team of motivated and skilled professionals made a big impact on how students were communicating and how everyone was learning and growing.

Reframing the Problem

Let's examine the steps that helped Abby's class move from struggling with listening to becoming actively engaged communicators. The initial framing of the problem that pervades our classrooms is that the kids weren't listening. Not listening can lead to a host of classroom management issues and might lead to punishment. Christine and her colleagues reframed the problem by using the lens of inquiry and seeking to understand how students could become better communicators. The reality is that this reframing approach can help us address any number of common challenges, both in and out of the classroom. In an article titled, "Are You Solving the Right Problems," in the *Harvard Business Review*, speaker and author, Thomas Wedell-Wedellsborg considers the implications for many "problems" and offers a strategy to think about reframing them.[60] The way we see the problem can prevent us from creating more effective solutions.

In the article, this example of how to reframe a slow elevator problem to uncover different solutions is provided:

> Imagine that you are the owner of an office building and your tenants are complaining about the elevator. It's old and slow, and they have to wait—a lot. Several tenants are threatening to break their leases if you don't fix the problem.

He notes that most people will identify solutions, such as replacing the elevator or fixing the motor. These symptomatic fixes provide solutions aimed at a perceived symptom or problem. These solutions address the assumption that the slow elevator is the problem.

When business managers, however, were asked to look at this problem, they identified a different solution. They suggested putting up mirrors next to the elevator and found that this diversion proved to effectively minimize complaints. Wedell-Wedellsborg found, "This simple addition proves wonderfully effective in reducing complaints about waiting for elevators because people tend to lose track of time when given something utterly fascinating to look at—namely, themselves."

You might note that the mirror solution doesn't address the stated problem. Rather than make the elevator faster, the solution comes by reframing the problem to find a different challenge to solve.

Now let's look at a common problem many educators face: You assign homework, and your students don't complete it and turn it in. Several students are in danger of failing due to their incomplete homework.

If you've ever dealt with this issue, you might have tried one of these common solutions: Call guardians and tell them about the

---

60   Thomas Wedell-Wedellsborg, "Are You Solving the Right Problems?" *Harvard Business Review*, Jan.-Feb. 2017, https://hbr.org/2017/01/are-you-solving-the-right-problems.

missing homework, give incentives for turning in homework, or hold students in for recess or after school until they finish it. These solutions assume that the problem is that students need to be more responsible and complete the homework.

If you look at the homework from another perspective, you might see a different reason for students failing to do their homework. For example, maybe homework is not as important as other things they have to do at home. Many students have siblings to care for, or sports or music practice, and some just need to move and play outside. Some have jobs, other interests and hobbies, and family to spend time with. If we move past the assumption that we have to give homework and instead look at what the learners need, we can then think about how to organize our time better in class to ensure that we are supporting learning and not just assigning and evaluating homework. Alice Keeler, teacher and co-author of *Ditch That Homework*, argues that learners need individual practice, and we need to make time for that during class so that we can give real-time, meaningful feedback to actually meet students where they are.

Recognizing the after-school demands on students and prioritizing the learning goals, some teachers have reframed the problem and created a more effective solution: reorganize the class schedule. Here is an example:

A teacher spent thirty minutes daily teaching isolated grammar skills and an additional thirty minutes practicing spelling words for the test on Friday. When she reorganized the class time to allow students to write about their own ideas and incorporated spelling and grammar practice in authentic writing tasks together, she created a thirty-minute block each day for students to receive personal support and practice based on their needs. That time frame allowed students to receive personal support from her and from their peers and to practice based on their needs, rendering homework unnecessary. This does not solve the problem of making students do homework at home as a means of teaching responsibility, but for this teacher, responsibility wasn't the goal of assigning homework; practice was. She reframed the homework problem by acknowledging her real intention for assigning it and found ways for students to use class time to practice the skills they needed to be successful. If we want to address the responsibility "problem," we could also look at a variety of ways to develop, practice, and reinforce desired skills without giving homework.

What's Preventing Students from Learning in School?

This notion of reframing problems made me think about many other challenges we face in education. In particular, I reflected on a recent workshop with passionate and caring leaders. They were discussing their dream for providing an education that prepared their students for college and career. They hoped to ensure their students were eligible for college, but they were frustrated by the seemingly insurmountable gap in their students' skills and where they needed to be. These leaders were all working so hard to prepare students for college and had been creating extra courses and opportunities for students to catch up, but in spite of their efforts to provide extra support, students were literally running out the doors to leave school and avoid the after-school support. Student apathy toward college preparation was the norm at this school, but the leaders hadn't considered why the extra classes and support weren't achieving their desired outcomes or that there might be another way.

Many of these leaders had been successful in school. They did not understand their students' lives or experiences. From their perspective, they were going above and beyond to help their students and teach them everything they needed to be successful. With a sincere desire to see their students succeed, they diligently implemented the district and school initiatives. They gave formative assessments, analyzed data in their professional learning communities (PLCs), retaught material, and provided extra classes and support. With all that, still fewer than 50 percent of their students were "proficient" on the standardized assessments, and fewer than 35 percent of them were eligible to attend college. They were doing all that was expected of them—and more—but it wasn't working, and they were frustrated.

One woman turned to me and asked, "What would you do with four hundred students who don't want to learn?"

Instead of assuming that students don't want to learn, could we ask, What is preventing students from learning in school?

I took a minute to process what she was asking and realized that one of the challenges they were facing was rooted in this very question. If we look beyond schools and at students' daily lives, we may well realize that they are learning more than we give them credit for. Many of them are learning to play video games; some are watching and learning from YouTube, and some are creating their own videos. We are innately curious as humans and are hardwired for learning. They are connecting and sharing things on social media; they are learning how to act and react by the models and interactions they have with peers and adults. I don't believe it is learning that they are against, but it is true that many aren't interested in how learning is prescribed in schools.

The hearts of these teachers and administrators are in the right place. They are committed to these kids, but their practices were not achieving the desired goal. What might happen if we reframe the question and look at this challenge from a different perspective?

Instead of assuming that students don't want to learn, could we ask, *What* is preventing students from learning in school?

Rather than assuming we know what they the learners need and why they are acting a certain way, we can better understand them and refine our practices as necessary when we honor diverse voices and empathize with them. IDEO, a global design company at the forefront of change and innovation, utilizes the human-centered design approach to meet the needs of their users. They define this approach as "building a deep empathy with the people you're designing for; generating tons of ideas; building a bunch of prototypes; sharing what you've made with the people you're designing for; and eventually putting your innovative new solution out in the world."[61]

This human-centered design approach runs contrary to the typical standardized approach taken by our current educational system that views learners through a deficit-based lens. In the standardized approach, educators must work to fill students with knowledge or skills to help them reach the desired goal, be it the next unit, the next grade, or prepared for college. Empathy for the end user (learner) lies at the heart of human-centered design; this essential skill allows the designer to better understand the end user.

To gather insight about how to better design their lessons and empathize with the learners, these high-school teachers and leaders interviewed their students. Throughout the thirty-minute interviews, educators asked students questions such as

- What is school like for you?
- Do you feel valued? By whom?
- When do you feel successful inside the classroom?
- When have you felt unsuccessful?
- How might you improve this school?

---

61 "What Is Human-Centered Design?" IDEO.org, http://www.designkit.org/human-centered-design.

In one-on-one or small-group settings and by asking open-ended questions and intentionally listening more than talking, they discovered a lot about their students. Through these interviews, teachers heard some ideas for improving their lessons, but what stood out most to them was that the schedules and class sizes contributed to the lack of meaningful interactions and that students felt insignificant in their classes. They also learned that students felt disconnected from their coursework. One student said he felt as if his classes and school were "irrelevant." These interviews made a huge impact on the teachers' ability to see school from their students' perspectives, and the insight allowed them to think differently about what they perceived as the problem. Although they had perceived the problem as poor behavior impacting academic achievement, they were genuinely surprised and saddened to realize that a significant percentage of their students were disconnected from their own academic experience and the reality of their not-so-distant futures.

Based on the students' responses, the teachers began to understand that relationships were at the heart of their challenges but could also be the solution. Students wanted to be seen as individuals and valued for their unique strengths. The teachers now understood that developing relationships had to come before developing the skills and knowledge necessary to put their students on the college and career path. This new vantage point allowed teachers to consider different solutions. Rather than adding more coursework and remedial programs, they began to brainstorm models for mentoring programs, advisory classes, student portfolios, and other opportunities that fostered relationships while making meaningful connections between learning and the students' personal interests. The student engagement that resulted reignited these educators' energy and passion by reminding them why they began teaching in the first place: helping students thrive.

These examples from Abby's classroom and the educators above provide insight into how reframing the problem can allow for learner-centered innovation to meet the needs of learners in your unique context. Taking an inquiry stance rather than just doing what has always been done can lead you to better solutions.

I certainly don't have all the answers. In truth, the "right" answers will vary based on the context and the learners. But I have no doubt that caring and talented educators can create new and better opportunities to meet the needs of those in their schools and classrooms by reframing the challenges and considering multiple perspectives. Reframing the problem is not to find the "real" problem, but finding a better problem to solve, and involving those who are doing the work in process. Looking at the challenges and the purpose of education differently can help us think about better solutions. Educator and author A.J. Juliani points out that "Our job is not to prepare kids for something; our job is to help kids prepare themselves for anything." If we use this goal as a starting point, reframing the problems we face might help us come up with novel solutions that better meet the needs of learners in a continually changing world.

Content Does Not Change Behavior

Imagine that, instead of interviewing students and creating the solution to meet the desired goals, the teachers spent their professional development time reading about advisory and portfolios. What if they explored the curriculum and learned about a new program for students to upload their work and were then asked to try these programs over the next month? How many do you think would actually take the time to do so? My guess is, not many. The new program would likely have been seen as adding something else to their already busy schedules and would have caused frustration and burnout rather than inspiring teachers to connect with their students. What made the difference for the teachers and students above was the connection made when they realized how and why the changes would meet their students' needs.

Professional development receives its fair share of criticism. Sometimes that criticism comes because the activities and the strategies don't connect with the teachers' classrooms or contexts. Sometimes it's because the new program or method makes more work for the teachers rather than helping them improve in their classroom.

> ## *The best ideas and finely tuned lesson plans are only as good as the impact they have.*

To be fair, at times, we love the learning and enjoy the professional development, but it doesn't translate to practice. Just think about a conference you went to that you loved or the awesome book you read. If you're like many people, you might have written down or highlighted a bunch of ideas, but you haven't put them into practice. We have no shortage of unused rubrics and frameworks and resources. The ideas might be excellent and could lead to powerful practices, but the content alone does not change behavior. Learners have to experience something. We all learn and change our behavior through cycles that include action, reflection, and revision that go beyond thinking, analyzing, and reading. What good are all those great ideas if they sit on a shelf or on a to-do list but never change how students learn? The best ideas and finely tuned lesson plans are only as good as the impact they have.

Enjoying the learning experiences isn't enough to shift practice for most of us. When I plan and facilitate professional learning, my goal is not that you like me or that you simply enjoy the day. Of course, I want people to like me, be happy, and enjoy the learning experience. I also know that isn't enough; learning must translate into action to make a positive impact on students. This point is illustrated by a teacher who, after she spent the day learning about the beaches and dredging sand with the Leadership and Professional Learning team at University of San Diego's Institute for Entrepreneurship in Education, shared with our team during a debrief, "After going through the process of experiencing fieldwork, listening to experts, researching, creating a presentation, and re-experiencing the day, *I found I was questioning more deeply.* I could see, feel, smell, and hear the knowledge and make a personal connection. *This was motivating because it was real and not just text.*"

Learning must translate into action to make a positive impact on students.

Her reflection brings a few thoughts to mind:

1. This teacher's shift in mindset and her response to her learning is powerful.
2. The learning experience she describes includes many of the standards that educators have to address.
3. How can anyone not want to provide opportunities for students to delve deeply into authentic experiences to make personal connections, gain new knowledge, and question deeply?

Moving from theory to practice requires action and opportunities to reflect, share, and refine in one's own context. We don't internalize learning as readily when we simply implement an idea that has been tested by someone else. When teachers experience hands-on, deep learning like this, they don't have to be told to teach kids differently; they *can't wait* to try their new ideas with their students.

If you are in charge of designing professional learning days, such as teaching in the classroom, you always have "so much to cover" in a short amount of time. You might be tempted to cram it all in instead of modeling the desired learning and teaching. In reality, personal and action-oriented learning experiences shift our practices to the desired learning and teaching. We too often know but fail to change how we deliver professional development and rely on telling teachers to do things, and it rarely translates to practice. We need to focus on offering professional learning that attends to and develops habits and behaviors, while providing ongoing practice and support.

While trends have emerged to "flip PD" and create more conference-based professional learning days in which educators have choices of sessions to attend, a lot of content is still being shared. But if content does not change behavior, perhaps it's time to take professional development a step further by creating opportunities for learners to *do* something. Conferences and workshops are a staple in professional learning. They can be motivating, and we learn so many new ideas, but if you don't take it further and they don't impact how students learn, what's the point?

Bias Toward Action

Have a bias toward action—let's see something happen now. You can break a big plan into small steps and take the first one right away.
—Indira Gandhi

At the beginning of any new idea, the possibilities can seem infinite and can lead to paralysis. New ideas might feel overwhelming if we don't break them into smaller steps. Prototyping is one of the most effective ways to jump-start our thinking and to guide, inspire, and explore an experimental approach. Using a prototype approach allows us to exert agency, start small, and learn from each step, making big ideas realities in the process.

Not too long ago, two teachers were sharing their excitement after attending a conference with me. What they learned didn't so much catch my attention, but the striking difference was in how they approached their ideas and next steps. The first teacher shared that she had learned some new applications and was so excited to practice and explore them further over the summer so that she could know the ins and outs of what was possible before she taught her new students in the fall. She clearly had the desire to learn and share new ideas with her students, but I knew that the need to figure it all out beforehand might prevent her from ever bringing these ideas into the classroom, where they could impact her learners. The reality is that new ideas pile up and go unused if we feel we need to become experts before implementing them. Overwhelm sets in, and the new ideas stay tucked away in our conference notes.

After the same conference, the second teacher described how she was inspired by the idea of Genius Hour. The following week, she invited parents to share what she wanted to try so that they would buy in and so they would support the project in the coming weeks. She was very upfront with everyone about not having all the answers, but she was eager to learn with her students, and she invited the parents to jump in and learn alongside their children.

The approach this teacher took—not knowing all the answers and outcomes first—might seem scary, but if we are asking students to take risks and learn new things, they need to see adults model that behavior too. Stepping out of our comfort zones and modeling risk-taking for our students can lead to new and better learning for everyone. You don't have to have all the answers to begin, a bias toward action will get you moving forward and help you figure them out—one step at a time.

Failure itself is not the problem; failing to learn from the process is where we can go wrong.

Educator as Researcher

Some of the biggest lessons I've learned that have shifted my practice in meaningful ways have emerged from inquiry-based projects, like the inquiry project Christine and her colleagues developed that I shared earlier in this chapter. Learning to better understand the challenges I am facing and then generating and testing new ideas has allowed me to own my learning and has provided me with a sense of agency. It is so empowering to see the results that come from putting what you are discovering into practice!

This approach to inquiry, commonly known as *improvement science*, aims to engage learners in rapid cycles of Plan, Do, Study, and Act (PDSA) to learn fast through action, fail fast, and improve quickly. This approach acknowledges that failure is part of the process and that failure itself is not the problem; failing to learn from the process is where we can go wrong.

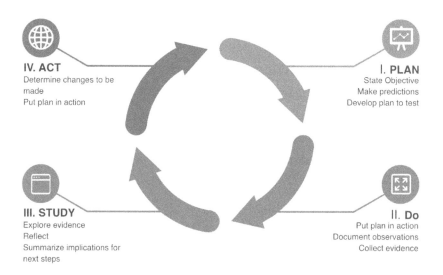

IV. ACT
Determine changes to be made
Put plan in action

I. PLAN
State Objective
Make predictions
Develop plan to test

III. STUDY
Explore evidence
Reflect
Summarize implications for next steps

II. Do
Put plan in action
Document observations
Collect evidence

Improvement science empowers learners to make tweaks as they investigate ideas. For educators, this model of discovery, exploration, and doing allows us to continually improve the way we serve the learners in our specific context. Amy Var, a middle-school teacher, engaged in an improvement science project to figure out how to enhance her peer-editing process by teaching students to give more thoughtful feedback. After learning about a variety of strategies, she thoughtfully implemented a few, including editing in Google Docs, to allow for more fluid commenting and editing. She found that this tool empowered students to invite outside collaborators to make comments on their writing. It also allowed her to collect evidence to determine the effectiveness of the tools. As Amy learned to use new tools and saw it working for her students, she let go of the control of editing and became more willing to allow her students to lead. The evidence she collected included student work, student feedback, and her own observations. She embraced the role of the learner and shared her thoughts with me on the process:

> More than anything, I'm looking forward to our next steps. I feel like I started by dipping my toe into the pool, and now I'm ready to dive head first into the waters of change and see where the tides continue to take me. It's such a good feeling, after eighteen years of teaching, to be this excited again![62]

I want to underscore her reflection. With so much focus on how to motivate and incentivize learners, Amy's personal learning experience illustrates that when what we are learning is directly tied to our own goals and is meaningful in our daily work, learning can be its own reward and can push us to want to know more. When learners are empowered to work through issues that matter to them rather than just going through the motions, the time and energy spent isn't a chore; it's productive because it improves both job performance and satisfaction.

When what we are learning is directly tied to our own goals and is meaningful in our daily work, learning can be its own reward and can push us to want to know more.

---

62   Amy Var, "Improvement Science Week 4-Study/Act—The Waves of Change," *Learning on the Run*, Accessed, Dec. 1, 2017, https://learningontherunblog.wordpress.com/improvement-science-week-4-studyact-the-waves-of-change.

There Is Not One Right Way

More often than not, research is viewed as something done by those in higher education to inform what educators in K–12 do. A great deal of research exists on mindset, brain plasticity, making mistakes, homework, and many more areas that impact education and learning. Despite this research, many practitioners experience a disconnect, and I have been thinking a lot about how we use research in education and the impact (or not) on how we innovate and improve. Too often, research and innovation are placed at odds. For example, I hear people challenge innovation in education because it is not evidence-based or proven by research. It often sounds like this: "We can't just experiment with kids and their future." Or "We have to know it works first." I certainly don't want to do anything to harm kids, but I also see how this can be used as an excuse to maintain traditions rather than looking at what's best for those we serve.

When I hear this argument of not experimenting on kids, I think of my experience as a parent and many parents I know. I can't think of a parent that hasn't "experimented" with their own kids in doing what is best for them. Just think of sleep schedules. Some research says that babies need to be on strict schedules and cry it out while other research says that you should cater to their every whimper and feed and hold them whenever they want. Research supports both sides (as is usually the case), but, as a mom, I tried out some things based on the research and made informed decisions about what I found to be some best practices. As I saw what worked, what didn't work, and the different needs and circumstances that emerged, I tried some different approaches. Sometimes it was better; sometimes it was not an improvement, and I learned what worked in my house, with my kids, and continually do so, daily. There is not one right way.

In the *Innovator's Mindset,* George Couros defines innovation in education as follows:

> A way of thinking that creates something new and better. Innovation can come from either "invention" (something totally new) or "iteration" (a change of something that already exists), but if it does not meet the idea of "new and better," it is not innovative.[63]

I also looked up the definition of research (and interestingly, you can find some different ones too). Here is *a* definition of research, according to Merriam-Webster:

> Studious inquiry or examination; especially: investigation or experimentation aimed at the discovery and interpretation of facts, *revision of accepted theories or laws in the light of new facts, or practical application of such new or revised theories or laws.*[64]

Essentially, the goal of research is to find new and better ways to do things and continue to do so over time. So really, research and innovation are actually in service of one another. As new findings emerge, we have to try them out in our classrooms, schools, and districts. Likewise, just because something has been proven as a best practice once doesn't mean it will always remain so, or just because it works with one group of kids doesn't mean it will work with another group. Through rigorous studies, we can document and generalize findings, but, as we learn from research, we will always need to attend to the context to ensure we are best serving the learners based on the desired outcomes, which continually requires innovation.

If we are honest with ourselves, many traditions don't serve learners, and research points to better ways, yet we fail to try

---

63   George Couros, *The Innovator's Mindset: Empower Learning, Unleash Talent, and Lead a Culture of Creativity* (San Diego, CA: Dave Burgess Consulting, Inc., 2015).

64   Merriam-Webster Dictionary, "Definition of Research," Accessed Dec. 1, 2017, https://www.merriam-webster.com/dictionary/research.

out new practices and innovate because they are at odds with long-held traditions.

Here are some examples:

Traditional Practice	Research Says	How Might We Innovate in Education?
Assigning homework to kids of all grade levels each night to teach responsibility and give extra practice.	There is no benefit to giving kids homework, especially in the elementary grades.	
Tracking students based on intelligence and standardized measures of achievement.	Beliefs in learners and their ability impact success. Students are capable of learning in effective learning environments.	
Value getting things right the first time, no make-ups, fixed view of intelligence.	Our brains grow with mistakes and make new connections between new and different ideas.	
Treat professional development for teachers as an event and expect fidelity in implementation.	Teachers thrive when they have opportunities to experience new learning practices, get feedback, and collaborate with peers to improve.	

I intentionally left the last column blank because, if we are focusing on the learners in our own context, the answers should vary. If you are asking what is best for each learner, determining what is already known through practice and research can help you decide what practices might serve them better. Try some things out, reflect, remix, and revise based on the learners you serve and determine your next best practice is for your context. Then, share so we can all learn and improve based on your experiences, innovative ideas, and lessons learned.

Innovative educators look to research and best practices and base decisions on the learners they serve in their contexts to provide new and better experiences to meet the desired outcomes. In service of creating better learning opportunities, we also have to understand that there is never just one right way, and change is a process.

Small Tweaks, Big Impact

In a district where I consulted, one the of areas of improvement was increasing the level of complexity of student work. To deepen our conversations about teaching and learning based on evidence from the classrooms and to better understand their current practices in relationship to where they wanted to be, we observe learning in action in multiple classrooms. It's important to note that this was not evaluative; we were looking through the lens of inquiry and seeking to understand that when we observed classrooms. (See more in chapter 11.) In one classroom, we saw students sitting in groups cutting and pasting the steps of a water cycle. As we talked to the students, we found out that the teacher had read the process aloud to the students; they watched a video clip on the cycle, and then she modeled the right order for students to arrange each of the six steps of the cycle on their individual papers.

While we debriefed what we were learning from our observations, one teacher noted that the students could complete the activity by simply following directions, but they were not necessarily demonstrating their understanding of the water cycle. Another suggested that if the teacher showed the video and had students read about the process and work collaboratively to figure out the right order, they would likely gain a better understanding of the water cycle. This small tweak shifted the lesson from compliance—following the step-by-step directions—to an opportunity to read, think critically, work collaboratively, and communicate with peers about the content to achieve the learning objectives.

Focusing on small tweaks can help your team understand what shifts are necessary to make a big impact.

Over and over, observations across campus stimulated similar conversations. In each case, as the team debriefed, we focused on the possibilities and what we were learning. Excitement about possible, small tweaks grew. Slight, easy shifts in the questions or the sequence of the learning experience made change seem doable. With this new perspective, the teachers revised their lessons to shift the cognitive load onto students, providing opportunities to engage in higher-level tasks and allowing students to drive the learning experiences. Observing classrooms and taking an inquiry approach to better understand the impact of teaching practice on student learning can illuminate opportunities for growth and fuel learner-centered innovation. As happened in this district, focusing on small tweaks can help your team understand in concrete terms what types of shifts are necessary in classrooms to empower learners and make a big impact.

Learning Is a Process, Not an Event

When professional development in schools and districts consists of a variety of isolated events, they fail the majority of the time to actually change how students learn in the classroom even under the best of circumstances. In an effort to be organized and cover all the new initiatives, I have seen professional development calendars scheduled to ensure they fit in time to review all the priorities. Teachers end up hearing about close reading strategies one day, accountable talk in the next session, and tech tools the following month. This leads to more overwhelmed teachers who feel pressured to fit even more things into their day.

The following cycle is not meant to be a step-by-step guide but to demonstrate the multiple steps that learning something new requires and the systems that need to be in place for ongoing, job-embedded learning. The teachers who observed classrooms gained valuable insights and ideas to shift practice, but this was only part of the process. We aligned the staff meetings and team collaboration time to ensure teachers had time to design new and better learning opportunities, try out some things, receive feedback, and continue to revise. If we value new learning and desire to see changes in our classrooms, we cannot expect it to happen after the school day or in two professional development days each year. Systems need to be in place that promote innovation to improve how teachers collaborate, learn, and teach on a regular basis.

These guiding questions will help you think about how to create time and focus to structure opportunities for collaborative work that empowers educators to create new ideas and share strengths and challenges of innovations to improve practices and achieve learning goals. This is an iterative cycle; these shouldn't be seen as linear but as a variety of connected opportunities and resources throughout the learning process to meet the needs of the learner in context.

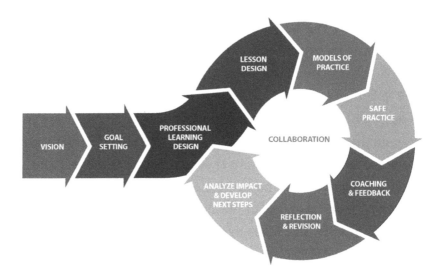

Personalized Professional Learning Cycle[65]

- **Vision**—Do you have a common understanding of what you want to accomplish? What is the vision for learning and teaching? How will you empower teachers?

- **Goal Setting**—What are your specific learning goals aligned to the vision? How will you assess impact?

- **Professional Learning Design**—How will teachers have opportunities to experience new learning? Who are the experts to seek out and from which to learn? How will your team develop new knowledge and strategies to achieve the learning goals?

- **Lesson Design and Models of Practice**—How can you open classroom doors and provide opportunities to see teachers in action? How might you provide models of the desired learning experiences?

- **Safe Practice**—How will you ensure teachers have opportunities to design new learning experiences

---

65 "Personalized Professional Learning Cycle," Institute for Entrepreneurship in Education. https://www.sandiego.edu/iee/partnerships/#tab-panel4.

and try out new ideas, take risks, and reflect on
new learning?

- **Coaching and Feedback**—How will all teachers
  receive feedback related to the vision and the desired
  shifts? Who will you solicit feedback from?

- **Reflection and Revision**—How will teachers reflect
  on their feedback and make necessary revisions to
  continue to improve practice?

- **Analyze the Impact and Develop Next Steps**—How
  will teachers assess the impact on desired student
  outcomes and determine next steps?

- **Share and Celebrate Growth**—At each phase, how
  will teachers have opportunities to share what they are
  learning? How might students share their process? How
  will growth be celebrated?

Concluding Thoughts

A clear understanding of the vision is critical, but shifting our
practice requires small steps to get there. Each tweak teaches us more
and allows for a continuous evolution of our practice. Changing
how students learn in the classroom is more about a series of small
tweaks rather than one dramatic shift. Effective teachers use ongoing assessments of their students and regularly create experiences
that meet the needs of the students they serve. They set high expectations and promote safe learning environments as they model and
guide diverse learners. To foster mindsets that empower creativity
and innovation, effective teachers also know they must step back
and let students grapple with problems so they can truly own their
learning. Likewise, by providing teachers time and support to
define the challenges or problems and leverage networks to identify, adapt, and develop new and better practices, we can effectively
scale up promising innovations in our schools.

Reflect and Connect Challenge
Share your thoughts, questions, and ideas using #LCInnovation

○ Take a challenge that exists in your school or classroom. How can you reframe the problem to create a better solution?

○ How could you leverage the insights and knowledge of administrators, community, teachers, or students to identify the "right" problems to solve?

○ Investigate your practice: Define a problem, plan for implementation, do something, collect evidence, and reflect and revise to improve. Share what you learned.

○ Demonstrate your bias toward action: What could you try today (or tomorrow)?

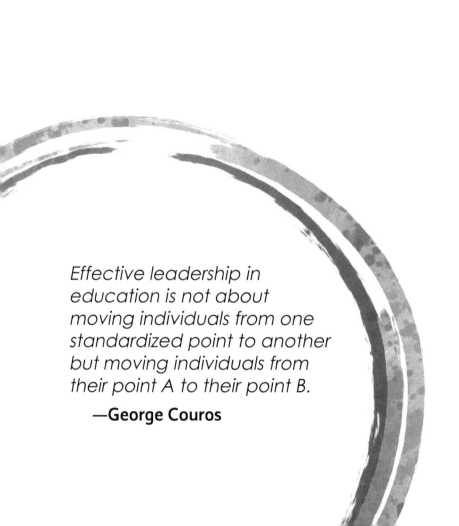

Effective leadership in education is not about moving individuals from one standardized point to another but moving individuals from their point A to their point B.

—George Couros

Meet Learners
Where They Are

DURING MY FIRST YEAR OF teaching, I was fortunate to have a great mentor who put relationships at the core of the work. I knew that my mentor, Anne Ashford, was special, but it wasn't until I realized how few teachers had a mentor or a coach, let alone one that was truly invested in their personal and professional growth, that I understood how lucky I was. She took time to get to know me and my goals before she talked about my behavior-management plan. She connected me to other new teachers and helped develop my professional network through some of her colleagues and connection. In fact, I met my husband and some of my best friends through her. You might not think that has anything to do with mentoring, but, in truth, it has everything to do with it. She took the time to get to know me, she was open with me, and we built a relationship. Because of all this, she earned my trust; she pushed me to achieve far more than I could have alone. She challenged me to do things that I didn't think I was capable of and was there to support me when I stumbled. Due to Anne, the growth I experienced from our work together, and the satisfaction that I felt as a teacher, I understand why an effective coach increases teachers' understanding of their content and instructional strategies, as well as their enjoyment of their work. As teachers learn with trusted colleagues and see the impact their learning has on their students, they become energized and eager to try new things.

At every stage in my education and career, I can pinpoint people who have been instrumental in my growth and have helped support and push me along my path. Much of my career has been focused on mentoring teachers and leaders, and because of Anne and others like her, I am cognizant of how it feels to be mentored. I'm also aware that many people hold the title of coach or mentor and that the title itself means very little. The influence mentors have is the result of strong relationships, regular access, connections, immense expertise, and ultimately high expectations, regardless of actual position.

> **Relationships**—The relationships with each mentor might differ, but at the core is the belief that the mentor cares about you and your work and is committed to helping you achieve your goals. Relationships are foundational. If you don't believe they care, you aren't likely to be open to their feedback.

> **Access**—Building trust and developing a relationship requires regular contact. You never know when you will come against challenges or need to talk through something, which is why mentors and mentees need regular access and

open lines of communication with each other. Ongoing, regular conversations create powerful opportunities for mentors to see patterns, highlight strengths, and expose some areas of growth. You can't do that effectively by dropping in or leaving a note with some next steps.

Expertise—Talking about your day or sharing experiences with friends and family can be helpful; however, you will notice a difference between talking to someone with a high level of expertise in your area and someone with little if any knowledge. The former is more likely and better-equipped than a friend or spouse might be to understand your challenges and unearth root causes to help you solve problems. Working with a coach or mentor that can push you to the next level requires knowing the context and having expertise in the area to guide next steps.

High Expectations—When I was studying the relationships between mentors and mentees for my dissertation, I found a lot of "buddy mentoring," with a focus on making the mentor feel good without pushing thinking or helping them to improve. It feels good to have someone tell you that you are doing great and praise your efforts; encouragement builds our confidence. But critical feedback is what really pushes a person's thinking. Everyone needs a mentor who is willing to point out weaknesses, encourage growth, and continually push for excellence.

Being mentored is not always easy, and it shouldn't be if it's about growth. Many times, we think of a mentor being there to support, but the best mentors push you to help you confront challenges and address blind spots that you might not see yourself. Being a mentor takes time and commitment, and I am grateful to my own mentors for the time they have poured into my development and growth.

To truly grow and learn, you have to be willing to be vulnerable, share your struggles, and invest in the work, and, when you do, both mentor and mentee grow.

Invest in People

Mark Cuban, entrepreneur and owner of the Dallas Mavericks, believes that one of his most important (and undervalued) innovations for the Dallas Mavericks basketball team was bringing in former players to coach current players. Today, this is a common practice in the NBA. But he recalls that he had to justify the practice to sports media. "We spent more on support of our personal computers and software than we did developing our most important employees: our players."[66] He says that bringing in players and specialists to help improve the skill sets of players is one of the key practices that led to the Mavericks' turnaround, a venture well worth the investment.

Likewise, Bruce Joyce and Beverly Showers[67] describe the impact of professional learning outcomes in their book, *Student Achievement through Staff Development* (3rd ed) and highlight that coaching significantly impacted the extent to which new skills and knowledge were transferred into a teacher's practice. Teachers who were coached practiced new strategies with greater knowledge and understanding and were more able to use strategies in their own contexts than teachers who simply learned about theory and practiced in isolated workshop contexts. The teachers who were coached in the classroom implemented 95% of skills over time compared with 5% of their peers that implemented instructional practices in their classroom without coaching. If we want to improve skills, knowledge, and their application in our classrooms, we must move

---

66   Adam Grant, "Mark Cuban Is Tired of Your 'Uber of Something' Pitch," *Esquire*, May 15, 2017, http://www.esquire.com/lifestyle/money/a55079/mark-cuban-gets-loud.

67   Bruce Joyce and Beverly Showers, *Student Achievement through Staff Development* 3rd ed (Alexandria, VA: Association for Supervision and Curriculum Development, 2002).

beyond one-size-fits-all trainings and curriculum and invest in the development of people.

Professional Learning Outcomes
Joyce & Showers (2002)

Components of Professional Learning	Concept Understanding	Skill Demonstration	Use in the Classroom
Theory and Discussion	10%	5%	0%
Demonstration in Training	30%	20%	0%
Practice & Feedback in Training	60%	60%	5%
Coaching in the Classroom	95%	95%	95%

To develop the skills, knowledge, and mindsets of others, coaches invest in people. Relationships are the most important investment we can make; the success or failure of your ability to grow and develop people hinges on personal connections and attention to the learning context. Checking boxes on an observation form, noting whether standards are aligned with the pacing guide, and collecting data on a spreadsheet are not helpful in moving people forward, nor are these activities coaching. These evaluations make people afraid, risk averse, and unhappy. Support that makes a difference is not about compliance to a standardized system; it is about knowing people, growing people, and unleashing talent.

Support Looks Different for Different People

I'm sure you have heard (and probably try to live by) the Golden Rule: Treat others as you want to be treated. We tend to expect people to treat one another with respect. The Golden Rule, or a variation of it, was a standard in almost every classroom or sport I ever participated in, and it was one of the rules that hung in my own classroom. If we see everyone as the same, and expect everyone to fit into a mold and act and do the same things, this rule makes perfect sense. But if we acknowledge that we all have a variety of strengths, interests, motivations, and experiences that shape our behaviors, we can see the Golden Rule's limitations.

To truly empower others and move from a culture of compliance to one that values creation and innovation, the Platinum Rule might serve us all better: Treat others as *they* want to be treated. Really, this rule makes perfect sense. When we honor the uniqueness of individuals and when people get what they need, they are more likely to be inspired to go above and beyond what is expected.

Many teachers, especially new teachers, have coaches both formal and informal who are well positioned to employ the platinum rule in professional learning by providing uniquely designed support based on the needs of the individual. Ingersoll and Smith (2004) found that teachers who were provided a mentor from the same content area in their first year of teaching, including planning and collaboration, were less likely to leave the profession after their first year. Effective coaches tailor support to the context and needs of the individual. They help teachers develop an explicit vision of quality teaching and learning and have skills and strategies to help teachers arrive there, such as inquiry-based questioning, frequent observations and feedback, and models of desired learning experiences. The guidance of an experienced teacher can allow teachers to make decisions as part of an experienced team rather than in isolation. This impacts student achievement as well as teacher job satisfaction.

In the article "I Am an Educator and I Am Desperate to Be Taught," one teacher shared her experience with two different types of coaches:

> While my previous coach had tracked things like percentage of student vs. teacher talk, rigor of questioning, and text complexity in her observations, my new coach was checking items off on a list, exactly the same as he had in every other class he visited: Were rules posted? Was there common formatting on worksheets? Did I have a behavior tracker on the wall? And most importantly, was there a standardized test question embedded in every lesson? The deep, personal inquiry into student learning was replaced with questions of compliance and testing.[68]

Monitoring teaching and learning compared with a standardized goal does nothing to grow people or make them feel valued, motivated, and inspired to learn to improve. To encourage learners to try new things and to be more innovative, we have to start from where they are, not from a checklist. If we embrace the platinum rule, we have to understand that the "right" support looks different for different people.

See Me. Know Me. Grow Me.

Treating others how they want to be treated requires that we know the learners first, which can include administrators, teachers, students, parents, and anyone we work with. These three questions from a visionary leader and great coach, Brandon Wiley, Chief Program Officer at Buck Institute for Education, can help us frame our thinking about how to best support a variety of learners: *Do you see me? Do you know me? Will you grow me?*

---

68   Anonymous, "I Am an Educator and I Am Desperate to Be Taught," *kiddom*, July 21, 2016, https://blog.kiddom.co/i-am-an-educator-and-i-am-desperate-to-be-taught-dc0dda41d4dc.

Do you see me?

Have you taken the time to get to know the person as an individual? Do you know their interests? What do they value or care about?

A teacher recently shared with me that he changed his beginning-of-the-year survey from standard questions, such as How many siblings do you have? and What are your favorite subjects? to an open-ended list of the "Top Ten Things I Need to Know about You." Instead of static answers, such as two brothers and art, he received responses like:

- It takes me an hour and a half to get to school each day.
- My parents just got divorced.
- It takes me longer to figure things out and so I am quiet but I really do care about school.
- I love drawing.

Teachers can connect and get to know learners in multiple ways to better support them, and often it begins with asking questions and being willing to listen.

Do you know me?

Can you name the strengths of this individual? Do you know their successes? What drives them?

When we see people for what's right with them and how they want to be treated, we build confidence and encourage people to focus on what they excel in instead of dwelling on challenges. I find that working on teams where we have taken the Strengths Finder assessment (StrengthsFinder.com) and been deliberate about building from our individual strengths has made a considerable difference in how we see one another and work together. (In case you are wondering, my strengths are: Woo, Relator, Activator, Positivity, Communication.) Acknowledging and building off strengths rather than focusing on weaknesses helps people feel seen and valued for who they are. As a result, I have found that individuals tend to take critiques less personally, are open about challenges, and are able to communicate about our competing or complementary strengths and work styles to collaborate more effectively.

When we know our strengths and share them with others, we can be transparent about our needs and openly discuss how to best work together to accomplish our collective goals.

Will you grow me?

Do you know the personal goals or aspirations of those you serve? How is your support connected to those goals and to who they are? What resources, pathways, or experiences are the best fit for each learner?

Supporting individuals requires moving away from the notion that we all need to (or even can) learn the same things at the same time. This doesn't mean that there aren't things that we all need to learn; rather it's an acknowledgment that the pathways we take, where we learn, and the resources we use might need to look a little different, depending on our individual strengths and weaknesses. As teachers and leaders, meeting the needs of diverse learners requires knowing the learners and their needs first and then finding new and better ways to support them.

I love the simplicity and power of these three questions. I try to think about them when I work with people in a variety of contexts, and I appreciate it when I receive the same in return. We are more willing and able to hear critical feedback when it is coming from someone who we perceive cares about us as individuals, sees our strengths, and is willing to invest the time to help us grow. The reality is that seeing, knowing, and growing people requires an intentional and significant investment in people's lives, but when we take the time, progress is sure to follow.

The Feedback Paradox

Feedback is essential to growth. I consistently hear from educators who say they want feedback. Just as consistently, I hear from administrators who say educators aren't receptive to feedback. Frequently, both are being truthful.

An example of this feedback paradox follows:

A needs assessment in one district overwhelmingly found that the majority of teachers sought critical feedback, not just high fives or kudos, to inform their practice. As the data were presented to the administrators, many became frustrated and recounted story after story of how they had been met with defensiveness and hurt feelings when they provided critical feedback to their teachers.

As I heard their comments, I reflected on my initial reaction when I felt that same resistance to feedback I was providing. My response was similar to that of the administrators I heard that day; I had quickly assumed that the recipients were just seeking positive accolades and didn't *really* want to grow. Upon further reflection and after some critical feedback from another colleague, I was reminded of a valuable lesson: *Feedback is best received within a relationship and when people feel valued.*

This truth extends to students in the classroom as well. In fact, research[69] highlights that achievement increased significantly when teachers gave feedback prefaced with, "I'm giving you these comments because I have very high expectations, and I know that you can reach them." When feedback was attributed to a teacher's high expectations and belief in student potential, "the intervention closed the racial achievement gap in this sample by nearly 40 percent."

---

69 David Scott Yeager, et. al., "Breaking the Cycle of Mistrust: Wise Interventions to Provide Critical Feedback Across the Racial Divide," *Journal of Experimental Psychology* Volume 143, No. 2, (2014): p. 804–824, Accessed Dec. 1, 2017, http://www.apa.org/pubs/journals/releases/xge-a0033906.pdf.

When it comes to effective feedback, what works in the classroom applies to all of us as mentors, coaches, leaders, and parents. Providing feedback that improves performance must be preceded by belief in and care for the individual. Without a trusting relationship, feedback feels like criticism, and people tend to feel misunderstood or as if they don't belong or are being judged. The kneejerk reaction to criticism is to feel defensive and blame external factors rather than persevere, but that kind of response rarely leads to improvement.

Feedback is best received within a relationship and when people feel valued.

Meet Them Where They Are

Dwight Carter, a principal and author, shared in a conversation how he received some negative feedback from a survey his first year as a principal at his new school. The feedback reflected a more challenging reality than he was aware of. He opened up about how devastated he was to learn that his actions weren't having the impact that he desired. He was working so hard and had the best of intentions, but, for a variety of reasons, he wasn't connecting with his staff or meeting their needs. The feedback, although difficult to hear, allowed him to have hard conversations with his staff about their perceptions and how he could improve.

Through this feedback, Dwight reflected and shared about the importance of moving beyond an "open-door policy" and going out of his way to meet people where they were without waiting for them to come to him. To do this, he moved his desk out into the hallway where he would see people, connect, and be visible on a regular basis rather than tucked away in his office. The reality is that most people won't tell you about challenges, especially if you have no relationship and the structures for feedback aren't in place. You have to deliberately make time to understand where people are to guide, support, and provide feedback. If you want to hear all the voices, you can't just invite people to the table, you have to bring the table to them.

I applied this lesson to my work with teachers; for example, as a new teacher mentor and instructional coach, I could have sat in my office and kept myself busy while I waited for someone to reach out for help. Instead of waiting for people to find time in their busy schedules to come to me, I blocked out regular check-ins to meet them where they were. Basing these meetings on the teachers' goals, it was more effective to have a regular structure that allowed meaningful reflection and support to address emerging needs before they became problems rather than wait for challenges to emerge. Creating the space to ask questions, provide guidance, and problem solve emerging challenges is a proactive strategy that helps people stay on track and may even stave off problems.

Radical Candor

Whether you are a teacher, a coach, or an administrator, your job is to develop the skills and knowledge of others, which often requires providing effective feedback. Although teacher evaluations are becoming more common, The Mirage, a report from the teacher training organization TNTP, found that, despite the investment in professional development, "school systems are not helping teachers understand how to improve—or even that they have room to improve at all."[70]

---

70   TNTP, "The Mirage: Confronting the Hard Truth About Our Quest for Teacher Development," *TNTP*, July 4, 2015, https://tntp.org/publications/view/the-mirage-confronting-the-truth-about-our-quest-for-teacher-development.

Examples of general feedback include, "You were a great presenter," or "You are my favorite teacher," or receiving an 'A' on an assignment. These positive accolades make us feel good, and that kind of encouragement is valuable but does not help us grow. It is kind to be nice and gives us the warm fuzzies when we are liked, but when we only give and seek feedback that soothes our egos, it can prevent growth. If we assume everyone wants to be the very best they can be, then we see feedback as an opportunity for growth. Central to providing useful and effective feedback is demonstrating you care personally while also challenging directly. Kim Scott, author of *Radical Candor* argues:

> *Caring personally* means embracing the full humanity of those we lead, and allowing them to embrace ours. Using phrases like "Keep it professional" or "don't take this personally" are insulting. They deny the truth that we are human beings with feelings, and our work is a *personal* expression of our identity. Caring acknowledges that we have lives and aspirations that extend beyond those related to our shared work. And caring demands that we find time for real conversations and get to know one another at a human level. Only when you actually care about the whole person with your whole self can you have a relationship.[71]

The second part of radical candor, *challenging directly*, involves telling people in caring, nonjudgmental language where they can improve. Great leaders let people know they care and are willing to have tough conversations to help people understand the truth about their performance so they can become better. I love this push from Steve Jobs: "Be a yardstick of quality. Some people aren't used to an environment where excellence is expected." Some people tend

---

71   Ron Carucci, "How To Use Radical Candor To Drive Great Results," *Forbes*, March 14, 2017, https://www.forbes.com/sites/roncarucci/2017/03/14/how-to-use-radical-candor-to-drive-great-results/#3bc5b89f4e23.

to avoid conflict and addressing areas for improvement because those kinds of conversations are uncomfortable. But as the TNTP report alluded to, ignoring practices of behaviors that may negatively impact student learning doesn't do anyone any favors. And unfortunately, when issues are left unaddressed, our students are the ones who suffer. As we seek to help others improve by demonstrating our genuine care and willingness to be forthright, we must give people high expectations to live up to *and* high levels of support to get people there.

Investing the time and energy to get to know people as individuals and to understand their strengths, goals, and aspirations is critical to supporting growth and development. The following excerpts from interviews with three teachers exemplify the importance of trust to their openness to feedback over the role or title of the person giving feedback.

> **Teacher 1:** Stacey reflected on the challenges she had with one of her mentors who was coming to observe her. "I figured out that I don't have a relationship with this woman, and I don't trust her to come into my room and observe me and really get what is going on because she hasn't been around." Stacey felt vulnerable being observed and receiving feedback from someone she did not trust nor whom she believed had her best interests in mind.

> **Teacher 2:** Similarly, Jeff desired more communication and feedback from his principal and explained that since he was halfway through the school year, "If my principal came in now, it would be the first time I ever saw him in here, and if he didn't like it, I would take it personally." Since he did not have consistent interactions with his principal and because he had not been in his classroom throughout the year, he didn't perceive that his principal cared about him or his

development. Therefore, if he had a critique, Jeff knew he would react defensively.

Teacher 3: Maria had a much different experience. She felt that her assistant principal had taken the time to develop a relationship, and, as a result, she expressed that she had become more receptive to mentoring as the year progressed. She perceived this mentoring relationship as her best support throughout the year. "She gives me a ton of positive feedback to the point that I am more and more open and honest about what I am doing and seeking feedback. So it has given me the confidence to try new things."

What this last insight on feedback highlights is the importance of radical candor: caring personally, challenging directly. These teachers connected both positive and negative relationships with the administrator, mentor, or coach to their openness to feedback. It is important to note that great protocols and questioning techniques allow for rich dialogue and powerful conversations, and these are vital to helping people move forward, but if you don't have a relationship, none of those tools or practices will be effective.

Create Ongoing Structures for Critique and Revision

This notion of radical candor is applicable to how we provide feedback to students as well. I often see extremes where the grade is the focus and, in the name of rigor, a student's work is marked up, seemingly without regard for the individual, and high expectations are upheld. On the other side, we conflate a positive culture with making everyone feel good and avoid addressing areas of growth or challenges because we don't want to hurt people's feelings.

I don't care how old or how successful you are, getting negative feedback, a poor performance review, or a page full of edits doesn't feel good. But just because it is hard doesn't mean we should avoid critique, because it's valuable to the learning process. It's both possible and necessary to value individuals and their efforts while also addressing skills and behaviors that need improvement. If you celebrate success and reflect on growth often, you can more easily address challenges in the spirit of improvement when people make mistakes or haven't quite reached the desired level of proficiency. This is also much more effective if you have regular opportunities and structures for feedback to address challenges and it is clear that it is an opportunity to learn rather than simply about a final grade for evaluation.

One of my favorite examples of this is the video clip "Austin's Butterfly," where Ron Berger details the journey of the project with elementary school students to highlight the impact of critique and revision. I love this video because it shows how all learners can move from an initial draft to a higher-quality product with guidance and support but also that even our youngest learners are capable of providing such support to one another. Austin, a first-grade student, was creating a scientific drawing of a butterfly for a notecard that was being sold to raise funds for a butterfly habitat. Over the course of six different drafts, Austin dramatically improved his drawing and accuracy based on the actual picture of the butterfly with kind, specific, and helpful feedback. This video is powerful, and, as the Models of Excellence website states, "The progress of the drawing from a primitive first draft to an impressive final draft is a powerful message for educators: We often settle for low-quality work because we underestimate the capacity of students to create great work. With time, clarity, critique, and support, students are capable of much more than we imagine."[72] When we raise our expectations and create the conditions where learners feel valued, supported, and expected to achieve, they will often go above and beyond.

---

72   Unknown, "Austin's Butterfly," *EL Education: Models of Excellence*, Accessed Dec. 1, 2017, http://modelsofexcellence.eleducation.org/resources/austins-butterfly.

Honor the Learning Process

Even as I have worked to became better at giving feedback throughout the learning process, I have always struggled with grading. I don't enjoy the feeling of simplifying the hard work of learners to a grade, a number, or a quadrant on a rubric. No matter how aligned you think you are to the standards or your target, grading is subjective. I want learners to produce their best, but reducing hard work, growth, struggle, questions, mistakes, revisions, or effort on an assignment to a grade or a number will never accurately communicate what the learner knows and the next steps. Even so, as a teacher, an evaluator, or a supervisor, I have to give a grade, and, the second I do, I know that becomes the focus rather than the learning. As an educator, I am always searching for learning and growth to matter, not the grade.

In addition to building in more time for reflection and revision throughout our days in the classroom, as a teacher, I specifically blocked off class time at the end of each quarter to reflect on the goals my students and I had set at the beginning of the quarter. Students documented evidence of their work that they were proud of, and each student did a 3-2-Q Reflection: three successes or things they were proud of, two areas that they wanted to improve, and a question that they had for further inquiry or growth. When students reflected on their growth, they led the process and took ownership of their learning and efforts to improve.

Much like grades and student evaluations, teacher evaluation and accountability systems can often feel like they are done to teachers rather than in service of growth, which can be frustrating. To create more transparency in our learning, I used this same self-assessment process with my team at the University of San Diego instead of following the traditional evaluation protocol. Individuals shared their strengths, opportunities for growth, and a question to guide their next steps. This reflection informed performance evaluations and ensured that the team had ownership in the process and collected their own evidence of growth and goals, rather than having all the feedback and goals come from the top down.

Making the learning process public and openly sharing personal goals and reflections provide a great way to highlight progress and move forward to the next level both individually and collectively. We still completed the obligatory paperwork for the evaluations, but the feedback and assessments were more authentic, and we all felt a sense of shared ownership in the process that made it a powerful learning experience, not just a task.

Put Away the Red Pen

I remember grading my students' essays and making comments, asking questions, probing for more, and then assigning the grade. I spent an inordinate amount of time as an English teacher providing feedback and grading essays. Then I would hand them back; my students looked at the grade, and very few paid any attention to the comments I had made. We quickly moved on. The process was painful. What I had done was the equivalent of an autopsy. The final product had already been completed, and I hadn't built in the time or the expectation to go back to revise or to improve it. I had invested a lot of time and energy giving feedback and writing really thoughtful comments at the most ineffective time in the learning process—after it was over.

What shifted my thinking about this is an analogy from Jan Chappuis, formative assessment expert and author, who compared grading in the classroom to making kids clean their bedrooms, both arduous tasks. Imagine asking your child to clean their room, and they don't. You ask again, and they put in minimal effort by throwing some clothes under the bed or in the closet. (Or maybe this is just my kids.) Imagine at the end of the week, you have guests coming, and the room is still not cleaned, so you go in and pick up all the clothes and clean the room the way it was supposed to be done. You tell your children, "This is what I expect of you next time." Another approach is to just close the door. In the end, your children's half-hearted attempts are reinforced, and they learn that you will do the work for them or just move on when they don't do what they were supposed to do.

Jan likened this approach to receiving a paper returned that looks like it has been massacred by the red pen, where a teacher grades an assignment and makes all the necessary revisions for the students. This approach reinforces to learners that they can wait out the teacher because the teacher will make all the corrections for them. If you require students to re-submit the corrections, they can just copy the revisions you made with minimal thinking or effort, or they just take a bad grade and move on, like closing the bedroom door. Either way, the teacher puts in a lot of effort but the learner experiences minimal effort and/or growth.

Instead of the teachers or the evaluators doing all the work, changing how and when we give feedback in school can have a huge impact on learning and growth when we create the systems where learners take ownership of the process rather than just being recipients of a grade.

Much attention has been paid to Stanford professor Carol Dweck for her book *Mindset: The New Psychology of Success*[73] and her work on growth mindset. Her research has helped us see that the brain is like a muscle and can grow with effort rather than seeing people as being naturally smart or lacking control over their own abilities, which she refers to as a fixed mindset. To maximize learning opportunities, we need to leave room for mistakes and put away the red pen and create more opportunities to reflect, revise, and improve.

---

73 Carol S. Dweck, *Mindset: The New Psychology of Success* (New York: Random House, 2016).

How do you find and celebrate the positive for students? Are people recognized for the talents and gifts they have? It's important to shine the spotlight on others, to notice efforts and acknowledge success, and target specific areas for growth. When learners experience success and are noticed for it, they are more willing and confident to persevere through the challenges. Similarly, when improvement happens gradually over time (as most does), it can be hard to see the growth. Being intentional about reflecting on growth and sharing both successes and lessons learned can build confidence and ownership.

Concluding Thoughts

When I first became an instructional coach, I worked harder to create lessons, design programs, and obtain grants to make it easier for teachers to deliver *my* lessons with lots of great new resources to *their* students. At the end of the year, we had some success, but my attempts to make their job easier by doing the work myself did not have the impact I had hoped for. Nor did it make their jobs any easier. Thankfully, I began to realize that we weren't going to make wide-scale change if I didn't involve teachers in the process by empowering them to create the lessons and to learn from their own implementation, reflections, and impact on student outcomes. Through that experience, I learned that the most significant impact on learning occurs when the learners (educators and students) are supported in their unique learning journey and empowered to take ownership of their education. Streamlining and standardizing might seem like an easier approach, but these practices deprive people of valuable learning opportunities.

Supporting individuals to deeply understand their practices, their goals, and their impact, to uncover their questions, and to remove barriers is at the core of how we can help make change possible in our classrooms. Figuring out the right strategy or better curriculum is not the challenge or the solution; the real change will come from the teachers who understand their students and have the deep expertise necessary to teach learners so that they continue to learn. In many schools, administrators, peers, teams, and other teachers serve as coaches and support one another's growth. Coaching, like all leadership, is less about authority or title and more about how you help teams and individuals become the best versions of themselves.

When you start from the individual and move backward from there, your chance of success rises exponentially because you are moving them from their strengths and needs, not trying to fix them. Leadership expert Peter Drucker states this beautifully:

> One should waste as little effort as possible on improving areas of low competence. It takes far more energy and work to improve from incompetence to mediocrity than it takes to improve from first-rate performance to excellence.[74]

When you look for the value in those you serve, you can more easily bring out what already exists instead of creating something from scratch.

---

74   Peter Drucker, "Manging Oneself." *Harvard Business Review.* January 2005. https://hbr.org/2005/01/managing-oneself.

Reflect and Connect Challenge
Share your thoughts, questions, and ideas using #LCInnovation

○ Reflect on the relationships you have with those you serve. How might you strengthen them? How do you build on the strengths of others to move them from their point A to their point B?

○ How might you create more opportunities for connecting and coaching those you serve?

○ If you don't have a mentor or coach that is supporting your growth and development, who might you seek out to help you improve?

○ How might you embrace Radical Candor— caring personally, challenging directly—to move people forward?

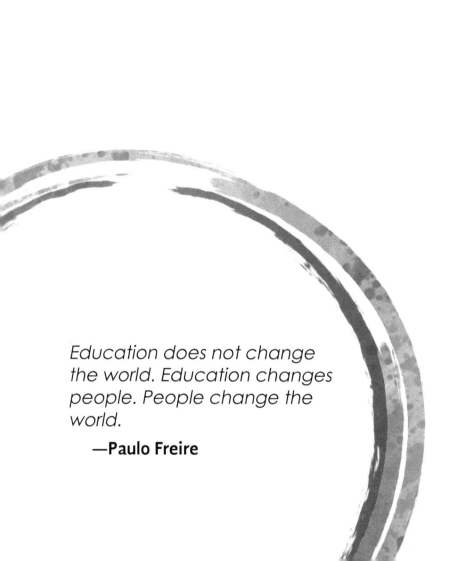

Education does not change the world. Education changes people. People change the world.

—Paulo Freire

Teachers Create What They Experience

HAVE YOU EVER LEFT A meeting, PLC, or any other professional development session wondering, *What was the purpose of that?* or *What am I supposed to do now?* If so, you are not alone. Traditional professional development is typically designed by someone who has determined the needs for the larger group. It's an isolated event where information is delivered, and teachers are then expected to implement new programs or standards or new curriculum without really understanding how to achieve the desired student outcomes or what the outcomes are supposed to be.

Creating a culture of effective collaboration, which includes professional learning, means that schools must leverage the collective genius of all teachers and ensure that everyone is equipped and aware of the what, why, and how of any new initiative. To get there, we need to address and correct some of the major pitfalls that prevent professional development from shifting practices in schools.

Five Reasons Professional Development Is Not Transforming Learning and How to Solve It

1. No Vision or Clearly Defined Purpose

Due to lack of a clear vision for learning and teaching, new initiatives are reduced to compliance of minutes or finishing units rather than focusing on improving teaching and learning to achieve the desired student outcomes. When teachers show up to meetings—not because they are excited to learn and grow but because they are expected to—creativity and innovation rarely ensue. Teachers have the final say regarding what actually happens in classrooms, so without teacher buy-in regarding the purpose of new initiatives, change is unlikely. Educators must have opportunities to develop a shared understanding of the vision and be empowered to drive their learning. When that happens, they will be able to create powerful learning opportunities for their students.

Try this:

As discussed in Chapter 3, creating a graduate profile is a great way to anchor conversations about teaching and learning in desired outcomes for learners. When a learning community is clear on the purpose, the conversations about strategies, resources, and expectations are grounded in what and how to achieve desired outcomes for students—not program mandates that may or may not be best for the learners in your unique context.

2. No Culture of Learning

This might seem ironic, but many schools lack a culture of learning. Schools have an expectation of doing a lot of things while what or how we are developing our practice of learning is rarely discussed. Early on in my career as a teacher, I ran out the door, grabbed a stack of papers to grade, and headed to the library for our weekly staff meetings. I was not alone. In fact, I learned this behavior from my colleagues who also had papers to grade, crosswords to complete, or newspapers to skim—during our staff meetings. My principal never challenged this behavior, and I quickly learned that distracted learning was the norm for educators.

Heads up, leaders: If teachers walk in with a stack of papers to grade in your staff meetings, you have a problem with your culture of learning. I have also been in meetings or workshops where the facilitator requires that we put away devices so that we can be present and pay attention. This overcorrection to demand attention is about as ineffective as ignoring those who are grading papers.

Try this:

A culture of learning must begin with a safe space for teachers to open their doors, share their practices, receive feedback, and relentlessly pursue opportunities to more effectively develop the knowledge and skills to create the desired learning environments. Instead of using staff meetings to convey information, make time for teachers to connect and share what they are learning and the impact of that on their students. Shared learning and meaningful connection boosts morale and creates a culture of learning.

3. Lack of Focus on (the Right) Student Outcomes

For some, *accountability* has a bad connotation because of the overemphasis on standardized test scores. So don't tune out. When I speak of accountability, I am talking about a much broader focus on student outcomes than a single standardized test. Teacher efficacy is defined as the belief in your ability to impact student outcomes. When teachers know they have an impact on the learners they serve, they are more efficacious and willing to try new things.

I have sat through countless planning sessions, curriculum mappings, and even great conversations about what twenty-first-century skills might look like in the classrooms, but if you never look at student work, observe learning in process, and analyze the impact on those desired skills, planning rarely changes practice. Instead, it wastes time and creates more documents that people forget to review. If we dedicate time and resources to collaborate and design better learning experiences for students, we need to hold one another accountable and support each other as we seek to improve.

Try this:

Look at examples of student work and their learning process connected to the desired student outcomes. To improve student achievement, we must focus the bulk of our energy on the collective analysis of evidence of student learning rather than the inspection of teaching.

4. Lack of Connection to Other Educators

Nothing is better than working with a group of committed people who support and push you to achieve more than what is possible on your own. When we work in isolation, we limit our potential to develop a full range of capabilities. In contrast, growth is accelerated by guidance and peer collaboration. Alone, it feels deceptively safe to do what has always worked and maintain the status quo.

If you aren't connected to other educators in your school, district, or globally, you are not likely exposed to new ideas or pushed to think about better ways of doing things. You can easily think that the way you have been doing it is the only or best way when you aren't seeing other models. So many resources and opportunities are available for educators to connect with and learn from one another. To continue learning and developing your practice, teachers need to get out of their classrooms both physically and virtually to leverage the collective genius of the many educators across the globe.

Try this:

Overwhelmingly, teachers prefer to learn from and with their peers, and we *all* benefit from regular collaborative learning opportunities with others. Put effective systems in place for teachers to connect and collaborate during the work day so that they can learn new strategies and increase their effectiveness and efficacy through the collective knowledge and support of the learning community. Teachers regularly suggest the following collaborative structures be embedded in the work day to facilitate their growth and development:

- Communities of inquiry to find and solve problems together
- Personalized opportunities to choose based on comfort, skills, and context
- Job-similar teams to design, reflect, and examine evidence of learning experiences

5. There's No Action

Obligation doesn't inspire a culture of learning, nor does it motivate teachers to take action on what they hear (or ignore) in meetings. Big change initiatives, particularly if they aren't well explained, can feel overwhelming; it's hard to know where to begin, so, instead, many educators just don't start. With that in mind, we need to set goals and start small with actionable steps that are about growth, not perfection.

Try this:

Put it all together to create action-oriented cycles. When teachers work together to design learning experiences, they can bring different perspectives and alternative methods to expand on what has always been done. Creating structured time for teachers to plan and reflect on possible impacts can help make the learning that happens in classrooms more public through focused conversations and intentional sharing. Sharing examples using a school hashtag or at a staff meeting makes learning and growth public and a shared process. Empowering teachers to design, implement, reflect, and revise can allow for ideas to turn into better practices. When teachers have clear goals to put ideas into practice or structures to share learning with peers, it inspires accountability.

Moving Beyond the Early Adopters

A common approach to new initiatives is to begin with a small percentage of teachers who are highly motivated, technically skilled, and eager to innovate. These teachers, referred to as the "early adopters," are selected to be the first to pilot new initiatives. In many cases, these early adopters also have access to training and support from instructional coaches or communities of practice to guide their ongoing professional development opportunities as they experiment with new approaches.

The theory of using early adopters to introduce innovative practices is that once they transform their classrooms, the new practices will trickle down into other classrooms. But what happens when the enthusiasm of early adopters doesn't ignite other teachers and instead ostracizes the rest of the staff? In many cases, this approach ends up creating a divide and categorizing people as techies versus non-techies, innovators versus traditional teachers. And when that happens, schools fail to build on the rich experiences and strengths of diverse educators.

When schools or districts empower select educators rather than leveraging the expertise and experience of all, the innovations only transform teaching and learning in a few classes, while the majority of classroom and learning opportunities for students remain unchanged. I get that it is fun and makes sense to work with the teachers and leaders who are eager and excited; early adopters tend to be technologically savvy and are willing to take risks in the classroom. It is well documented that these leaders can provide models for what is possible, but to cross the chasm and realize the type of learning that is needed in our schools, the push must be to move *everyone* forward. Only then can we ensure that all students have the benefit of the best instructional practices and learning experiences. As Ira Socol, Director of Learning Technologies and Innovation in Albemarle County Public Schools, notes, "we must move innovation ahead quickly. Not scaling up, but scaling across—moving the big ideas to every school and every classroom, but leaving the specifics/the creativity/the special match with the kids to the teachers."[75] Teachers (like all learners) thrive when they have a clear understanding of the vision and know where they are going yet have the autonomy to get there in a way that meets the needs of the learners in their classrooms.

Few teachers would allow a student who didn't like math or who didn't want to write to simply opt out of participating and learning. But, as adults, we can get comfortable with how things have always been. We work hard to maintain the status quo because it can be uncomfortable to try something new, especially when the results are not guaranteed. Teachers are professionals and should be treated as such, but part of being a professional is working to meet the goals and expectations of the larger system. If we wouldn't allow our students to opt out of learning or trying something new, why is it okay for educators? More importantly, as educators, we should be modeling and sharing our learning, not just telling others to do it.

---

75   David Socol, "Dallas Dance, Pam Moran, and the nature of successful school
     leadership," *Medium*, April 21, 2017, https://medium.com/age-of-awareness/
     dallas-dance-pam-moran-and-the-nature-of-successful-school-leadership-c48abc8f4be2.

A common refrain I hear in light of our changing world is, "If you're not progressing, you're regressing." That's scary—because it's true. So it is critical that we seek to continually learn and develop our practice. When leaders permit others to stay in their comfort zones, the stagnant educators drag everyone else down and limit the success of the whole team.

Balancing the System Goals and Personal Growth

Students need to grapple with problems and own their learning, and the same holds true for educators. The rally cries are clear: If we want to see learner-centered practices in the classroom, we need learner-centered professional learning. Educators are looking to develop their skills, particularly in areas based on their own content area, skills, and goals. Providing voice and choice honors the needs of educators as professionals. To support personal pathways, many districts and individual schools are moving away from the large-session, one-size-fits-all format and allowing learners a choice in a variety of sessions. I have also seen some alternatives to stand-and-deliver sessions and information-heavy staff meetings, such as flipping faculty meetings or providing choice options for an all-day professional development event for the district. This focus on voice and choice can lead to more engagement in sessions. But we can't stop there. To integrate new ideas into practice, we can't just change the format of meetings to make them more exciting or find a different way to share information. We will not see these instances of isolated training translate to better outcomes for students if we never create the time and space for teachers to learn and try out that learning with their students in their unique context— based on their needs and goals.

Creating opportunities for teachers to engage as learners in more authentic and personal ways can impact the experiences teachers create for their students. But when learning opportunities are either too standardized or, on the other extreme, too open-ended, it rarely creates a culture that shifts practices that move the system forward or impact learning for all students. The following table identifies some common characteristics of professional learning:

Too Standardized	• Learning is designed for one size to fit all • Focus on fidelity to programs, not learners • Designed for the "average," meets the needs of few • Externally designed path and pace • Lack opportunities for voice and choice of the learners
Just Right	• Develops desired skills and knowledge based on the needs of the learner • Builds on strengths and interests • Allows for creativity and passion to drive diverse learning experiences • Honors individuals and allows them to progress from where they are • Models desired teaching and learning
Too Open Ended	• Lack of clear learning goals • Passion runs high for some, and others become paralyzed by too many choices • No one is sure what is expected of them • Many left to figure it out on their own • Little follow-through and lack of cohesion on a team or staff

When Professional Learning is Too Standardized

Discussing the possibilities in schools today, a district leader shared some really innovative programs in the district and acknowledged that the leadership was isolated from the day-to-day teaching in most of their classrooms. When I asked about what professional learning opportunities teachers had to learn more about these approaches that he believed were truly new and better than what was happening in most classrooms, he said, "We just don't have time for that. All of our 'PD days' are taken by training on our new curriculum. All teachers attend three days of the same training at the district office to ensure that they all know how to implement the new curriculum."

This focus on the stuff, not on the people that can make the changes in education, is what Antwon Lincoln, an EdTech coordinator in Chula Vista Elementary School District, calls "Product-Based Learning." This common approach ends up focusing on programs; the goal is to ensure everyone is *trained*, not necessarily to ensure that everyone has *learned to better meet the needs of those they serve*. If you expect teachers to be innovative and create better opportunities for their students, the professional learning they experience should provide them opportunities to interact with and explore new possibilities.

When Professional Learning is Too Open-Ended

Opportunities that are too open-ended might start with good intentions and still fail to have the desired impact. In an effort to support teachers' individual needs and make sure they learned what they wanted, one district offered teachers $1,500 to determine their learning goal, document the hours and resources they used to learn, and share what they did as a result. Sounds awesome, right? To the administrators' surprise, a very small percentage of teachers actually followed through. Although teachers sought support to improve in their practice, this personal learning plan was too open-ended, and teachers were overwhelmed by the choices. They didn't know how to navigate the learning path on their own. With a lack of clear objectives, resources, and structure for the learning, many shared that it was hard to imagine what this new model of professional learning looked like and chose not to take advantage of the opportunity to create a personal learning plan for their professional development.

When Professional Learning is Just Right, It's Based on Competency, Not Seat Time

For professional learning to be just right, it has to allow for personal pathways that are guided by clear goals and structures for learning. Traditionally, we focus on what educators attend and ensure that everyone has been trained rather than on what skills have been developed and how educators are developing their practice as a result. In *Learning Transformed*,[76] Tom Murray and Eric Sheninger acknowledge that "hours-based accountability, which is the metric that many—if not most—districts use to weigh professional learning expectations, indicates absolutely nothing about the growth of an educator's instructional practice."

A competency-based system allows educators to demonstrate proficiency in areas where they excel and seek support and guidance for specific areas of growth. Similar to demonstrations of student learning linked to mastery, competency-based professional learning allows leaders to identify the expectations, co-construct the goals, and create personal paths to develop and demonstrate mastery of desired competencies based on needs and the context in which the educators teach.

---

76 Eric C. Sheninger and Thomas C. Murray, *Learning Transformed: 8 Keys to Designing Tomorrow's Schools, Today (Alexandria, VA: Association for Supervision and Curriculum Development, 2017).*

Led by Superintendent Pat Deklotz, Kettle Morraine School District in Wisconsin has been a pioneer in this work at the district level. The administration worked with teachers to listen to their needs as they moved toward a new vision of teaching and learning. Pat shared, "We took deliberate and thoughtful action, listening to our teachers, and aligning their interests with our system's need to attract and retain high-quality staff. We wanted to provide opportunities to recognize the differences in the professional development needs of our educators and for them to experience personalized learning themselves, in a competency-based model."[77] By offering personal pathways and using a micro-credential system to assess, track, and reward the development of desired competencies, teachers have been empowered to drive their own professional growth. In a blog, Mr. Anderson, a teacher in Kettle Morraine, shared that "micro-credentialing has changed, for the positive, how educators are viewing their own professional development and career path— it has enabled educators to personalize what it means to be a career educator for themselves and their classrooms."

By maximizing the multiple and diverse resources available, we can rethink the traditional model of professional learning and support by establishing clear expectations for all and empowering diverse teachers to design professional learning pathways to reach their goals and chart unique pathways. The essential lever of valuing the differences in teachers and immersing them in learner-centered experiences will allow educators to design similar learning experiences for the students they teach.

---

77   Digital Promise, "Transforming the Classroom with Micro-credentials," *Digital Promise*, March 16, 2016, http://digitalpromise.org/2016/03/16/transforming-the-classroom-with-micro-credentials.

Training versus Learning

A school leader shared with me that, although she felt her school offered ample professional development, she was frustrated that they hadn't seen a dramatic shift in the classrooms. She had hoped to see an increase in students solving authentic problems and using applications for deeper learning experiences. Instead, students used technology to upload and share information or to complete assignments that looked very similar to the work they had done without technology. In response, I asked the leader to describe a typical professional learning day. She told me that, in every after-school meeting, she showed teachers how to use different apps; in fact, she constantly shared tips on new apps and tools she came across. What puzzled her is that the teachers seemed encouraged in the meetings and even shared their own ideas.

As we dug deeper into why the training wasn't translating into the classroom experience, she realized that her teachers were doing exactly what she had modeled for them: they were using new tools to do the same activities and teach the same content they always had. Although they liked learning about new tools, they hadn't been modeled or used in a way that connected them to student applications for different or deeper learning.

I always cringe when I hear the word *training* used to describe educator professional development. Training happens *to* or is thrust upon people. *Learning*, on the other hand, is a process of developing knowledge through authentic and relevant experiences. If professional learning is ever going to be effective in bringing about change for students, it must shift away from something done *to* educators toward a process of creating a culture of continuous learning cycles and problem solving. There is a time to learn new skills or specific programs, but professional learning can't end with information; content is only the beginning. The following table depicts common experiences that differentiate training from learning.

Training: The action of teaching a person or animal a particular skill or type of behavior	Learning: The acquisition of knowledge or skills through experience, study, or by being taught
Needs or focus externally designed	Individually or collectively determined based on goals or needs
Isolated events	Ongoing cycle of learning, application, and reflection
Implement new skills	Situated in teaching and learning context
Presentation by "experts"	Facilitated by reading, connecting, practicing, reflecting, and networking with colleagues and experts
Objective is a desired behavior or skill	Objective is improving practice
Transmission of knowledge or skills	Engage in activities that deepen knowledge, skills, and application of new learning

Brad Gustafson, a principal and author of *Renegade Leadership*, shared a great example of how he shifted a traditional professional development day to model the type of teaching and learning he wanted to see in the classroom. He started by collaborating with his staff to design a day built on the school goals and priorities. Together, they leveraged research-based practices and gave teachers choices on the topics they wanted to grapple with based on challenges that were most meaningful to them. This learning experience, which took place within a four-hour period, focused on relevant topics and built on previous learning to sustain momentum and go deeper. The goal was to drive the change they wanted to see in their school.[78] This intentionally crafted day of learning provides a great example of balancing the system goals while allowing for individuals to receive what they need.

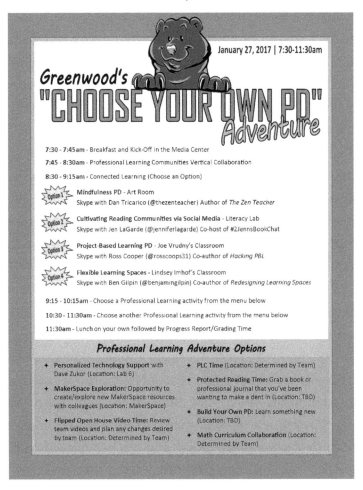

78   Brad Gustafson, "He Said, She Said...Can We Talk About PD?," *Adjusting Course*, Jan. 23, 2017, https://www.bradgustafson.com/single-post/2017/01/23/He-Said-She-SaidCan-We-Talk-About-PD.

Shifting the Focus from Teaching to Learning

In education, we have a lot of systems that run smoothly because we have been doing them for years. The problem is that when we work with the same people, doing the same things, ineffective practices are rarely challenged or changed. Traditions and habits don't inspire new ways of thinking for educators or for students.

Here is an example, and I apologize to any English teachers reading this, but I have been in too many conversations about whether *The Outsiders* is an eighth- or ninth-grade book and have mitigated arguments between seventh-grade teachers about whether or not to teach *Farewell to Manzanar*. And if you know English teachers, these conversations can become heated. This same scenario plays out in many contexts, whether it is the play that is done every year or the unit that has to be taught in the fall because it has always been that way. One of many problems with these arguments is they are about territory and preserving the status quo, not kids, what they are learning, and why. If the comfort and preferences of adults become the priority rather than what's best for learners, students miss out on powerful learning opportunities connected to their goals, questions, and interests.

As a result of doing what had always been done, when I was the literacy coach for our school, we noticed that many students were going through their day without the opportunity or expectation to read. Many students were performing below grade level on standardized tests and struggled to read the textbooks and assigned novels. Attempting to support students, teachers had resorted to creating PowerPoint presentations to summarize and convey key facts; books were read aloud, and teachers played recordings of novels so everyone could follow along at the same pace while short passages and multiple-choice worksheets were widely used to assess comprehension. We came to the realization that, if our students never read on their own or made meaningful decisions for themselves in school, they were going to struggle with these things out of school. While we grappled with this very real issue, our professional learning consisted of disparate events that offered no help. The English language arts department wanted to do better for our students, but I also knew that if they knew a better way, they would have been doing it already. We needed to learn new strategies to improve, and we had to shift the culture to focus on our desired student outcomes and align how we were designing and facilitating the learning experiences.

To achieve our goal of increasing reading practice and ultimately literacy, our English department had to shift our meeting structures from examining what *we wanted* and what *we were teaching* to reviewing student work to find out what *they were learning*. We wrote a proposal to our principal to purchase a copy of the book *7 Strategies for Teaching Reading* for each teacher in our department and requested stipends for the teachers to meet regularly after school for eight weeks. The total cost of our request was less than $1,000 ($100 per teacher and $20 for each book). We read the book and came together after school to engage in collaborative conversation that allowed teachers to experience the new strategies in their own reading and learning. We then planned ways to support students in their diverse classes. Each week, we independently read about a new strategy, rotated modeling lessons for our colleagues, and collaborated on a plan to put the new ideas into practice. One distinction here is that we did not create a plan for one specific lesson; we thought about how to integrate the new strategy across various lessons and develop multiple iterations of the strategy to inform our practice. To ensure we were working to close the knowing-doing gap, we partnered up each week to observe each other and learn from the variety of methods we were each putting into practice. At the beginning of our weekly meetings, we shared what we were learning. The open reflection not only allowed us to create a culture of transparency in our team but also pushed us to try out new ideas and build off one another's successes and challenges.

We shifted our conversations from what content and page number we were teaching that week to what we were learning and how we could impact student outcomes. This also meant that we had to bring evidence of learning from all students connected to our desired outcomes. We had to move beyond the spreadsheets and percentages to actually understand what was happening in our classrooms. We spent our time digging deep into our problems of practice, looking at student work, and interrogating our practices to ensure we were truly meeting the needs of the learners.

While our English department worked together to create better learning experiences for our students, reading about and discussing new ideas was critical for our growth. As we explored these new approaches and ideas, we began to rethink the traditional teaching of a class novel. We created more opportunities for choice and designed opportunities for students to grapple with text to make sense of it. We moved from designing learning experiences based on the content and page number we were teaching that week to how to design learning experiences that empowered our students and helped them develop the skills to become better readers, writers, and speakers. By being willing to make changes in the way reading and literacy had always been taught, we improved outcomes for our students.

In spite of the pressure to focus on short cycle passages and tests to assess comprehension skills in isolation, we continued to let students choose books that interested them, read and discuss books and other types of text with peers, and further investigate relevant questions. Given what we learned during those eight weeks, we maintained our relentless focus on learning, experimenting, refining, and analyzing the impact our new methods had on students as the year progressed. We were empowered educators who were moving beyond standards and scripted curriculum. At the end of the following year, we continued to work together to improve our practices, and as a result, we almost doubled reading proficiency on the yearly standardized test from 34 percent to 66 percent, which has continued to improve in subsequent years. Most importantly, we learned that we could break a cycle and redesign a system to achieve better outcomes for our students and our teachers.

Based on what we learned as a team and how we worked together, we showed our principal what was possible and how effective collaboration and learning could improve student outcomes. As a result, the following year, as a school, we rearranged our schedules to support job-embedded collaboration to facilitate our iterative cycles of learning for all teachers. This learning cycle didn't require adding more learning time; it required changing how we used our time. We looked at the existing time and adjusted priorities to align our work in staff meetings via grade-level collaboration. The clear priorities provided a focus for administrators and coaches who worked with the teachers.

Learner-centered innovation is not just about creating something new but doing something that yields better outcomes because of what we have created. With that in mind, we asked questions like, "How do we know that our idea is working?" and "What is the impact on desired student outcomes?"

When we focus our efforts on what we want to accomplish, not simply the metrics or data from an isolated test or standards but on the type of student we want to create, we might find that our meetings and our learning experiences become more impactful.

Concluding Thoughts

The reality is that every educator needs to know certain things, some of which must be covered for compliance measures; for example, like it or not, we have to train on CPR and bloodborne pathogens. Not everything can be like the "Choose your Own Adventure" stories. But we can (and should) limit the standardization to times or topics necessary for safety and the functioning of systems. Not all standardized professional learning is negative, but organizing all professional learning in a standardized way will not help us meet all learners and allow them to reach their potential. When at all possible, educators (and students) should be empowered to engage in learning based on their personal goals and passions.

In his book, *Where Good Ideas Come From*,[79] Steven Johnson notes that, "innovative systems have a tendency to gravitate toward the 'edge of chaos': the fertile zone between too much order and too much anarchy." If we want innovation in our schools—and we should—we have to create systems that live in this fertile zone. When we are too rigid and demand compliance, we leave little room for creativity or opportunities to be innovative. On the other hand, when we lack the vision and support to get there, many feel lost without a clear direction and revert back to what they have always done. To balance the goals of the system and the personal growth of the individual, we need to provide a clear vision and the structure for individuals to learn in a way that aligns the system goals and personal goals.

---

79   Steven Johnson, *Where Good Ideas Come From* (New York: Penguin Group, 2010).

Reflect and Connect Challenge
Share your thoughts, questions, and ideas using #LCInnovation

O   How might you create systems that minimize training and foster a culture of learning? What would you add or modify in the chart shared?

O   How might you align your staff meetings and collaboration time to support iterative cycles of learning connected to desired student outcomes or goals?

O   What are shifts you can make to support personal growth aligned to systemic goals?

PART 3:
Share Your Learning

Teamwork is the ability to work together toward a common vision. The ability to direct individual accomplishments toward organizational objectives. It is the fuel that allows common people to attain uncommon results.

—Andrew Carnegie

Better Together

I ONCE JOINED A PROFESSIONAL learning community (PLC) for their bi-monthly afternoon meeting. Educators walked into one of the teacher's classrooms a few at a time, where they chatted about the day until everyone had arrived. Once the meeting started, one of the teachers pulled up a document with four questions on it to record the minutes. The four questions were:

- What do we expect our students to learn?
- How will we know they are learning?
- How will we respond when they don't learn?
- How will we respond if they already know it?

They collectively began to fill in the answers, searching through the pacing guide to indicate which standards they were supposed to be teaching that week, which assessments they were giving, and how they were going to differentiate the lessons. Their goal was clearly to complete the minutes to turn in and move on. At the end of the meeting, they had completed the task, but not one teacher kept the information for themselves; it wasn't seen as useful in their daily classroom practice. This PLC was driven to complete a task, and although they wanted students to succeed and do well on the desired learning objectives, the meeting and conversations were focused solely on answering questions and submitting the minutes required.

How much more useful could that meeting have been had the focus been on using their questions to delve into ways to improve their practice? The questions they asked are great *if* they are used to guide and investigate practices and to collaboratively explore new and better ways to meet the learners' needs. But simply answering these questions and filling in worksheets won't change how students learn or how teachers teach. The team I had observed had fallen into a routine and, based on compliance demands, had developed a performance orientation that led these educators to focus on seeking the "right answer"—the answer they thought would please (or, at the very least, appease) their administration. This compliance/performance mentality rarely inspires people to take risks. In fact, it most frequently results in surface learning and stunted innovation. Learners and teachers alike are motivated when they have ownership over the work they are doing and can solve problems that are meaningful, not filling in worksheets.

Linda Darling Hammond, Stanford professor emeritus and president and CEO of the Learning Policy Institute, has done extensive research on professional learning and added a tremendous amount to the field of education. Much of my own work is grounded in her research, so I push on how some these best practices from her research translate to professional learning in our schools with a great deal of respect and admiration.

This excerpt from the report "Professional Learning in the Learning Profession" summarizes the research on ideal professional learning:

> Teachers meet on a regular schedule in learning teams organized by grade-level or content-area assignments and share responsibility for their students' success. Learning teams follow a cycle of continuous improvement that begins with examining student data to determine the areas of greatest student need, pinpointing areas where additional educator learning is necessary, identifying and creating learning experiences to address these adult needs, developing powerful lessons and assessments, applying new strategies in the classroom, refining new learning into more powerful lessons and assessments, reflecting on the impact on student learning, and repeating the cycle with new goals.[80]

As the report points out, having learning *teams* that engage in ongoing, job-embedded professional learning cycles is key to shifting practice. Using this research as a directive has led to many educators spending precious collaboration time going through cycles to analyze data from benchmark tests, focusing on ensuring that all students have content memorized or know how to pick the author's message from four multiple-choice options, or sharing strategies and resources to reteach and improve test scores. These are often compliance-based professional learning cycles, in which the agenda is externally set, and analyzing data and filling out forms, rather than learning, can quickly become the focus.

When these cycles of learning are focused on the wrong goals, we end up going through the motions to collect data and revise lessons hyper-focused on narrow skills. The data might even show we improve, but to what end? Do the professional learning

---

80   Linda Darling Hammond, et al., "Professional Learning in the Learning Profession," (National Staff Development Council, Stanford University, 2009), https://learningforward.org/docs/pdf/nsdcstudy2009.pdf.

experiences align with what we believe is best for learners and help move toward the larger goals or ones that are easy to measure?

For professional learning experiences to move educators, classrooms, and the world forward, we must make the critical shift from compliance-based cycles to cycles of learning that empower teachers to improve their practice and meet the needs of learners. Imagine the same cycle, but instead of focusing on the right answers, teachers have opportunities to experience new models of learning and shift their thinking about what is possible in the classroom. Based on new experiences, teachers work together to select goals and research what works in their classrooms with their learners. They determine the best evidence to gather and analyze based on their goals. Teachers collectively provide and receive peer feedback and support to improve based on the shared vision, their goals, and the needs of their learners. This kind of cycle ensures that the vision and goals for learners remains the driving force for professional learning.

If teachers don't experience models of professional learning that shift the mindset from compliance to empowerment, we might be focused on getting better at the wrong things. The goal of professional learning and development shouldn't be to just get better at what has always been done; it should be to better meet the needs of learners in your classrooms and move forward. Working effectively in learning teams helps move these new ideas and methods out of isolated pockets of innovation and into school- and district-wide cultures that foster learner-centered innovation for all.

(Effective) Teamwork Makes the Dream Work

A group of talented individuals working together does not make an effective team. For people to work together and move forward as a team, they must have a shared purpose and shared norms. This requires constant attention to ensure individual efforts align and support the vision; if each individual works independently, they end up moving in different directions. When teams are effective, every member of the team (as well as others whose work the team influences) benefits. But in many cases, teams cause more frustration than improvement and might fail even to achieve desired results.

So how do we ensure that our professional learning teams are effective? Google researchers studied 180 teams for more than two years and found that the most successful teams share the following five traits:[81]

1. **Psychological Safety**—An environment in which everyone feels safe to take risks, voice their opinions, and ask judgment-free questions is a prerequisite for effective teams. In a psychologically safe culture, managers create safe zones so that employees can let down their guards and speak and brainstorm openly.

2. **Structure and clarity**—High-performing teams have clear goals with well-defined roles within the group.

3. **Dependability**—Team members get things done on time and meet expectations.

4. **Meaning**—The work has personal significance to each member.

5. **Impact**—The group believes their work is purposeful and positively impacts the greater good.

When I read these findings, I immediately recognized that these five traits align with Maslow's Hierarchy of Needs.[82] Maslow's hierarchy builds on the foundation of physiological needs, safety, love and belonging, self-esteem, and ultimately, self-actualization.

---

81 Michael Schneider, "Google Spent 2 Years Studying 180 Teams. The Most Successful Ones Shared These 5 Traits," *Inc.*, Accessed Dec. 1, 2017, https://www.inc.com/michael-schneider/google-thought-they-knew-how-to-create-the-perfect.html.

82 A. H. Maslow, *Motivation and Personality*, 3rd Edition (New York: Harper & Row, 1987).

Similarly, you can't have high-functioning teams that achieve great success if people are afraid of sharing their ideas or challenging existing norms.

Katie Martin   @KatieMartinEdu

If we are honest, adult collaboration often mirrors the frustration we experience in group assignments in classrooms: one person does all the work, more arguing than productive dialogue occurs, and disengagement is more prevalent than empowerment. In effective teams, all team members play a critical role in collaboration and improvement. To get to this place of support and forward momentum, I have learned that the individuals on any team need to do the following for the team to be successful in its endeavors:

1. Spend time getting to know yourself and your team

2. Create structures that ensure equitable voice and choice

3. Create structures that empower team members to collectively learn and build on strengths

Know Yourself and Your Team

Have you noticed that there are certain people with whom it is always a struggle to work? I had one team member with whom I constantly felt frustrated. Every time I threw out an idea, her first reaction was to offer a long list of "yeah, but . . . " arguments. I took offense to her naysaying and stopped sharing ideas with her. I started to do the work all on my own, which created a whole new set of problems. Her negativity and my response obviously impacted our effectiveness and our relationship. We finally hit a turning point when we participated in an activity that I thought would be a silly ice breaker that ended up completely changing our team dynamics. The activity, Compass Points: North, South, East, and West,[83] from the National School Reform Faculty, helped define group work preferences. Our school's staff members individually read and reacted to four statements and, based on our initial reactions, picked the statement that resonated most with our preferred work style. (Although people might not fit perfectly into a single category, the exercise works best if you follow your first instincts.)

The four workstyle statements follow:

- **North**—"Let's do it!" Likes to act, try things, plunge in.

- **East**—Speculating. Likes to look at the big picture before jumping in.

- **South**—Caring. Likes to know that everyone's feelings have been taken into consideration and that their voices are heard before acting.

- **West**—Paying attention to detail. Likes to know the who, what, when, where, and why before acting.

---

83   Sue Horan, "Compass Points: North, South, East, and West; An Exercise in Understanding Preferences in Group Work," *School Reform Initiative*, June 2007. http://schoolreforminitiative.org/doc/compass_points.pdf.

Based on our responses we moved to different corners of the room. Then, within each of the four groups that formed, we discussed the following five questions.

1. What are the strengths of your style?
2. What are the challenges of your style?
3. With which group do you have the hardest time working?
4. What do you need other groups to know about your style?
5. What do you value about the other groups?

Each group discussed the questions and then shared with the other teams. A critical part of the activity was for the larger group to come together again and discuss what people noticed about the distribution of the people, noting any surprises or *ahas*. Equally important was that we took time to consider implications for collaborative work and what the next steps might be.

In this activity, I found out that I am "north," also known as an "activator" for those of you who are fans of StrengthsFinder. I become antsy without action and prefer to try things and learn by doing. I am comfortable adapting in the moment as needed. Come to find out, the person I thought of as a roadblock was "west," which meant that her tendency was to focus on details and make sure she considered everything before taking action. Our approach to work and life were essentially on the opposite ends of the spectrum. This realization was a game changer. Aware of our different perspectives, I understood that she wasn't trying to argue or dissuade progress. Instead of assuming that she was just trying to be difficult and didn't want to do anything, I discovered that her personality could be leveraged as a strength to help me think through things before acting. I also found out that my tendency to act on everything irritated her and had been a barrier for collaboration. Through understanding our dispositions, we could work better together. This understanding didn't mean that we instantaneously began to agree on everything, but it did enable us to have a much better working relationship—and that allowed us to be more effective as a team. Labeling our dispositions helped me reflect on my impact on the team and work better with team members. In the end, we were empowered to create better solutions because we no longer acted alone.

In addition to learning our workstyle preferences, intentionally creating a culture based on strengths rather than focusing on deficits can have a dramatic impact on how people interact and feel about their work. The reality is that people are more confident, passionate, and do better work when they focus on what is right with them instead of what's wrong with them. To ensure everyone felt valued, as I shared earlier, everyone on our team took the Gallup StrengthsFinder assessment to identify our top five strengths. The StrengthsFinder premise is that there are thirty-four research-based strengths. The assessment provides a common language to understand individuals' unique strengths. When people are aware of their strengths and are empowered to leverage them to do their best work, everyone benefits.

The point is that to lead and collaborate well with others, you first must understand yourself and your own strengths. Only when we each know our best traits can we maximize the talents of the entire team. If you haven't already taken the StrengthsFinder assessment, you can access the test here: gallupstrengthscenter.com.

Whether or not you take the StrengthsFinder assessment, it would be worth your time to reflect (individually and as a team) on the following questions regularly:

- What are your personal strengths?
- How did you build on your strengths this week?
- Were there times your strengths were not utilized?

- How can you continue to leverage your strengths to support the team?

As a leader, having these conversations with your staff will help you understand how they see their influence and areas where they might feel undervalued or want to be more involved. It will also allow you to learn more about each person, maximize their talents, and build more effective teams. These questions can also be used as discussion topics for teams and would also be powerful to ask students.

Ensure Equitable Voice and Choice

Staff meetings, PLCs, and department or grade-level meetings are common in schools, but I often hear that they aren't as effective as they could be. For example, one teacher expressed to me that his team meetings were really frustrating: the forty-five-minute weekly meetings had little structure or facilitation and ended up being pointless venting sessions. Can you relate?

Another teacher shared with me that her principal had carved out significant time for collaboration, but she felt like they accomplished relatively little because their teams lacked focus and clarity of purpose. As a result, they wasted a lot of time.

Even though collaboration is at the top of every list of essential skills that students need to develop—and on every list of desired skills that employers want—it is infrequently taught or modeled. Part of the reason why it is so infrequently taught is that we lack models of effective collaboration in our own practice. Yes, we need time for teachers to collaborate. (That principal was taking a step in the right direction.) But we also need to invest time in learning how to collaborate more effectively. Too often, we endure the norm of bad meetings instead of taking steps to improve them. With poorly structured and facilitated meetings and a lack of goals or clarity of purpose, teams waste time, which negatively impacts morale.

Early as a team leader, I really wanted our collaboration to be different. I read up on how to improve meetings and did everything I thought I was supposed to do. I created an agenda and set times and stuck to them. I identified who was responsible for each task necessary for achieving the goals I'd set. I was motivated by my "activator" strength and wanted to overhaul everything about the way we held meetings. But in the end, I realized all those efforts were about me and what I wanted. I had great aspirations and positive intentions; I was seeking change in service of our students. I thought my good intentions justified my approach, but I failed to involve the team in the process. In turn, the team was compliant; they showed up and sat through meetings and filled out necessary paperwork but rarely offered up suggestions, pushed back, or built on anything we discussed. We survived our weekly team meetings, but they were not a place of deep learning and growth.

Over the next few years, I benefitted from exposure to different approaches that helped me make our meetings better and effectively changed the culture. I learned about cognitive coaching and facilitative leadership, and I developed skills and a new mindset that allowed me to more effectively facilitate meetings and lead more collaboratively. Instead of pushing my way through an agenda, I learned the importance of establishing community guidelines as a team, and I learned to ask better questions and use protocols to provide more structure for equitable voice in our discussions. Most importantly, I learned that, if I wanted our team to provide more voice and choice for their students and let them lead their learning, telling teachers to change wasn't going to cut it; we had to create the space for all of us to learn.

Create Structures to Empower Learners

Many schools and districts provide time during the school day for educators to collaborate. Districts have shortened school days, utilized guest teachers, or creatively configured the schedule to allow for non-teaching time to be built into the day. This is positive; however, just providing the time isn't always enough. When valuable collaboration time is spent reacting to events rather than delving into the real challenges teachers are facing, we aren't maximizing learning opportunities. The activities that teachers engage in during the allotted times vary greatly, as does the impact on teaching and learning.

Seth Godin puts it this way: "There's a queue of urgent things, all justifiable, all requiring you and you alone to handle them. And so you do, pushing off the important in favor of the urgent."[84] It's so true! As busy educators, we *must* remember that if we are always reacting to the urgent, we will never have time to improve. Teams must be on the same page about what needs to be done, but we can't expect to collectively get better if we spend most of our time together focused on updates, logistics, and completing tasks imposed by others.

While some leaders overburden their staff with urgent expectations, others swing too far in the other direction. For example, one principal told me she trusted her teachers to meet and do what they need. When I asked the teachers about how they were using the allotted collaboration time, several told me they were frustrated because some team members showed up late or not at all. Without clear expectations or any facilitation or structures in place, the teams found it difficult to work together effectively.

Trust is imperative to empowerment, but it should not be confused with abandonment. On the other hand, overly structured agendas and monitoring of collaboration time can be stifling. Operating under too many constraints zaps creative and innovative thinking and inhibits teams from accomplishing what they need to do.

---

84   Seth Godin, "The why of urgent vs. important." *Seth Godin*, February 26, 2017. http://sethgodin.typepad.com/seths_blog/2017/02/the-why-of-urgent-vs-important.html.

For effective collaboration to thrive in our teams, we have to find the balance between structure and freedom. We need clear goals and reasonable facilitation to ensure that we are learning and improving the right things. As you consider how you want your team meetings and collaboration time to look, make sure you're doing these five things:

1. Celebrate

So much happens throughout the week, making it easy to become bogged down by the challenges. Focusing on the positives and celebrating one another makes such a positive impact on culture. Taking five minutes to highlight what you notice in others and what is going well helps build up people. Intentionally create rituals that ensure that individuals feel seen and valued so that they are inspired to make a difference.

2. Set Goals and Reflect on Progress

Most of us have personal and professional goals that are probably written down somewhere on an evaluation sheet or that we set at the beginning of the year. Creating goals is not hard; sticking to them is the problem. If we don't focus on our goals and track their progress, we probably won't reach them. Carving out time to share updates on our personal and collective goals creates transparency in learning and helps to hold people accountable and provide support as necessary.

3. Peer Teaching

As teachers, we spend a lot of time teaching our students, but we rarely teach our peers. That's unfortunate, because we learn so many lessons and strategies each day that impact our learners and could impact so many more if we took the time to teach our peers. Likewise, we could all benefit from the collective wisdom of a group when facing challenges. Formal professional development sessions and conferences shouldn't be the only ways we learn something new. In fact, the most useful learning can come from a peer who is teaching the same groups of kids and who understands your context. Teaching one another is an important element of successful learning communities. Take turns teaching a new strategy, tool, or lesson learned, read articles, and try something out.

4. Critique + Revise

Presenting challenges, providing feedback, and creating actionable next steps are all valuable exercises that help improve learning experiences. Teachers can benefit from presenting a lesson idea or project on which they are just beginning to hear feedback. Midway through a project you can seek feedback to help improve and determine next steps. In my experience, one of the best ways to understand and provide feedback to improve teaching and learning is to look at student work samples from your own projects. When educators look collectively at student work to determine strengths and implications for designing learning experiences, we can learn a great deal about our impact on desired learning outcomes and discover ways to improve. In chapter 11 we will explore tools to facilitate this process.

5. Problem Solving

Creating the space for people to put problems of practice on the table for the group to collectively solve builds capacity and trust in a team. When team members take turns sharing a problem of practice, they can leverage the expertise of the group to collectively solve challenges. And although each problem might be specific to one person, they usually have implications from which the rest of the team can learn.

Collective Efficacy

I truly believe we have unlimited power to innovate learning and help students thrive. But we must first create the right kind of culture, which requires prioritizing time and experiences that help us learn and improve. To do this, we need to make time for celebration, goal setting, reflecting on progress, teaching each other, learning together, critiquing, revising our work, and problem-solving. This kind of collaboration not only develops expertise but also builds the community and develops shared norms and belief that impact both teaching and learning. The power in the collaborative time is not in the time alone; the power lies in the opportunity to network, engage in meaningful conversations, and to generate new ideas.

Structuring the time to learn together and focus on common goals helps to develop collective efficacy, the belief in our ability as a team to make an impact. Collective efficacy depends on the values that are developed and shared by community members. When the community trusts its members and can effectively cooperate to learn, reflect, and grow, it is more likely to create a safe and trusting learning community for the educators and the students. Even more so, when instructional leaders promote a culture of continual learning, teachers enjoy their work and are more successful. Mark Benigni, an *EdWeek* "Leader to Learn From," acknowledges that his job is to inspire risk taking. As such, he has made concerted efforts to let teachers lead in his district. He says, "Collaboration is about recognizing that the best ideas don't always come from the superintendent's desk. Sometimes it comes from our students or our families, and many times it comes from a great teaching staff."[85]

---

85   Holly Corbey, "Want to Improve a District? Let Teachers Lead the Way," *Edutopia*, May 3, 2017, https://www.edutopia.org/article/want-improve-district-let-teachers-collaborate-holly-korbey.

The Power of a Network

New ideas and connections are the basis for creativity and innovation. If we want to continue to evolve and create schools that meet the needs of all learners, educators need to connect with diverse people in business, their community, other schools, and districts to build networks that inspire new ideas. While networks are critical to idea generation, networking can be seen as "sleazy" in traditional education circles. Many have built personal and professional identities around being educators, which has been, in some ways, categorized as opposite of jobs in business or industry. In education, we pride ourselves on being about learning and growing people, serving others but not ourselves. Many educators characterize business as being about sales and individual rewards, and, thus, doing what is the norm in business is shunned in many education circles. For too long, networking has had this connotation as being a part of business that is self-serving and unnecessary for educators. In fact, I have had many colleagues say, "I don't network. I'll just keep to myself and focus on my work" and "I don't care about developing a network; I just want to be a good teacher." I too saw the world of business and education as opposite in some ways until I read *To Sell Is Human* by Daniel Pink. The book helped me see that, whether our "offer" comprises ideas or products, we are all in the business of sales. Pink notes that, "The ability to move others to exchange what they have for what we have is crucial to our survival and our happiness."[86]

When we build a network and create connections with people who offer divergent ideas, we have more opportunities to learn and evolve in our practice. Some educators might not like the idea of "networking," but we can't argue against something that makes us better and happier in our work. As Tim Sanders, former Yahoo!

---

86   Dan Pink, *To Sell Is Human: The Surprising Truth About Moving Others*, (New York: Riverhead Books, 2012).

director, has been known to say, "Your network is your net worth."[87] We improve when we open ourselves up to learning from others, share our ideas, and work together to create something better. And when we improve, our students benefit. So let's look at a few ways to expand your network.

> *Ideas are in fact manifestations of a complex network of neurons firing in the brain and new ideas are only possible when new connections are formed.*
> **—Steven Johnson**

Communities of Practice

Tools and resources won't improve education; new and better ideas we create and share with one another will be the levers that change schools now and in the future. *Communities of practice* are composed of groups of people that share a concern or a passion for something they do, and they interact regularly to learn how to do it better. Set outcomes or deliverables are not required for communities of practice, but these groups are more than simply community that coexists because of their three defining characteristics: a domain, community, and practice.[88] The Innovator's Mindset Massive Online Open Course[89] (IMMOOC) is an example of a community of practice where educators around the world have

---

87   Greg Linnemanstons, "Top 10 Lessons from Tim Sanders on Building Relationships," Weidert Groups Sales and Marketing Blog. September 17, 2013. https://www.weidert.com/whole_brain_marketing_blog/bid/118463/top-10-lessons-from-tim-sanders-on-building-relationships.

88   Etienne and Beverly Wenger-Trayner, "Introduction to communities of practice," *Wenger-Trayner*, 2015, http://wenger-trayner.com/introduction-to-communities-of-practice.

89   George Couros, "Innovator's Mindset Massive Online Open Course." Accessed December 16th, 2017. immooc.org.

connected based on the book *The Innovator's Mindset* and built on the connections and ideas that have shifted mindsets and practice.

The domain: A community of practice goes beyond a bunch of friends or a network of connections between people. It has an identity, and, just as the IMMOOC brought together educators who are interested in innovation in education, communities of practice share a defined interest. Membership is pursuant to a commitment to the group and is maintained through actions and by what you give and receive from the group. By nature, those who put more time and energy into it receive more from the group.

The community: Activities and interaction build relationships and create bonds among participants. Although the IMMOOC was entirely online, weekly live hangouts, Twitter chats, and a community Facebook group allowed people to connect to the community through multiple channels while also creating relationships among individuals who found deeper connections and affiliations within the community.

The practice: Members of a community of practice regularly engage in an iterative process of learning and doing in their work. They create shared resources through their stories, their examples, through trial and error, and through sharing the process so that everyone can learn from one another.

These interconnected networks of people come together because of shared interests or goals, and the learning communities are built over time with sustained interactions and shared spaces. Whether online or in person, communities of practice are about developing new and better ideas.

Anne Krolicki, a high-school English teacher, summed up how she felt being part of the IMMOOC community:

Over the last few weeks, I have noticed a huge change in myself, both as a person and as an educator. It is amazing what fueling your passion can do for all aspects of your life. I have had more energy for my family, for my students, and for myself, and it hasn't been an energy burst—like the kind I need for a week or two when I have a lot going on. That type of energy isn't sustainable, and when the busy weeks are over, you're left feeling empty— drained. The energy I feel now fills me up and keeps me constantly pushing for more.[90]

Communities of practices have the power to renew and rejuvenate us with purpose and passion, but you have to invest in them to reap the rewards.

I know what you're thinking: *I don't have time for networking.* I get it. At times, it can feel almost impossible to add even one more thing to your busy life. But I have found that networking, connecting with those who lift you up and push you to be better, is well worth the investment. In the book, *Crossing the Unknown Seas,*[91] this passage sums up the power of a community that builds up one another so work can be taken on with purpose and joy.

"You know that the antidote to exhaustion is not necessarily rest?"

"The antidote to exhaustion is wholeheartedness."

Educators are busy with life and work, and, no doubt, our plates are full. But when we find our tribe and connect with others to engage, learn, and grow, we can be filled with a sense of "wholeheartedness."

Critical Friends

Just like you never want to buy the nicest house on the street, you might need to start pushing yourself to seek out people who

90   Anne Krolicki, "#IMMOOC: The Gift That Keeps on Giving," *The Second Year Teacher,* Sept. 16, 2017, https://thesecondyearteacher.wordpress.com/2017/09/16/immooc-the-gift-that-keeps-on-giving.

91   David Whyte, "Crossing the Unknown Sea," *A Network for Grateful Living,* Accessed Dec. 1, 2017, http://gratefulness.org/resource/crossing-unknown-sea.

push your thinking and challenge you if you are always the smartest person in the room. Motivational speaker Jim Rohn has been known to say, "You are the average of the five people you spend the most time with."[92] So, if you subscribe to this provocation, of course, it matters who you surround yourself with and who is pushing you (or not) to be better. You want to surround yourself with people who will raise your average, not bring it down.

You need people—students, teachers, administrators, industry partners, and the surrounding community—who will challenge you and make you better. In a world where you can find "facts" to support any opinion or point of view and where the information that comes into our lives via social media and social circles is curated to fit our perspectives, we need to seek out opposing perspectives more than ever. The power in engaging with critical friends is not just spending time together or finding people who will support you. While that is important, true learning and growth requires being pushed out of your comfort zone.

Although you might not be able to surround yourself physically with the top in your field, you can choose to spend time with those who elevate you, and, when you can't, ensure that you seek out points of view that push your thinking. For example, I used to only read books on education, but I once I started reading books on leadership, business, entrepreneurship, and psychology, I began to see so many connections to the world of education. I also noticed my blind spots. I began to see the conversations in the world that were not happening in my close-knit education circles, which pushed my thinking and practice.

Challenging our thinking and expanding our circles helps us not only in education but also in life. Now I intentionally seek out

---

92   Melia Robinson, "Tim Ferris: 'You are the average of the five people you most associate with," Business Insider, January 11, 2017. http://www.businessinsider.com/tim-ferriss-average-of-five-people-2017-1.

divergent viewpoints to try to better understand counter arguments and think about blind spots that I might miss when I only talk with those who share my same point of view.

Accountability Partners

Brady Venables, technology integration specialist, and Shawn Clark, a transformation specialist, are prime examples of people who push each other to be better. They take this a step further to rely on one another as accountability partners—you know, the friend you make plans to go to the gym with so that you actually go because you don't want to let them down. Shawn wrote about the power of their partnership on the blog *Classroom Confessionals*, which they regularly co-write:

> Finding your accountability partner requires you to know yourself first and identify your own strengths and weaknesses. Allowing yourself to own your growth areas allows you to begin the journey to find a partner who complements your practice and who can help fine tune competency in your role. I admit there are times when I am scared to pick up the phone or text Brady because I really don't want to face what she has to say to me. Her incessant questioning sometimes hurts my head and my heart but I absolutely come out the other side a better and brighter and more thoughtful person who is never allowed to not put students first.[93]

When you find a person who pushes you, encourages you, reflects with you, and challenges you to always be better, you can't help but improve. It's easy to find people who will make you feel good about staying with the status quo. Finding those who will invest the time into helping you become the best version of

---

93   Shawn Berry Clark and Brady Venables, "Accountability Partners: Finding Your Professional Soulmates," *Classroom Confessional*, April 27, 2017, http://www.venablesandclark.com/single-post/2017/04/27/Accountability-Partners-Finding-Your-Professional-Soulmates.

yourself is not as common, but those are the relationships we *need*. Taking risks ensures that there will be challenges along the way, so seek partners who will pick you up and help you learn from the experience while keeping you on your path to achieve your goals.

- Do you have people who challenge your thinking and push you to do better?
- Do you challenge others or maintain the status quo?

If your answer to either of these questions is no, I challenge you to find a critical friend, accountability buddy, or community of practice to push your thinking and help you achieve your goals.

Balancing the Smart and Heart

At the beginning of soccer season, I attended the typical parent meetings for both of my kids. Both coaches had the same goals and same content to share, but the vibe was very different in these two meetings. One coach read from a list of what we needed to accomplish and parents signed up, packed up the kids, and headed home to the million other things that they needed to do. In the other meeting, however, the coach introduced herself and talked about why she wanted to coach the kids, along with her background and philosophy. Then she had the parents introduce themselves and share a little bit about their families. We felt an immediate energy as we all talked and connected with one another. We went out for pizza later. Throughout the season, we continued to get to know each other as we had fun conversations on the sidelines and supported our kids as a team. On the other team, I still don't know the other parents. We made it through the season, awkwardly acknowledging one another each Saturday at the field.

Whether on the soccer field, in the classroom, in team meetings, or in large conference sessions, building and sustaining community connections matter. For the members of a group to be able to learn from and with one another, they must first build connections. I have never been a fan of ice-breakers. Too often, they seem like fluff, activities that steal from valuable learning time. That said, I have come to realize that intentionally designing activities that properly set the stage for connection (and even relationships) can allow learning to go so much further because they allow for people to find common ground. Typical, cheesy icebreakers aren't the only way to get people interacting. Sometimes games are fun, and sometimes fun can come with intentionally designed play or activities. When people feel connected, they let down their guards; that's when we really start to learn from others and begin to work together. If you create purposeful opportunities for people to build relationships, new connections and ideas often emerge as a result.

Rich Thome, a former superintendent who is one of my mentors, has always pushed me to balance the smart with the heart. He reminds me that just because you have the greatest ideas or are smart, people don't care unless you connect to the heart and build personal connections. Yes, it takes a great deal of work to do, and there never seems to be enough time. But even a few minutes spent having fun together and playing can be a great investment in your community. Play energizes people, and fun activities allow people to bond as they work together toward a common goal even if that goal is simple or silly. Through the formed connections and relationships, we can accomplish so much more than what is possible alone.

Play Paves the Way for Creativity and Innovation

When tensions were high and everyone was stressed, our team at the University of San Diego decided to start our staff meeting with some time to learn something new. We had just gotten some Makey Makeys and Google Cardboard virtual reality viewers, and we wanted to explore the possibilities. As we read and followed the step-by-step directions, we began to work together to "make it work."

I expected to learn how to set up the Makey Makey, how it worked, and to play a few tunes on a banana piano. I did those things and learned a lot from others on the team, but the best part of the experience far exceeded what I learned about the tools. When we let go and just played, we began learning together in a safe environment with no other expectations but to experiment and have fun. Through these interactions, we generated so many new ideas and forged deeper connections with one another.

As I reflected on the connections made through exploration and play, it became clear that the opportunity to have unstructured fun was extremely productive. We created new knowledge about the products, ideas, and people. Our shared experiences resulted in new bonds. Ultimately, as we problem solved, communicated, and laughed, we connected in a way that enabled us to work better together. After spending a significant amount of time playing with my coworkers, I have become convinced that sometimes you just need time and space to explore, tinker, and play. What really fuels creativity is taking breaks and creating the "white space" to allow for ideas to formulate and emerge.

How often do you make time to play or learn something with your students or coworkers? How do you model taking risks and being vulnerable? Being a learner is foundational to being a leader, and sometimes learning requires a little play.

Concluding Thoughts

You can have all the right structures in place, but if you haven't built the relationships and created a community with shared goals where the individuals feel valued, none of it matters. If we don't invest in the relationships and build connections between people and our ideas, we limit the potential of what we all can achieve together. High-functioning teams value the team as a whole and understand that relationships are at the core of the work. They ensure they invest time in building those relationships to best serve the team so that they accomplish the desired goals. A willingness to ask for and receive input characterizes the best teams. That vulnerability shows that the team members respect one another's opinions and are willing to incorporate diverse viewpoints to become more productive and efficient. In schools where empowerment and collaboration are norms, teachers often have higher morale and stronger commitment as well as the desire to remain in teaching.

This quote from Henry Ford captures the difference in *calling yourself* a team and *working together* as a team: "Coming together is a beginning. Keeping together is progress. Working together is success." We have become accustomed to showing up at team or staff meetings and counting that as our duty, but showing up is not success. Showing up is the first step. Coming together as a team and pooling our expertise to develop ideas that will improve outcomes for all learners is what we should be working toward every day. We have too much to do, and the stakes are too high to go at it alone.

Reflect and Connect Challenge
Share your thoughts, questions, and ideas using #LCInnovation

O How might your team better understand each other's strengths? Try the Compass Points activity with your staff and share the workstyle preferences of your team. How can you use this information to work better together?

O How else might you grow your network or find an accountability partner to push you?

O How might you make time to play and build relationships? What other strategies do you have to build community?

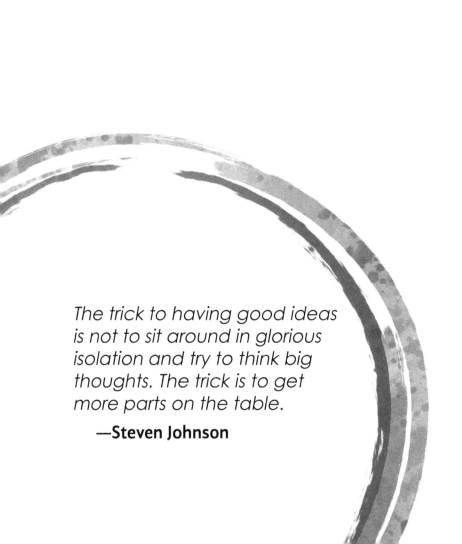

The trick to having good ideas is not to sit around in glorious isolation and try to think big thoughts. The trick is to get more parts on the table.

—Steven Johnson

Make Learning Public

WHEN IS THE LAST TIME you observed one of your peers?

Almost every time I ask a group of teachers this question, I hear the following responses: "never," "it's been a long time," or "we used to do that." One teacher shared with me that she still relies on many strategies she learned from observing her amazing cooperating teacher *twenty years ago*.

Observation is a powerful component of how we learn and should be an ongoing part of how teachers continually improve. Preparation programs, on-the-job experiences, as well as the observation of their previous teachers, all include observation as a major part of how teachers learn. Dan Lortie, a sociologist, coined the term *apprenticeship of observation* in his book, *Schoolteacher.*[94] He

---

94   Dan C. Lortie, *Schoolteacher: A Sociological Study*, (Chicago: University of Chicago Press, 1975).

argues that students observe their teachers throughout school and create mental models based on their experiences. "The net result of this highly influential period of observation is that teacher education courses are said by many to have a weak effect on student teachers. This limited effect and the reported tendency for novice teachers, once they have entered the profession, to revert to their default model can lead to teachers teaching as they were taught." Seeing new and better models of desired learning environments helps deepen one's understanding of how to organize instructional time and effectively teach. If the last time you saw another person teach was when you were a student, your mental model is becoming increasingly outdated. The world has evolved, and our teaching and learning models need to keep up with the times.

It's not uncommon for teachers who have taught next to one another for years to have never seen each other teach. When this happens, assumptions are made about what is and isn't working. Closed cultures encourage and perpetuate ineffective practices and prevent better ideas—strategies that could have a positive impact on the school as a whole—from emerging. In an article titled, "I Lie About My Teaching,"[95] Ben Orlin, a math teacher, wrote about the disconnect in between how we *talk about* teaching and learning and what *actually happens* in our classrooms:

> Teachers self-promote. In that, we're no different than everyone else: proudly framing our breakthroughs, hiding our blunders in locked drawers, forever perfecting our oral résumés. This isn't all bad. My colleagues probably have more to learn from my good habits (like the way I use pair work) than my bad ones (like my sloppy system of homework corrections), so I might as well share what's useful. In an often-frustrating profession, we're nourished by tales of triumph. A little positivity is healthy.

---

95   Ben Orlin, "I Lie About My Teaching," *The Atlantic*, July 9, 2014, https://www.theatlantic.com/education/archive/2014/07/why-teachers-lie-about-their-classrooms/375099.

> But sometimes, the classrooms we describe bear little resemblance to the classrooms where we actually teach, and that gap serves no one.
>
> Any honest discussion between teachers must begin with the understanding that each of us mingles the good with the bad.

To build capacity and develop a shared understanding of what powerful teaching and learning looks like, sounds like, and feels like, educators need to get into classrooms and observe (not just talk about) teaching and learning. Too often, we make decisions based on assumptions, as well as on our own beliefs and perspectives, rather than on what is currently happening in classrooms. In many cases, this ideal of teaching and perfectionism is protected by the silos we maintain in our schools and districts. More is asked of teachers than ever before. The standards, resources, and expectations have all changed. And because classroom doors stay closed, teachers are left to their own imagination to figure out how it all fits together—and those silos stunt everyone's growth. As Tony Wagner, Harvard professor and author of *The Global Achievement Gap* says, "isolation is the enemy of improvement."[96]

The challenges of time, workloads, and demands are great in our profession, but resources to help you deal with these challenges abound if you are willing to open your physical and virtual doors. Maybe you've already tapped into the expertise of the next-door teacher. Or maybe you, like thousands of others, are stepping out and broadening your network through live conferences, social media, virtual chats, and meetups. However you choose to do it, I encourage you to break down the silos and make every effort to figure out how to strengthen current practices and, as necessary,

---

96 Tony Wagner, *The Global Achievement Gap: Why Even Our Best Schools Don't Teach the New Survival Skills Our Children Need—and What We Can Do about It* (New York: Basic Books, 2010).

create new and better experiences. With increasing access to information and people, we have the opportunity to be more connected than ever.

Behaviors are learned through social interactions. People learn from one another, through observation, imitation, and modeling. We learn how to act and react to situations from others. We foster schoolwide achievement through the organization of schools to facilitate positive learning models and the strategic design of interactions to promote learning for everyone. Both research and our own experiences tell us that the most powerful learning requires personal connections, relevance, and experiences that allow for productive struggle. Even with that knowledge, educational traditions and systems that favor the efficiency of standardization have led us to ineffective methods of structuring learning experiences in schools.

We create meaning from our own perspectives and experiences, and we need different models to build our repertoire of new strategies and practices. When you look beyond your own classroom or school, you will see vast differences in how classrooms are organized, how teachers interact, and how students learn. Setting up systems that invite people to observe in nonthreatening ways is a great starting point. Pineapple Charts have become popular because they allow teachers to pick specific times that people can observe a practice or idea. This is bound by what you invite others to watch, with a focused goal. Jennifer Gonzales's blog post, "How Pineapple Charts Revolutionize PD,"[97] describes the process and provides some great examples.

> In case you haven't heard of or used a Pineapple Chart, this system allows teachers to invite one another into their classrooms for informal observation. The chart is set up in some location where teachers

---

97   Jennifer Gonzalez, "How Pineapple Charts Revolutionize Professional Development," *Cult of Pedagogy*, Sept. 25, 2016, https://www.cultofpedagogy.com/pineapple-charts.

go on a daily basis: the teacher's lounge, the copy room, or wherever teacher mailboxes live in your school. On the chart, teachers "advertise" the interesting things they are doing in their classrooms, activities they think others might want to observe. The activities might be as complex as a science lab, a history simulation, or a Skype session with a school in another country. Or they might be as simple as a read-aloud or a lesson.

Posting (and using) a Pineapple Chart in a school is a great step for those who need a push to step into another classroom or to invite other teachers in to see a practice or strategy that they are proud of.

If we really want to shift practice, we have to move beyond showcasing our "best." We need to collaborate on the challenges of trying something new. You can take the pineapple chart observation a step further by sharing feedback with those you observe. The learning is then reciprocal, and both teachers learn and grow as a result.

Team teaching is another step on the bridge to innovation. Paige Couros, an elementary school teacher, shared with me in a conversation, "For teammates who are hesitant to try something new, team teaching provides a safety net; for example, if the camera/microphone doesn't work or if students needed different supports during literacy stations, another teacher is present to help out. In my experiences with team teaching, my partners and I plan the lesson together, and then I bring my class to theirs, and that teacher tries it out. If something went wrong, which inevitably it did, we served as one another's backup. Additionally, a debrief after the lesson to discuss next steps deepens the learning experience for teachers."

Working together to support one another and improve is different from showcasing your best work or creating the illusion of a "perfect" classroom. I truly believe that breaking down silos and sharing real challenges are the only ways that we will continue to improve. If we become so wrapped up in making sure everything is perfect, we eliminate opportunities to take risks and step out of our comfort zones. When we want everything to be perfect, we can miss out on additional opportunities to grow and improve lessons because we are so narrowly focused on a preconceived notion of how learning should look.

Perfection is the enemy of progress
—Voltaire

Keep in mind that the first versions of any new idea or teaching method will likely be inferior. But the process of practicing and going through iterative cycles leads to learner-centered innovation. Sharing that process with other educators provides even more powerful learning experiences—experiences that ultimately lead to better practices. Another powerful movement that builds on this notion of feedback and growth is #ObserveMe, where teachers post a sign on their door to let people know they are welcome in the classroom. A common template to guide the observation and solicit feedback on specific practices includes the following:

- Identify what you want feedback on
- Consider including a guided observation tool to make it easy for observers to give you actionable feedback on your specific goals
- Print out the sign and put in on your door or window
- Then, take a picture of it and tweet it out using the hashtag #ObserveMe

At El Camino High School in Oceanside, California, teachers had been exploring a variety of new teaching strategies and seeking an authentic way to both showcase what they had learned and get feedback on their evolving practices. Each teacher posted an #ObserveMe sign on their door describing what they were working on and what they wanted feedback on. Doug Kriedeman, the principal, arranged for teachers to be free to observe others. He also visited classrooms to celebrate the powerful learning of both teachers and students. The teachers shared what they were observing across the classrooms and with others on Twitter, using the school hashtag #SchoolIsReal. Doug shared that "#ObserveMe day was empowering for teachers. Opening classroom doors gave us an opportunity to celebrate the amazing things happening in classrooms every day and inspired great ideas across our campus." As teachers began to share and they developed a greater understanding of their own teaching, what was happening across campus, and they were increasingly more willing to take risks and try new things.

There is value in visiting educators within one's own school to develop a shared understanding of what teaching and learning looks like in the context of your community. Visiting other schools provides great benefits by allowing teachers to see new opportunities created by different methods and teaching styles. Teaching has long been an individual profession behind closed doors, and shifting that paradigm is not easy. It requires vulnerability to open classroom doors. Pineapple Charts and #ObserveMe signs provide systems that allow leaders to take the first step and encourage others to step out of their comfort zones to make the learning process more transparent.

Focus on Learning, *Not* Evaluation

Educators at Palmquist Elementary in Oceanside, California, were focusing on the 4 Cs: collaboration, critical thinking, creativity, and communication. They planned lessons together as teams and shared ideas about what integrating the 4 Cs into their classrooms could look like, but no one had ever seen this in action except for the principal. The principal shared how proud she was that teachers were shifting from whole group instruction to small groups; group work was increasingly more thoughtful and effective, and many teachers were integrating science, technology, math, and engineering through hands-on, project-based learning. But she acknowledged that none of her teachers had been able to see what was happening across campus. In order to spread these great practices and help teachers learn from their colleagues, we scheduled two days to observe classrooms and celebrate the positive. In lieu of the scheduled grade-level collaboration, I worked with the principal to organize-grade level visits to all classrooms on campus. To ensure that teachers felt supported, we set up a scavenger hunt to find and celebrate examples of the 4 Cs they saw in each of the classrooms. Teachers brought their phones and took pictures to document and share examples and ideas to take back to their classrooms. Using these pictures, we put together a montage for teachers to see the best examples of communication, collaboration, critical thinking, and creativity evident across the campus. The video documented what was happening on campus, validated the school's progress, and served as a catalyst for growth.

What is important to highlight is that this wasn't about evaluation but about learning from one another. Perhaps that was the reason people were willing to be vulnerable and let others in. It allowed the educators to deepen their connections, ask questions, and build off the examples and models they had seen in practice. As you can imagine, after seeing twenty-five classrooms and different ways of organizing the classrooms, explaining concepts, transitions, giving feedback, and so much more, everyone had so many questions and new ideas that they couldn't wait to try. Opening the classrooms was a critical first step to inspiration and innovation. If we are going to see changes in our schools, we will have much more success if those leading the way are empowered and excited to inspire change. Providing opportunities to see what is possible is critical to shifting mindset.

I have grown so much as an educator from the vast amount of amazing teachers I have observed and interacted with, and I know the same is true for others. When we focus on what is going well and create opportunities for reflection, observations prompt reflection about our own practice—both validating and stretching thinking. Nothing puts educators on edge or inhibits innovation more than "evaluators" inspecting classroom practice from a deficit perspective. Opening our classroom doors is a key step in school improvement and is inspiring when it is more about creating a culture of learning and innovation than it is about doing it right. Observing teachers for an evaluation or coaching has a different focus than learning about trends on campus and getting into classrooms to learn and improve your own practice. Know your purpose and make sure that it's clear to those you are observing as well. Open communication and transparency about what we are learning and how we are improving is at the core of shifting practice to improve learning, teaching, and leading. If you want to create a culture of learning and innovation rather than evaluation, start by putting down the checklist and celebrating success.

Feeling nervous about administrators, educators, or even parents being in our schools and classrooms often comes from the fear of being judged. This is a common fear, but as Aaron Hogan, administrator and author of *Shattering the Perfect Teacher Myth*, says, "Vulnerability is the prerequisite for all innovation, creativity and change."[98] If you have a great idea but are afraid to try it

---

98   Aaron Hogan, *Shattering the Perfect Teacher Myth: 6 Truths That Will Help You THRIVE as an Educator*, (San Diego, CA: Dave Burgess Consulting, Inc., 2017).

because you aren't sure if it will work or you are afraid of what others will say, the status quo will prevail. When innovative practices are celebrated and shared, great learning can spread through schools and the world. If we only tell the stories of the good or gloss over the challenges instead of sharing the hurdles that are part of learning, we miss the power of the learning process. The culture of learning and risk taking can make great ideas and practices spread through schools and communities like wildfire or keep them hidden behind closed doors.

Curating Student Work

As a new teacher, I gave my seventh graders a couple of days to complete a writing assignment. I don't even remember what the assignment was about, but I do remember receiving sloppy paragraphs rife with poor punctuation, misspelled words, and incomplete sentences as their final drafts. For a moment, they actually had me convinced that they couldn't do any better and that we needed to go back to the basics. In the midst of my plans to revisit how to write a paragraph, I happened to visit a friend at the nearby elementary school. When I brought up the challenge I was having, she showed me some of her student's work, and then we found a few of my students' old portfolios that never made it home at the end of the year. As I reviewed their previous work, I saw beautifully written stories and thoughtfully constructed sentences punctuated and edited in a big construction paper envelope. The learning was essentially buried away in the corner of an old classroom, and I didn't know it was there to build on. The transition from elementary school to middle school is challenging in a lot of ways, but that didn't mean my students had all of a sudden lost the skills they had developed. Their lack of excellence on the current assignment, however, did reveal to me that I hadn't brought out those skills. I had not had models of the work they were capable of, and I had a very limited view of what quality seventh-grade work could really look like in my school or my community. As a result, I hadn't created the expectation that they would have better writing. My students acted as if they were starting over with their writing skills instead of building on what they had learned in years past.

After I compared the past and present examples of student work and had a model of what was possible, my students quickly closed the gap and began to move beyond where they were in sixth grade as a result of our new and shared expectations. This experience taught me two things: 1) Looking at student work is powerful for educators and students, and 2) portfolios are great, but if students don't own the process and don't continue growing from grade to grade, we all lose. If I could have picked up from where each student was in sixth grade when they started seventh grade and if students were responsible for curating and sharing their work, we would have gone so much further, much faster. George Couros has pushed the conversation around digital portfolios. He explains that a student's digital portfolio empowers the learning process because "it gives the creator of the space an opportunity to showcase learning while building a digital footprint that will be beneficial long after their time in schools. It also allows students multiple ways to showcase their learning since basically anything I can see or hear, I can now make digital and link into their space. The possibilities are endless."[99] I couldn't agree more. I think about how different our conversations and the quality of student work would be if it were documented and shared with teachers from year to year. Instead, students lose a lot of time, essentially starting from scratch as the teacher gets to know them in each new grade level. And as my own students did, sometimes they even regress. This backtracking could

---

99   George Couros, "Resources on Blogs as Digital Portfolios," *The Principal of Change*, Accessed Dec. 1, 2017, https://georgecouros.ca/blog/presentation-resources/resources-on-blogs-as-digital-portfolios.

be avoided (or at least significantly reduced) if students curated and built on their work over the years. What if students could continue working from their best thinking and ideas and show their progress over the course of their education rather than chunk their learning by grade level or teachers? What if students owned their portfolios, and we, as educators, created the experiences to add to them with new ideas and learning, their questions, and diverse projects? When students curate their work and are invested in the learning process and goals rather than turning in assignments, they take ownership of the work and create quality products.

Protocols for Critique and Revision

A fairly common practice is to share activities and showcase the final products produced in classrooms, but when it comes to delving into what is working and what is not, many teachers are not used to this level of transparency in their practice. Only when we are open to exploring the challenges we face can we develop better experiences for those we serve. To improve teaching, we have to focus on what students are learning. To go beyond discussing lesson plans and curricula, looking at student work helps educators understand how students apply what they are learning and focus on the actual impact of the teaching.

To truly understand the current reality requires that educators are open about their practice and allow themselves to be vulnerable to expose both strengths and challenges. An open culture, where the norm is sharing and learning, is easier said than done and is often more successful with facilitation and clear protocols to help guide the process and help people move beyond their comfort zone. The use of protocols is increasingly spreading to workshops, PLCs, and staff meetings, with the understanding that the right constraints can ignite creativity and innovation. Here is a brief explanation of why protocols work:

Thus, protocols have been adapted countless times in many settings and for diverse purposes. They are popular too because each implicitly teaches one of three rare but important skills: the first, how to give and receive safe and honest feedback; the second, how to analyze complex problems carefully and without rushing to judgment; and the third, how to ground interpretations of complex texts— for example, student work or school data—in close "readings" of the texts.[100]

The Power of Protocols provides a variety of protocols to guide effective collaboration, which eases the discomfort and leads educators through new processes. The development of shared norms and structured protocols helps educators focus on teaching and learning without putting people in a position where they feel threatened or judged. When protocols are used effectively to guide collaborative groups, educators can not only gain ideas from the models, but also benefit from the experience and expertise of their colleagues.

The Looking at Student Work protocol is helpful in providing educators a structure to share their lessons, student work, and even challenges they face. This protocol has been adapted and used widely since 1992, when it was first used by the Coalition of Essential Schools.

It usually takes between thirty and sixty minutes to complete. It is ideal in groups of four to six and with the help of a facilitator and timekeeper.

---

100 Joseph P. McDonald, et al., *The Power of Protocols: An Educator's Guide to Better Practice, Third Edition (the series on school reform)*, (New York: Teachers College Press, 2013).

Looking at Student Work Protocol

Step 1: Overview (three to five minutes)

Facilitator reviews norms and provides an overview of the protocol and steps to all participants

Step 2: Presentation (three to five minutes)

Presenter shares an overview of what the presenter tried that they are seeking feedback on and provides examples of student work to examine, including:

- Objectives targeted in the learning experience
- Examples of student work
- A burning question or wondering to focus the dialogue

Step 3: Individual Reflections about the Student Work (three minutes)

Each group member jots down some notes about what they see in the artifact and what they wonder based on the presenter's question. This should include both warm (strengths) and cool (areas for growth) feedback.

Step 4: Discussion (ten to twenty minutes)

The group discusses their thoughts and feedback. They should note warm and cool feedback and questions that arise for them. The presenter is encouraged to listen to the discussion and take notes without responding. Questions to guide the discussion might include:

1. What do you notice about the student work?
2. How might the learning be deepened or extended?
3. What insight can we provide to the presenter about the burning question?

Step 5: Reflections from Presenter (two to five minutes)

The presenter shares reflections and implications for next steps and further study.

Steps 6: Implications for Practice (five to ten minutes)

Looking forward, discuss as a group: What might be some next steps or implications for your practice or context?

—

This protocol can also be adapted for use in a variety of ways. It's best to use actual work from the students you teach; however, if the group is not quite ready for that level of vulnerability, beginning with other examples can help scaffold the process. These models can help people become comfortable talking about teaching and learning. When this is done in collaborative groups, educators can not only gain ideas from the models, but also benefit from the experience and expertise of their colleagues. Some great examples of student work and authentic projects can inspire teachers to explore different kinds of learning experiences and have conversations about the implications for their own classrooms. As discussed in chapter 10, teachers can benefit from presenting a lesson idea or project on which they are just beginning for suggestions on how to enhance the approach. It is also useful midway through a project to help improve and determine next steps. The process can also be used for feedback on a challenge. When we solve problems collectively, we can learn a great deal about our impact on desired learning outcomes and continue to improve. Teams benefit when their collaboration is focused on presenting challenges, providing feedback, and creating actionable next steps. Protocols provide valuable structure that help improve learning experiences to positively impact students.

Share the Process

Have you ever come across a series of Pinterest #craftfails? I remember a few that had me laughing hysterically—not *at* the person who'd had a #PinterestFail but *with* them because I have had my fair share and can definitely empathize with these fails. In addition to making me laugh, seeing those flops made me feel better. I remember that I am not the only who doesn't just whip up a batch of perfect cake balls on the first try (or second or third). This sparked my thinking about our classrooms, and how, as I shared earlier, we are so quick to share the positives and what goes well. This constant comparison to perfection can cripple people who don't have success on their first or second try or who feel so far away from the ideal.

When a gap exists between where someone perceives they are and what they see as someone else's practice, the pathways can seem vague or unclear, and the first steps futile. Additionally, when people lack a tangible next step or compare themselves to an idea of perfection rather than the reality, they can become defensive.

Our natural reaction to failure is to protect ourselves, which can prevent everyone from moving forward. Educators are often thought of as selfless because of the desire to serve others and make an impact in the lives of children. Although that servant's heart drives many teachers, we are not immune to the influence of our egos. The desire to be perfect and have everyone think that we have it all together can prevent learning and innovation if we don't take risks to step out of our comfort zone.

The ego, a sense of self-esteem or self-importance, is a part of the physiological system that develops your self-concept. When your ego is threatened, it can protect you from clearly seeing reality. For example, you might think that your team teacher has better relationships with her students; the students are learning more in another teacher's class, or you feel shame because you didn't complete tasks that were expected of you. In other words, the ego makes up its own reality to protect itself from the shame or areas for improvement and can create a false reality that can cause defensiveness or create barriers that hinder progress and ultimately limit success. This manifests itself in such comments as "this is the way we have always done it," "I learned it this way, and I am fine," or a version of "my students(or teachers) can't do that."

Instead of asking what to do with teachers who are unwilling to share, ask yourself, "What is holding them back?" Effective leaders, at all levels, understand that everyone is in a different place and strive to meet people where they are instead of expecting everyone to have already arrived.

If you find yourself saying, "my kids can't do that," or "yeah, but . . ." consider how you could reframe your fear and take a small step forward to take a risk. I often see classroom walls filled with signs that celebrate failure, such as, FAIL: First Attempt in Learning. These statements help promote the growth mindset in students as they acknowledge that failure is part of the learning process. It is great to see teachers promoting this mindset in students, but if we don't model this among our colleagues or with students in our classrooms, what message are we actually sending? Are you opening yourself up to take risks and share what you are learning as you expect your students to do, or are you just paying lip service to the notion? If we paint a glossy version of what our ideal classrooms should be or what we want people to see, we will continue to isolate ourselves and our practice in service of an ideal rather than embrace the messiness of learning and innovation.

In thinking about this gap between where we want to be and where we are, I was reminded of a conversation I'd had with an amazing teacher who was having trouble with her colleagues. She was named the teacher of the year at her school, but she felt isolated and ganged up on by her peers, who were trying to prevent her from creating a website to showcase her students' work. She was devastated because she was working so hard and wanted to share what her students were doing. Her colleagues were giving her flak for going above and beyond. As we talked about the situation, she realized that she had only let her team teachers see her success; she had emphasized what was going well and downplayed her challenges. Ultimately, the picture-perfect image she had presented created jealousy and resentment among peers.

We naturally hide our fails, but doing so doesn't build community; in fact, that fake persona prevents connection. Although it is important to share your work and highlight the positives, we shouldn't omit shining a light on the process that got us there so that others can join us.

As I talked with this teacher about how to bridge the divide between her and her colleagues, she decided to share her process, how she could create such amazing projects with her students, and what she had learned along the way. Once she shared how she had struggled, the challenges she faced with her team teachers, *and* offered to highlight their students on her website, the walls began to fall. Her team started bringing her in to ask for support instead of closing their doors.

Many times, when educators feel that they are isolated from their peers or when their colleagues are giving them a hard time about going above and beyond, they might have shared very little of the process and added to the misperceptions and divisions.

Create a Hashtag, Build a Community

Districts and communities of practice can connect and share their ideas, questions, and student work without ever walking into a classroom. Creating a hashtag allows individuals to curate and share their story. With a simple hashtag, individuals can share what is happening in their classrooms on social media to connect with educators locally and globally. In *Hacking Leadership,* Joe Sanfelippo and Tony Sinanis[101] relate that "using a hashtag helps students and staff exercise their voices on their terms." In Fall Creek, where Joe is the superintendent, the #gocrickets hashtag is full of tweets about Fall Creek life. It streams to the school's website and serves as a way for the local community and beyond to share and see the amazing things happening every day.

Taking this type of connection a step further, Matt Arend, principal at Sigler Elementary, creates a video each year to capture the highlights and share the journey. As he watches his teachers and students grow and develop over time, he acknowledges that, "The most important step we had to take was one I took first. I, the principal of the building, had to get comfortable with not being the only one sharing. I had to let go of the control and let the teachers/staff share right along with me. Since then, we have not looked back." Now, each grade level has their own hashtag, and they have a school hashtag, #siglernation, to which everyone contributes. As a community, Matt says, "We share, we tweet, we learn. Most importantly, we tell our story."[102]

Even beyond our own school communities, educators today can have more access to one another, which can give light to many new ideas and practices in schools and beyond. In *The Innovator's Mindset,* George Couros poses the question, "What if all teachers tweeted once a day about something they did in their classrooms and took five minutes to read other teachers' tweets?"[103]

---

101 Joe Sanfelippo and Tony Sinanis, *Hacking Leadership: 10 Ways Great Leaders Inspire Learning That Teachers, Students, and Parents Love (Hack Learning Series Book 5),* (Cleveland, OH: Times 10 Publications, 2016).

102 Matthew Arend, "My Thoughts, My Reflections, A Principal View: Tell Our Story." *Matthew Arend,* Accessed Dec. 1, 2017, http://matthewarend.com/2017/06/04/tell-our-story.

103 Couros, George. *The Innovator's Mindset: Empower Learning, Unleash Talent, and Lead a Culture of Creativity* (San Diego, CA: Dave Burgess Consulting, Inc. 2015).

Kyle Hamstra took this idea and created #hashtag180 to share what is happening in his classroom and connect with other classrooms based on specific learning objectives to improve practice connected to standards and learning objectives that teachers are expected to teach. He describes the goal on his blog. "The #hashtag180 Challenge was originally designed for educators to access and share learning resources very specifically by tweeting life and classroom experiences, hashtagged with learning objectives and #hashtag180. Where does it go from here? The possibilities are endless . . . ."[104]

He was right, and many educators have built off this idea to share but have also turned this into a way to open classroom doors to parents and the community. Bill Ferriter decided that, if he was going to post something every day, he wanted it to be manageable and also to serve a variety of purposes. He creates short videos intended for his students that are linked to specific curriculum standards. He also cross posts the videos that he shares on Twitter to his own blog that serves as a digital portfolio to highlight what he is teaching and how it connects to his state standards. #genius

Bill reflects in his blog, "By creating videos, I knew that I was also creating interesting content that my students and parents might be interested in watching, too. That turned each #hashtag180 post into more than just a learning opportunity for me. Each post is now a learning opportunity for me *and* a review tool for my students *and* a communication tool for my parents." By taking five minutes a day to create a short video for students connected to a specific learning objective, parents and the community can also see it and connect or add their ideas, and a digital portfolio is created to document the learning in his classroom over time. Teachers around the world can see how different teachers design learning experiences tied

---

104 Kyle Hamstra, "Join the #Hashtag180 Challenge!" *#HamstraHighlights*, April 15, 2017, https://kylehamstra.com/2017/04/15/join-the-hashtag180-challenge.

to specific standards and share their own ideas. Imagine if every teacher did this? I'd say that's a pretty strong example of making powerful learning go viral.

The Power of an Authentic Audience

When students have an authentic audience for their work, it communicates that they matter and that their work has value. Creating opportunities for students to share their work with the community promotes conversations about what they are learning and can prompt reflection and application of learning in their future. Having an authentic audience is equally important for educators. When teachers become learners and take on new learning experiences, they often become more aware of what is possible and create better experiences for their students. Annick Rauch and I co-wrote a blog[105] about the benefits of blogging for professional learning, highlighting the impact we experienced as a result of sharing and reflecting openly. One of the educators featured was Kristen Edwards, who shared that she uses her blog to spark conversations with teachers and models the evolution of her thinking over time to help teachers she works with embrace their own learning process. The best educators are learners first. When educators take risks and embrace the process, they are better able to understand the experiences and opportunities that exist for learners. Another educator, Cariann Cook, acknowledges that,

> It [blogging] also helped me relate to my students who "can't think of anything to write about." It's been good for me to put my thoughts on paper (on my computer) to really internalize the thoughts going around in my head. I like the intentionality of it and after only three weeks of blogging I've started thinking, Ooh, I could blog about this!

---

105   Katie L. Martin, "The Power of Blogging for Professional Development #IMMOOC," *Katie L. Martin*, March 24, 2017, https://katielmartin.com/2017/03/24/the-power-of-blogging-for-professional-development-immooc.

If you are a leader (or teacher) and have never blogged or used social media, how can you tell others to do something you are not willing to try yourself? If we expect people (adults or kids) to try new things and share what they are learning, we have to be willing to lead the way. Annick acknowledges that teachers are busy; it's safe to say that reflection (and even more so, open reflection) is pushed to the bottom of our priority list even if that's not our intention. Most teachers, however, understand the value of reflection and how it helps us improve. Blogging and even quick shares on social media provide an opportunity for self-reflection and then takes those reflections public, where others can read, critique, and learn from us. It also gives us an authentic audience and level of accountability that pushes us to think through our ideas even more and to be open to accepting feedback in order to push our own thinking. Knowing that we have a wider audience to critique and support us empowers us to try new things, and take risks, and hopefully leads us to innovate to create better experiences in our schools and classrooms. Don Sturm, an innovative teacher, expressed that blogging "allows me to step outside of my bubble by making my ideas public for all to read and comment on. That authentic audience is an important part of blogging."

LCI Tip:

If you are a leader, foster collaboration on a regular basis by creating spaces and opportunities for teachers to share their work and what they are learning. Carving out time during staff meetings or planning time is a great way for teachers to share. But to move beyond the school, encourage teachers to share their learning in real time in online communities with a school or district hashtag.

After a yearlong partnership with a group of leaders, teachers, and administrators in between the University of San Diego's Entrepreneurship for Education and Fallbrook Union Elementary School District, I was walking around, beaming about how many teams were talking about the great stuff that was happening in their schools and how they had been sharing their work. At the culminating professional learning day, my teammates Kim Cawkwell and Emily Roth facilitated opportunities for site-based teams to reflect and share their learning journey over the year. As I listened to the teams discuss how they could continue to document and share their work not only at the site and district levels, but also expand their impact through blogging, Twitter chats, websites, Instagram, and Facebook pages, I was brought back to the beginning of the year, when the conversations were much more guarded and learning was private. Because the administration at the school had wisely created the space and structured opportunities for learning and sharing, these educators had been introduced to new ideas and methods. Although they had begun by looking at models from other educators beyond their school, within a year, they were implementing the ideas they learned and designing new and better experiences and sharing with others in their district and beyond. These collaborative practices helped them peek inside other classrooms and open their doors too.

Concluding Thoughts

Whether inviting someone in to give you feedback or checking out a different classroom, push yourself to explore new models and look for how to grow rather than simply affirming what you already do. Be aware of your bias and go into observations to look for opportunities to try new things. If you are open, you will be amazed at what you can learn.

It is difficult to change our practice without clearly understanding what teaching and learning could or should look like. Designing powerful experiences that meet the diverse needs of the individuals in your classroom is rarely a matter of finding the right curriculum or the best program. It is much more about knowing your students and having a clear sense of the skills, knowledge, and dispositions that need to be developed. This is not something that can be scripted in a textbook, and very skilled teachers have different ways of doing this effectively. By breaking down walls and making learning public, seeing other teachers becomes a common practice, and we regularly share what is happening in classrooms—the good and the bad. In the article "I Am an Educator and I Am Desperate to Be Taught," the author reflects,

> I am eternally grateful to the teachers who voluntarily gave up lunch breaks to meet with me, who welcomed me into their classrooms, and allowed me to question their methods with a generosity of spirit that made me the educator I am today. Their lesson plans, their teacher voices, and their passion for the true work of teaching lives in every class I have ever taught or PD session I have led.[106]

I have heard teachers say over and over how impactful observing other teachers can be, yet this practice is so rare. When we build time into the school day for educators to observe one another, we set an expectation for how the staff should work and grow together. It also affirms that observation and sharing the process of learning is valued at our schools. The growth and development of a staff should be a priority, not an option or what we do during lunch hour.

---

106 Anonymous, "I Am an Educator and I Am Desperate to Be Taught," *kiddom*, July 21, 2016, https://blog.kiddom.co/i-am-an-educator-and-i-am-desperate-to-be-taught-dc0dda41d4dc.

Reflect and Connect Challenge
Share your thoughts, questions, and ideas using #LCInnovation

O   Find a way to visit five classrooms or another school. How can you celebrate and share what you see? What might be the implications for your own practice?

O   What are you learning? How will you model and share what you are learning? Share using your existing school, district, or community of practice hashtag, or create your own.

O   How might you support those you serve to share their learning with an authentic audience?

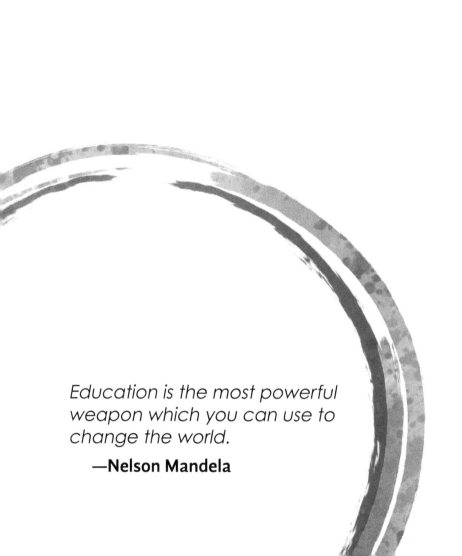

Education is the most powerful weapon which you can use to change the world.

—Nelson Mandela

Unleashing Genius

WHILE PUTTING MY SON TO bed one night, I noticed he seemed uncharacteristically sad. When I asked what was wrong, he said, "I don't know what I want to be when I grow up." This is not what I expected to hear from my six-year-old, and it broke my heart to know that he was upset and ashamed because he didn't know what he wanted to be. After a bit more conversation, he shared that he had been asked a few times by family members and at school what he wanted to be when he grew up and had felt pressured to have an answer. I told him that I never knew what I wanted to be growing up and tried to assure him that he doesn't need to know either. Realistically, the job he will end up doing probably doesn't exist yet.

This conversation has been on my mind a lot lately. It's made me more aware of how I talk to kids (my own and others) about their futures. Asking kids what they want to be when they grow up seems to be an easy way to get to know their interests, but the question is also used to categorize them. Countless units and projects from preschool on up are designed to ask kids to identify a future career path, and every kid is expected to pick something. I am guilty of doing it myself, even though I always hated it when adults asked me this question.

Although we ask this question with the best of intentions, it can end up having a lasting impact on how kids see themselves. Early messages about what is valued and what is accepted in both family and social circles are translated by reactions to the answers to this question. Career theorist Linda Gottfredson says that the career aspirations of children are influenced by the perceptions of what is appropriate for one's gender and class rather than more private aspects of their self-concept, such as their skills and interests. At this early age, kids are forming their self-concept and identity by attaching value to what adults like and find acceptable based on what is positively reinforced.[107]

How Can You Aspire to a Career That You Don't Know Exists?

I can empathize with my son. Growing up, my mom was a teacher, and my dad was a car salesman. This was all I really knew about careers or all that I really saw as a career path. I had very little exposure to any other jobs aside from a career day at some point in high school that I probably treated as a day off rather than an investment in my future. I remember thinking, *I don't really want to sell cars, so I guess I will be a teacher.*

We are influenced by our surroundings and what we experience, which can limit our understanding of the world and especially the possibilities that exist. My friend Ed Hidalgo, who spent years hiring talent at Qualcomm, a Fortune 500 company, and now

---

107 The Careers Group, "Circumscription and compromise," https://careersintheory.files.wordpress.com/2009/10/theories_gottfredson.pdf.

is the Innovation and Engagement Officer in Cajon Valley Union School District, poses the question in his TEDx Talk, "How Can a Child Aspire to a Career They Don't Know Exists?"[108] He argues that the key to changing a child's trajectory is providing diverse experiences early on to understand who they are—and to allow them to see themselves in the world of work and see new possibilities for their future.

Rather than narrowing the path for kids and pushing them to think about a career disconnected from their passions and interests, Jaime Casap, Education Evangelist at Google, urged in a keynote talk, "Don't ask kids what they want to be when they grow up but what problems they want to solve." I think this is a great way to reframe this typical question, and it made me think about what else we could ask kids instead of, What do you want to be when you grow up? What if we asked kids questions like:

- What are you interested in?
- What do you love to do?
- What makes you happy?
- When do you feel like you are successful?
- How do you like to work/play with others?
- What comes easily to you?
- What do you want to learn more about?
- What is important to you?

Because my children are young and developing their identity, I want them (and *all* children) to have opportunities to understand who they are and what makes them unique. I want them to have opportunities to build on their strengths, explore their passions, and be empowered to solve problems that matter to them while

---

108   Ed Hidalgo, "How Can a Child Aspire to a Career They Don't Know Exists?" *YouTube*, July 1, 2015, https://www.youtube.com/watch?v=yRQLj2erYPk.

also learning about problems that matter to others. I want them to see the world as full of opportunities, where they can create their path rather than pursue what they perceive as the right job. This pressure and early guidance toward certain paths has led to an increasing number of disengaged workers.

I began this book by highlighting the Gallup poll and how engagement plummets from fifth grade to twelfth grade to about 35 percent. Students indicate they have few opportunities to build on their strengths or do something they enjoy in school. Unfortunately, this trend continues into the workplace. The 2015 Gallup poll found that, on average, 32 percent of workers are what they consider engaged in their jobs. The majority are not engaged, and 17.2 percent are categorized as actively disengaged. They elaborate on what this means in the report:[109]

> Most U.S. workers continue to fall into the disengaged category. These employees are not hostile or disruptive. They show up and kill time, doing the minimum required with little extra effort to go out of their way for customers. They are less vigilant, more likely to miss work and change jobs when new opportunities arise. They are thinking about lunch or their next break. Not engaged employees are either "checked out" or attempting to get their job done with little or no management support.

This reality is startling for me, and hopefully it is for you too. If only 32 percent of the workforce is engaged, while 17 percent are disengaged, imagine what is possible if we doubled the amount of engaged workers. What if our workforce were not only engaged but empowered? As has been mentioned many times in this book, the world today needs creative, passionate, and skilled individuals. To harness the power in each of us, we need to create systems that tap into the strengths and potential of each individual. I believe this

---

109 Amy Adkins, "Employee Engagement in U.S. Stagnant in 2015," *Gallup News*, Jan. 13, 2016, http://www.gallup.com/poll/188144/employee-engagement-stagnant-2015.aspx.

begins with what students advocated in a change.org petition in which they asked the administration to broaden the narrow path of success defined by test scores and college acceptance. In this petition, shared in the *Chicago Tribune,*[110] the high school students begged the administration to "start defining success as any path that leads to a happy and healthy life. Start teaching us to make our own paths, and start guiding us along the way." If we are honest, isn't this what we all want—to be happy and healthy and do work that gives us purpose and joy? The education system was designed by people, and the only way it will change is for people to change it. Thoughtful leaders in 1892 created the rules and the systems that made sense for the world then. Today, it is up to us to believe in our collective future enough to make the changes that are necessary for tomorrow. That means you and I must be part of the solution.

Mischievous or Genius

In the *Captain Underpants* movie, George Beard and Harold Hutchins, two young troublemakers, wrote a comic book about a superhero named Captain Underpants. The mischievous pair hypnotize their principal and turn him into the superhero they created, and endless adventures ensue. In the opening scenes of the movie, they compare the elementary school to a penitentiary where students are expected to memorize dates while falling asleep and moving through school like zombies. When the bell rings, they rush home to their treehouse full of inventions and drafts of stories and books they have created on their own. As I watched this movie with my kids and heard them laughing at all the silly antics, I couldn't help but see the creative genius in these boys who are always in trouble for their latest prank or invention. Although this

---

110   Suzanne Baker, "Student petition says too much pressure to succeed at Naperville North," *Naperville Sun*, April 14, 2017, http://www.chicagotribune.com/suburbs/naperville-sun/ct-nvs-203-naperville-north-petition-st-0414-20170413-story.html.

is a cartoon, the message from Dav Pilkey, the author, comes from his own experience as a young student. He was diagnosed with ADHD and dyslexia and was often in trouble in school. He created *Captain Underpants* in the hallway where he was usually sent to be reprimanded for his behavior in class. Dav took his experience and created something amazing. I left the theater wondering, *How often do we squash the dreams of students and miss out on great ideas when we label creativity and innovation as mischievous instead of genius?*

We need to create the conditions that empower learners to find the right questions rather than simply providing the answers.

What if we focused on deliberately crafting better questions to elicit and expand on the ideas of the learners rather than planning how to transfer information? By bringing learners' experience and questions into the classrooms, we can solve meaningful problems and ignite passions to learn from the amazing ideas and insights that students have. When the learners are asking the questions, they are more invested in figuring out the answers. But if we insist on managing our classrooms as if static content is the goal, we will undermine the genius that exists in our students and educators. We need to create the conditions that empower learners to find the right questions rather than simply providing the answers.

Great leaders, like David Miyashiro the superintendent of the Cajon Valley Union School District, understand that the power of student voice has created opportunities to showcase it in the schools and throughout the larger community. TedXkids@ CajonValley, an independently organized TEDx event, empowers students to share their ideas and what they are doing to make an impact in their communities. In his district, he has created a venue where students were not only inspired to explore their strengths, interests, and values, but also encouraged to do something about it. As I was sitting in the audience at this amazing community event, I was struck by the power of their ideas. One of the talks featured twin brothers who shared stories about bullying, so they created a club to help others who are feeling alone. Another student shared what she learned about the impact of littering and how she is working to save the environment. She is leading by example and encouraging others to help and commit to picking up five pieces of trash (that aren't yours) a day.

My favorite presentation came from two fifth-grade boys who shared that they frequently got in trouble until their assistant principal, with whom they had spent a lot of time, helped them make their idea of building a garden a reality. "Once I told her my idea, she did it. Not like in a few months, like in two days!" They described how they take care of the garden and what they are growing. They are even learning how to cook and are eating healthier foods as result. Thanks to the garden and someone who believed in their ideas, these two students now go to her office for encouragement, not when they're in trouble. They shared, "Sometimes all you need is a garden to get you on track." Their story serves as a reminder that we can each make an impact on others and their life trajectory if we can look past the bad to find the good that exists in all of us.

During this event, students of all ages with diverse passions and experiences got up and shared their ideas. It's pretty impressive, considering all that goes into giving a TED-style talk. They not only had great ideas, but they also had to organize their thoughts, put together compelling visuals, and learn to communicate effectively with a live audience. The skills that students demonstrated align with many of the skills we aspire to develop in students to help them to be successful throughout life. Beyond the skills, and possibly even more important, is that the students were able to see that their ideas matter. By putting ideas out in the world, they begin to understand the power of asking better questions, generating new ideas, and believing they can actually make a difference.

Genius lives in all of us, and it will be uncovered only if we make time to pursue our interests and wonderings to explore new and better ways rather than seeking the right answers. Too much control and guidance takes the thinking out of problem solving. And at the other extreme, being too hands-off leaves them flailing like the students Ted Dintersmith, coauthor of *Most Likely to Succeed*,[111] talked about in a keynote at Buck Institute for Education's yearly conference, PBL World. When an eleventh-grade English teacher asked students to pick a topic they were interested in to explore independently, half the class immediately did a Google search for, "What should I be interested in?"

After years of being told what to learn, students don't magically own their learning just because we schedule time for it in our lesson plans. We have to cultivate ideas and nurture questions and wonderings; otherwise, imagination dies. When we don't make space to think deeply and reflect and place value on more questions and new ideas over the right answer or a quick response, we stifle curiosity. Eventually, many stop asking questions, either because they fear they will be wrong, or because they are unsure about their ideas. As mentioned throughout this book, we are clearly held accountable to standards and expectations, but as we evolve as educators, our responsibility is to be creative within our given constraints and find ways to be innovative instead of trying to recreate the system—a task that might not be within your sphere of influence. With that truth in mind and given your constraints, how

---

111   Tony Wagner and Ted Dintersmith, *Most Likely to Succeed: Preparing Our Kids for the Innovation Era,* (New York: Scribner, 2015).

might you create the space for learners to wonder, question, and explore? Where are there opportunities for learners to expand on *their* ideas? Here are four simple questions to ask those you serve that can get you started:

- What problems are you interested in exploring?
- What do you already know or think on this topic?
- What are you wondering about?
- What do you want to learn?

One of my favorite lines from Google's video, "Rubik's Cube: A question, waiting to be answered" is ". . . when the right person finds the right question, it can set them on a journey to change the world." The images of kids conducting experiments, building robots, playing in the mud, and even blowing up things always make me smile at the thought of what is possible when learners are inspired and have the support to explore their ideas, questions, and passions in and out of school. (If you haven't seen it, take a minute and watch it! bit.ly/lci_question)

From Accountability to Collective Responsibility

Accountability is not bad. Management and leadership experts tout, "what gets measured gets done" for a reason. In her book, *Better Than Before,* habit expert Gretchen Rubin identifies four tendencies that explain how individuals respond to inner and outer expectations.[112] She identifies these as upholders, questioners, rebels, and obligers. The upholders don't like to let anyone down, including themselves, and can easily form new habits. Questioners only worry about internal expectations and do what makes sense instead of following arbitrary rules. They don't try to please others.

---

112 Gretchen Rubin, *Better Than Before: What I Learned About Making and Breaking Habits--to Sleep More, Quit Sugar, Procrastinate Less, and Generally Build a Happier Life,* (New York: Broadway Books, 2015).

Rebels push back on everything and are the least common. Most people fall into the obliger category. They are held accountable by external forces to make sure they actually follow through and meet expectations. An obliger needs a buddy to go to the gym with them to make sure that they actually go.

In life, we all prioritize that for which we are held accountable; it is for this very reason that systems are set in place to check homework, take attendance, and make sure the curriculum is taught. But accountability gets a bad rap because things like standardized tests, grades, and other data that are easy to capture are measured (and prioritized above) what we say we actually care about, such as creative thinking, complex thinking, problem solving, communication, and innovation.

There's only so much time in the day, so it is important to hold each other accountable and support those we serve in order to achieve the goals that we all collectively determine are valuable and worthwhile. Over the past twenty-five years, I have seen this transition while watching my mom's progression as a teacher. I have vivid memories of visiting her classroom throughout my childhood. Her first, second, and third graders were always in centers, working on a variety of hands-on and thoughtful tasks to learn to read and write. They did Webquests on her old Apple IIe computers and created things out of cardboard and other random household items. They were always in a variety of rotations, working on meaningful activities so that she could pull and work with small groups. Her classrooms always embodied what we now know as blended learning, personalization, and makerspaces. These practices have always been part of her teaching—as they have been for many teachers who have been intentional about learning and innovating to meet the needs of their students. Her classroom was always a place where kids worked together to create, develop, and build on and apply foundational skills. I have always looked up to her and learned so much by watching how she designed learning experiences for her students. To say she is an amazing teacher is an understatement, but her decision making and the power she had as an educator has changed dramatically during the past ten years.

In 2006, three years into No Child Left Behind, I noticed a distinct change in her classroom from years earlier, when kids as young as first grade were leading much of their learning. In the grade-level team meetings, she and her colleagues began talking about how to teach kids to distinguish between two- and three-syllable words and to ensure they could choose the right answers in the benchmark test. Admittedly, she is an "obliger" and began to prioritize what she was held accountable for. I was shocked at how their collaboration and instruction changed. As she lost more ownership of the curriculum and focused more on high-stakes test measurements, the learning shifted from something enjoyable and meaningful to what was easy to measure.

Standardization has allowed for efficiency, which works for rote processes, but when it comes to teaching, learning, and growing people, it won't allow us to innovate in our schools or to develop the unique talents and skills in diverse individuals. Joe McCannon and Becky Kanis Margiotta from the Billions Institute have supported wide-scale change and caution that, "we cannot plan transformative change in advance; it is the product of opportunism and agility that, over time, moves whole industries and sectors."[113] When those doing the work have the freedom to make informed decisions and are empowered to do what is right for those they serve, we will all benefit from the wisdom and efficiency of their decisions.

---

113 Joe McCannon and Becky Kanis Margiotta, "Inside the Command Center," *Stanford Social Innovation Review*, Jan. 21, 2015, https://ssir.org/articles/entry/inside_the_command_center.

Are You Going to Focus on Ranking Kids or Learning?

Despite the incessant focus on sorting and ranking, good grades in school don't always equate to the highest levels of success. Shawn Achor's research at Harvard reveals that college grades aren't any more predictive of subsequent life success than rolling dice. A study of more than seven hundred American millionaires showed their average college GPA was 2.9.[114] When we focus on the grades and scores rather than on the skills, and, more importantly what students can do with those skills, we miss the point, and our students miss out on meaningful learning. As Laszlo Bock, CEO and co-founder of Humu and the former Senior Vice President of People Operations at Google, said in an interview for *Time*, Google no longer relies on GPAs or test scores when hiring talent.

> After two or three years, your ability to perform at Google is completely unrelated to how you performed when you were in school, because the skills you required in college are very different. You're also fundamentally a different person. You learn and grow, you think about things differently. While academic environments tend to be more artificial. People who succeed there are sort of finely trained, they're conditioned to succeed in that environment. One of my own frustrations when I was in college and grad school is that you knew the professor was looking for a specific answer. You could figure that out, but it's much more interesting to solve problems where there isn't an obvious answer. You want people who like figuring out stuff where there is no obvious answer.[115]

---

114 Eric Barker, "Wondering What Happened to Your Class Valedictorian? Not Much, Research Shows," *Time*, May 18, 2017, http://time.com/money/4779223/valedictorian-success-research-barking-up-wrong.

115 Eric Barker, *Barking Up the Wrong Tree: The Surprising Science Behind Why Everything You Know About Success Is (Mostly) Wrong*, (Harper: HarperOne, 2017).

Similarly, in *Barking up the Wrong Tree*, Eric Barker highlights research from Karen Arnold, who followed eighty-one high school valedictorians and salutatorians from graduation to see what happened after high school. These top performers are "reliable, consistent, and well-adjusted, and by all measures the majority have good lives." But these high achievers rarely go on to change the world as many expect. Arnold identifies the disconnect in the trajectory of success, "School has clear rules. Life often doesn't. When there's no clear path to follow, academic high achievers break down."

Many would argue that it is not bad to strive for "a good life"— that "normal" or "middle class" is a fine goal, which has traditionally been true. But times have changed. Thomas Friedman points out in his book, *Thank You for Being Late*, that the promise of the middle class no longer exists.[116] So many of today's educators followed a traditional path and are living out the expectation that came with going to school, following the rules, and getting a job, but that path is becoming more of a distant dream. Many of today's kids will have to *create* their jobs and forge a new path. The world has changed so dramatically and will continue to do so at an exponential rate, and, to best serve our students, educators and institutions must evolve with it, or we will leave our students behind. According to Friedman,

> Today's American dream is now more of a journey than a fixed destination—and one that increasingly feels like walking up a down escalator. You can do it—we all did it as kids—but you have to walk faster than the escalator, meaning you need to work harder, regularly reinvent yourself, obtain at least some form of post-secondary education, make sure that you are engaged in lifelong learning, and play by the new rules while also reinventing some of them. Then you can be in the new middle class.

---

116 Thomas L. Friedman, *Thank You for Being Late: An Optimist's Guide to Thriving in the Age of Accelerations*, (New York: Farrar, Straus and Giroux, 2016).

When we become so focused on improving test scores and following the rules, the larger goals of developing learners who can think, communicate, and generate novel ideas is overlooked. We can't ignore tests because our system exists, and that is how kids get into college and get degrees, but neither should we succumb to and mindlessly move through a system that squelches our children's ability to think, create, collaborate, and innovate. Just as I noticed the change in my mother's teaching, parents and employers notice the impact this system has on our students. I was shocked by the clarity with which those outside of education see this dilemma when, on my way to the airport one morning, my Uber driver asked about my family. I told her that my kids were finishing first and second grade, and she casually said, "Their magic is slowly being cloaked. They are still young and haven't been indoctrinated into the system yet . . . just wait." I was speechless.

Are you okay with this "cloaking of our children's magic" as the accepted norm? I'm not! As a parent, I am not okay with this happening to my own children, so as an educator, how could I be comfortable with this happening to *any* children?

Why do we accept disengagement as the norm? Are we really okay with being zombies, going to work day in and day out with little purpose or drive? I am not, and I certainly don't accept that this is the life for which my kids are destined. My guess is that you want bigger and better things for yourself, your staff, and your students than what the current system perpetuates.

The good news is that we can create experiences and design schools in ways that prepare students to be critical thinkers, communicators, and problem finders and solvers. With these skills, they will be more able to tackle standardized tests and other, more important tasks in their lives. But make no mistake: If we continue to focus on ranking students by grades, following standardized curriculum, teaching to the test, and valuing compliance over learning and innovation, we will continue to struggle to meet this low bar and fail to develop learners who can find employment and lead meaningful, productive lives. We can do better than that, and it's not about adding more; it's about looking at the time in the day differently, revising and updating our roles, and unleashing the genius that exists in each individual.

> *How we spend our days is, of course, how we spend our lives.*
> **—Annie Dillard**

If we spend our days preparing for a test, then testing, and then reviewing the tests to master the basics—without setting our sights on a greater purpose for authentic learning—testing is all we will be about. If all we talk about in schools is the data and achievement on tests or the programs and the latest and greatest reform, we forget about the people who matter. And when that happens, our educators' and students' unique passions and talents—the greatest assets we have—will not just go undeveloped; they will be diminished. If, as leaders, we spend our days in meetings, writing emails, and reacting to problems rather than in classrooms, we make assumptions about what is actually happening in schools and fail to really learn about the strengths and challenges of the students and educators we serve.

Why Believing in Others Matters

When I hear educators say, "I have the worst class I've had in years," "These kids can't do it," or "*They* don't want to learn," or principals and administrators say, "These teachers won't . . . . " my heart breaks for the students in their classes and the teachers in their schools. Creating an education system that meets the needs of diverse learners in a changing world is complex. The work is hard and seemingly never ending. I will never minimize that, but the reality is that, if we don't believe in our students and staff *and* in our own ability to impact their trajectory, we simply won't.

Have you heard of the Pygmalion Effect, also known as the self-fulfilling prophecy? This comes from research by Rosenthal and Jacobsen[117] that demonstrated how teacher expectations influence student performance both positively and negatively. They found that when we expect certain behaviors of others, we are likely to act in ways that make the expected behaviors likely to occur. When teachers have positive expectations, they influence performance positively, and, likewise, negative expectations influence performance negatively. This is a reinforcing cycle, where beliefs shape expectations, which, in turn, shape actions and behaviors that impact outcomes for better and worse.

●●●●●

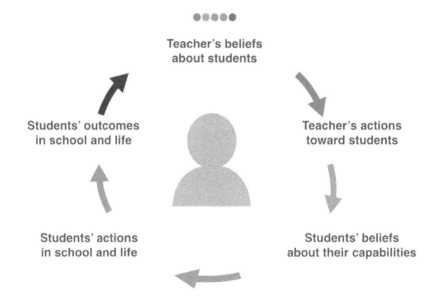

---

117   Robert R. Rosenthal and Elisha Y. Babad, "Pygmalion in the Gymnasium," *Educational Leadership*,1985, p. 36-39.

If we really want to create learning environments where all learners are valued and seen as capable of achieving desired outcomes, we have to begin with the belief that they can. One of my professors and mentors, Dr. Paul Deering, pushed my thinking early on in my career regarding the terms we often use (and confuse): ability and achievement.

- *Ability*: talent, skill, or proficiency in a particular area
- *Achievement*: a thing done successfully, typically by effort, courage, or skill

Our beliefs about these two terms and how we view our students is linked to Carol Dweck's work on growth mindset. If we believe that intelligence is fixed and don't see opportunities to grow or develop learners' skills and talents, we aren't as apt to try. On the other hand, when we believe we can learn and improve through hard work and effort, we work to create the conditions and experiences that lead to increased achievement and improved outcomes.

Do You Practice What You Preach?

It's one thing to say that we believe in students, but, when there is a lack of congruence with what we say and what we do, actions always speak louder than words. Katie Wright, Director of M.Ed Programs at High Tech High Graduate School of Education, highlights this in her blog post "Do as I Say, Not as I Do."[118]

> A teacher may say aloud to students, "Mistakes help your brain grow!," but then in the next breath that same teacher might praise rapid responses from students instead of allowing for sufficient wait time. Here, students discern the teacher prefers a fast response and does not place value on grappling with tough questions or making mistakes. Another

---

118 Katie Wright, "Do as I Say Not as I Do: Mindset Discerning in the Classroom," *Institute for Entrepreneurship in Education*, May 3, 2016, http://sites.sandiego.edu/ieeblog/2016/05/03/470.

> example: if a teacher intervenes quickly when a
> student is struggling to reply to a question (with the
> positive intention of helping that student to save face
> in front of peers), the student *discerns* the teacher
> actually has a low estimation of her or his ability.

This same thing happens when administrators tell teachers and students to take risks but fail to try new things or share what they are learning and how they are learning it with those they serve. When our words don't match our actions, what we do speaks much louder than what we say.

Creating the climate for success begins with aligning beliefs, actions, and expectations. As researchers Rosenthal and Babad note, "When we expect certain behaviors of others, we are likely to act in ways that make the expected behavior more likely to occur."[119]

We hear a lot of talk about creating opportunities for students to interact and have more voice and choice in their own learning, but I also hear teachers who hold back because they aren't sure their students would actually be capable of this type of work. I've also had administrators that tell me that voice and choice for educators sounds like a great idea for other administrators, but that their teachers aren't ready for this. We hold people back based on our assumptions and our fear rather than believing in their ability to try, learn, and grow.

I saw this play out while working with a group of experienced teachers to shift to more authentic, project-based learning. We explored a variety of new approaches, collaborated on new ideas, and everyone was excited—in theory—but offered a variety of reasons for why it wouldn't work in their classrooms. Teachers were facing challenges of pacing guides, time, resources, the population, testing, and more. All of their excuses were true, but I didn't let them off the hook. Each of the teachers tried *something*

---

119 Robert R. Rosenthal and Elisha Y. Babad, "Pygmalion in the Gymnasium,"
     Educational Leadership, September 1985, p. 36-39.

new in their classrooms. Depending on their comfort level, there was a wide range of implementation. Some tried a new strategy; others tried a whole lesson, and others implemented larger projects. With the exception of one teacher out of twenty-five, each teacher shared about how their students had "exceeded their expectations." The following teacher's reflection summarizes the group's collective experiences:

> Although I had faith that my students would produce quality work for this assignment, what they produced exceeded my expectations. Perhaps I should not have been surprised; for when you give students a sense of ownership and choice over their learning the creativity this unleashes often leads to great results. The results of this assignment make me want to develop similar projects in the future.

I am often asked how to change teacher mindsets. The reality is that you can't just change what people believe. The best way to change beliefs is by creating conditions and experiences for teachers to try new things and see what is possible. I can tell you all day long that the learners (administrators, teachers, or students) in your context are capable, but you probably won't believe me until you experience it. You are just going to have to take a leap of faith and try something to see for yourself. I believe in you!

What Is Your Impact?

The messages we send extend far beyond the beginning-of-the-year speech, the syllabus, the vision statement on the letterhead, or even the strategic plan shared at staff meetings. There is a big difference between plastering a vision on walls or your website or a beautifully crafted strategic plan and actually *living out* the core values and mindsets that guide your beliefs and how people lead, learn, and teach. And when our vision and core values are misaligned, it creates tension. Defining your core beliefs is important, but living them is the only way to make change happen.

In *To Sell Is Human*, Dan Pink shares the following:

> At every opportunity you have to move someone—from traditional sales, like convincing a prospect to buy a new computer system, to non-sales selling, like persuading your daughter to do her homework—be sure you can answer the two questions at the core of genuine service. If the person you're selling to agrees to buy, will his or her life improve? When your interaction is over, will the world be a better place than when you began? If the answer to either of these questions is no, you're doing something wrong.[120]

As educators, we have the power to influence the trajectory of lives every day. When students come in our schools and sit in our classrooms, we must ask the following every day and through each lesson:

- Am I improving their lives?
- Am I working to make the world a better place by creating more thoughtful, compassionate, creative, and skilled individuals?
- Am I providing opportunities to contribute positively to the local and global communities in which they interact?

What we do in school and what students learn only means something if students continue to love learning, remain curious, strive for something better, and ultimately find their place in the world. It only takes one person to take those steps and spark change, and I, for one, am encouraged and hopeful that, together, we can continue this movement. The future is created through the honest

---

120 Dan Pink, *To Sell Is Human: The Surprising Truth About Moving Others*, (New York: Riverhead Books, 2012).

and open reflections of our past, but if we want something better for the future, we have to create it. This doesn't mean we ignore the past, but it also means that we can't simply go on recreating the experiences we had as students for our own children. They live in a different time with opportunities that did not exist when we were children. We would be remiss to allow our apprehensions to hold back their aspirations.

Reflect and share your thinking and learning with others. As you do so, we will all continue to evolve, and the future of education will be brighter.

Onward.

Reflect and Connect Challenge
Share your thoughts, questions, and ideas using #LCInnovation

O What shifts can you make to move from accountability to collective responsibility??

O What is your impact on those you serve? What can you do to make the lives of those you serve better?

O How will you create experiences and unleash genius? Share your story!

THIS BOOK IS THE PRODUCT of the lessons I have learned from my family, friends, teachers, coaches, and so many colleagues along the way. I can't begin to thank all the people who have contributed to this journey but I am forever grateful for the impact of so many in my life.

To my husband, Matt—From the moment we met, you believed in me and supported me to follow my dreams. I love how you inspire our kids and those you teach to try new things and find the joy in learning. You and the kids are the greatest joys in my life, and I am so thankful for our life together and all we have ahead of us.

To my parents, Lori and Don Hughes—Thank you for celebrating my passions and always seeing the best in me and others. I admire you both so much and am grateful for your love, guidance, and support throughout my life. None of this would have been possible without you!

To George Couros—You have both pushed and pulled me at every step of this journey, from nudging me to blog and share my ideas to encouraging me to write this book. Thank you for believing in me and your unwavering support along the way. I am forever grateful for your friendship and guidance.

To the past and present team at the University of San Diego's Institute for Entrepreneurship in Education—It was the greatest honor to work alongside you all. I learned so much from all of you and the many partners that we were able to work with. Katie, Dave, Kim, Andrew, it was truly one of my greatest joys to get to work with such an amazing team and even better people. Thank you for all that you have taught me and for your amazing friendship along the way.

A special thank you to Paula Cordeiro and Scott Himelstein for your vision and leadership that has allowed us to do such meaningful and innovative work in K–12 schools and districts.

I have had the opportunity to work with some of the most amazing leaders in education. Many thanks to Devin Vodicka, Kaleb Rashad, Eric Chagala, Doug Kriedeman, Ed Hidalgo, David Miyashiro, Katie McNamara, Candace Singh, Annie Wolfe, John Cahalin, Elyse Burden, and the entire team at the Buck Institute for Education. You all inspire me by your vision, dedication, and desire to do whatever it takes to create schools that build on the strengths and talents of all. Above all, I am grateful for your friendship throughout this journey.

To all the educators who push me to be better each day from near and far, some who are highlighted in this book and many who are not, thank you for pushing boundaries, trying new things, and sharing what you are learning so we can all be better.

I have been fortunate to have mentors at various stages of my career who have been instrumental in shaping my trajectory. A special thanks goes to Anne Ashford, Paul Deering, and Rich Thome for caring for me as an individual and supporting me at distinct parts of my life to find my place and exceed my wildest expectations.

To my Hawai'i Ohana—although we are all over now—learning, teaching, and growing with you in the early years of our careers through our PhDs and as new moms, the friendship and life lessons have made me a better person. Lisa, Steph, and Jenn share my passions in life and work, which made our long drives back and forth to classes something to look forward to and memories that I will never forget.

Thank you to the IMPress and DBC publishing team—George, Paige, Erin, Dave, and Shelley—for taking my ideas and helping me to create the best book possible. We all benefit from your commitment to sharing the stories and ideas of passionate educators and ultimately creating better schools for all.

Bring Katie Martin to Your School or Event

KATIE MARTIN IS AN ENGAGING speaker and workshop facilitator who customizes learning experiences for your specific context. Katie's heartfelt perspective as a mom and her experience as an educator working with leading schools and districts have shaped her view of not only why we must change how we learn in school but how we can create a culture where learning and innovation are the norm. Katie's mix of research, personal stories, and practical examples will challenge you and your team to create learning experiences that develop the type of learners, workers, and citizens who will thrive in a changing world. Her workshops will inspire you to think about what isn't working, consider what is possible, and to lead change in your classroom, school, or district.

Popular Topics from Katie Martin

- Learning, Teaching, and Leading in a Changing World
- Learner-Centered Innovation
- The Evolving Role of the Educator
- Creating Experiences That Spark Curiosity, Ignite Passion, and Unleash Genius
- Creating a Strengths-Based Culture
- Leveraging Technology to Create Learner-Centered Experiences

To book Dr. Katie Martin to speak at your event, visit IMPressBooks.org.

IMPRESS

Empower

What Happens When Student Own Their Learning

By A.J. Juliani and John Spencer

In an ever-changing world, educators and parents must take a role in helping students prepare themselves for anything. That means unleashing their creative potential! In **Empower**, A.J. Juliani and John Spencer provide teachers, coaches, and administrators with a roadmap that will inspire innovation, authentic learning experiences, and practical ways to empower students to pursue their passions while in school.

Katie Martin

DR. KATIE MARTIN is the head of partnerships for the Western United States at AltSchool. Her work has centered on developing partnerships with diverse districts to learn and share how to create the conditions to support the evolving role of the educator. Her focus is on shifting pedagogy to inspire deeper learning and leveraging technology to ensure the best possible classroom and life experiences for all learners.

Katie has a bachelor's degree and master's degree in middle school education, and her PhD specializes in new-teacher induction and ongoing support to impact teacher efficacy. She has served as middle school English language arts teacher, instructional coach, and led the district new-teacher mentoring program; additionally, she enjoys teaching graduate classes in diverse education programs.

A leader, teacher, and speaker, Katie's experience in research and practice guide her belief that if we want to change how students learn, we must change how educators learn. She aspires to do that by creating experiences that empower all learners to develop knowledge, skills, and mindsets to thrive in a changing world. As a mom, she wants her kids to have learning experiences in school that build on their strengths and interests, and she is passionate about making sure educators are equipped to that for all kids.

Connect with Katie

- KatieLMartin.com
- Twitter @KatieMartinEdu